LITERARY CRITICISM IN THEORY AND PRACTICE

LITERARY CRITICISM IN THEORY AND PRACTICE

R.N. SHRIVASTAVA

ATLANTIC

PUBLISHERS & DISTRIBUTORS (P) LTD

Published by

ATLANTIC

PUBLISHERS & DISTRIBUTORS (P) LTD

7/22, Ansari Road, Darya Ganj, New Delhi-110002
Phones : +91-11-40775252, 40775214, 23273880, 23275880
Fax : +91-11-23285873
Web : www.atlanticbooks.com
E-mail : orders@atlanticbooks.com

Branch Office: Chennai
Phones : +91-44-48531784, 28291383
E-mail : chennai@atlanticbooks.com

Printed & bound in India by Atlantic Print Services

In Memory of
R.S. Crane and Chicago Colleagues
of
the University of Chicago

Preface

Advanced students of literature must be conversant with the theory and practice of all major schools of modern literary criticism so that they may be able to evaluate and appreciate literary works independently. I have attempted an in-depth study of the Chicago school of criticism because it is a critique of contemporary criticism particularly New Criticism, which largely dominated the critical scene of the second-half of the twentieth century of both America and England. Thus, this movement in literary criticism provides the necessary critical tools to sharpen the critical sensibility of literary critics.

The present book is designed to acquaint the readers with the powers and limitations of all the prevalent critical methods of our times. The basic intention of the Chicago Critics was to restore the nature of literary criticism as a form of enquiry free from the bias and prejudices of the New Critics who had reduced criticism to the level of a geometrical theorem in which a hypothesis is finally proved. For example, Cleanth Brooks believes that the chief attribute of poetry is paradox and invariably searches it out in all the close readings of the text. In such practical criticisms, literary criticism ceases to be an act of exploration, a form of free enquiry.

The aim of the Chicago Critics was to make all the discerning readers 'His Own Critics' as explained in chapter six of this book—an independent explorer.

The objective of this book is to train students in the mechanics of critical methodology by giving them an idea of the Chicago School of criticism. As we know that criticism is essentially a discipline concerned with the analysis and evaluation of particular literary works in the light of general principles of aesthetics this book will be of great help in shaping advanced students of literature as self-sufficient critics.

The book will also help them in removing confusions with regard to apparent contradictions among the critics. The concept of critical pluralism of the Chicago Critics explains that there is no contradiction among critics unless they talk about the same aspect of literary work. The semantic theory of R.S. Crane resolves the crisis of apparent contradictions in the light of Edward Sapir's linguistic observations. Critical pluralism of the Chicago Critics, in brief, is an attitude that welcomes the diversity of critical approaches and recognizes the powers and limitations of each critical method. According to them, a pluralist critic permits the use of more than one critical method. Such an attitude is bound to end the "tyranny of ruling hypothesis," or dogmatism and "critical monism" that plaqued the contemporary criticism.

Thus, this book would go a long way in restoring the health of criticism and putting the house of criticism in order, as the Chicago approach was basically remedial in character.

I am grateful to the following American scholars who took immense interest in completion of my study on the Chicago School of criticism: Dr. Gwin Kolb, Wayne C. Booth, Robert Marsh, Bernard Weinberg, all from University of Chicago, W.R. Keast (former President Wayne State University, Michigan), M.H. Abram (New York), Walter Davis (California), Warren G. French (Kansas city), John Caroll (Toronto), Owen Jenkin (Minnesota), Goldwin Smith (Ithaca), Bruce Bashford (New York), Mrs. Julia Crane (widow of R.S. Crane) and other eminent scholars of America who gave me valuable suggestions and information from time to time. The American Study Research Centre, Hyderabad (India) also helped me in a number of ways. Among Indian scholars I am highly indebted to Dr. S.K. Prasad (Magadh University), Dr. S.S. Prasad (Patna University), Dr. P.S. Sastri (Nagpur University), Dr. Raj Nath (University of Allahabad), (Patna University), Dr. C.L. Khatri (Magadh University) and Prof. Visharvaranjan (Bihar University) for suggesting necessary changes and co-operation in writing in this book.

My special thanks are also due to my wife Dr. Arati Shrivastava and my children Jyoti Kalash, I.A.S., Amrit Kalash, I.P.S. and Rimijhim Varsha who have always been a source of strength and inspiration to me.

RAVINDRA NATH SHRIVASTAVA

Abbreviations

The humanities	:	*The Idea of the Humanities.*
LCSP	:	*Languages of Criticism and Structure of Poetry.*
PMLA	:	Publications of the Modern Language Associations.
ASRC	:	American Studies Research Centre.
CIEFL	:	Central Institute of English and Foreign Languages.

British spelling have been used in the text.

Contents

1

Introduction of the Chicago Critics

I

The critics, who were most influential in America between the two World Wars were the Formalists or the New Critics. Therefore, it is rightly held that "the most influential critical method of our time is formalistic."[1] It is an admitted fact that every new movement is born out of a sense of dissatisfaction with the existing situation. What in America came to be known as New Criticism came into being out of a strong reaction against "the Victorian and Neo-Humanist emphasis on the moral uses of literature, the academic interest in historical and literary tradition and the biography of the author, and willingness of impressionists to make of each literary experience an odyssey of the critic's personality. It is also likely there was some reaction against the Marxist's stress on social values, and the psychological stress on the neuroses of writers."[2] "The New Criticism," as M.D. Zabel points out, made a clean sweep of existing critical conventions. In support of his argument, he quotes a few important sentences from Joel Spingarn's famous address, entitled "The New Criticism," at Columbia University in 1910, which is as follows:

> We have done with all the old Rules.... We have done with the genres, or literary kinds.... We have done with the comic, the tragic, the sublime, and an army of vague abstractions of their kind.... We have done with theory of style, with metaphor, simile, and all the paraphernalia of Graeco-Roman rhetoric.... We have done with all moral judgment of art as art. We have done with the race, the time, the environment of a poet's work as an element in criticism.... We have done with the "evolution" of literature.... We have done with the old rupture between genius and taste.[3]

Such a powerful critical explosion was bound to produce a chain-reaction. As in the event of nuclear explosion, the conscientious scientists feel alarmed about the hazardous effect of the radio-active fall-outs, so a section among the formalists started protesting against the excesses, limitations and perversities of the formalistic method. John Crowe Ransom, the founder of the Formalist school of criticism protested, in commenting on Brooks' *Well Wrought Urn* that the technique of analysis has been used to such an extreme there that "the sense of the whole is lost in the study of a part."[4] R.P. Blackmur, another representative New Critic, also protests that the formalistic method deals chiefly with "the executive technique of poetry (and only with a part of that) or with the general verbal techniques of language." T.S. Eliot, L.C. Knights, F.R. Leavis have also accused the New Critics of having "isolated one part of the work of art for examining, forgetting the poem as a totality."[5]

In the mid-thirties, R.S. Crane vigorously campaigned for the reform of the literary study at the University of Chicago. At that time, he felt happy in the company of those university professors who championed the cause of criticism by minimizing the importance of historical scholarship in the teaching of literature. But soon a quarrel among the reformers of literary study started. R.S. Crane favoured a "progressive-conservative"[6] reform and others a "radical reform." The second group of reformers set up a sharp antithesis between historical scholarship and literary criticism, R.S. Crane gradually grew disgusted with this trend. The "family quarrel" among the reformers of literary study led to a parting of ways. In course of time the "radical reformers" came to be known as the New Critics and the "progressive conservative" reformers as the Chicago Critics. As the New Critics and the Chicago Critics have a common heritage, Wilbur Scott rightly says that "both are chiefly concerned with the 'internal' analysis of a work of art, eschewing social, moral, philosophical, and personal material as irrelevant; both insist on-close textual study."[7] But the two groups of critics soon turned into "irreconcilable antagonists." The attacks on the New Critics assumed a polemical character in the writings of the Chicago Critics.

Thus it can be said that the 'Chicago School of criticism' was born out of a reaction against the New Criticism. Therefore it may be regarded as a splinter group of the Formalist critics.

II

The beginning of the Chicago School of criticism, can be traced back in the publication of R.S. Crane's revolutionary essay "History Versus Criticism in the Study of Literature" which has roots in the educational reforms launched by Robert Hutchins and Mortimer Adler who introduced a new kind of "general education" at the University of Chicago.

R.S. Crane and Richard Mckeon, the co-founders of the Chicago School of criticism were largely influenced by the re-evaluation of educational methods that took place at the University of Chicago in the late 20's and 30's. One of the central concepts of the 'general education' which was introduced over there in order to redesign the curriculum in English was an emphasis on the study of 'first principles.' R.M. Hutchins, the then President of the University of Chicago, explaining the aim of the 'general education,' observes: "The fundamental problems of metaphysics, the social sciences, and natural sciences, are, then, the proper subject matter of higher learning.... I have used the word metaphysics to include not only the study of 'first principles,' but also all that follows from it about the principles of change in the physical world, which is the philosophy of nature, and about the analysis of man and his production in the fine arts including literature."[8] He further says that "By constructing a university in this way it can be made intelligible. Metaphysics, the study of first principles, pervades the whole."[9]

By Metaphysics, as Richard Mckeon explains, the Chicago academicians meant "the study of methodological starting points, not the establishment of statements about the nature of the world which are true in some absolute sense."[10] He says "that metaphysics provides the basis for the higher learning in America."[11]

Catching the main spirit of the higher education of their time R.S. Crane, and his other colleagues gave the highest importance to the study of principles. In Chapter 2, I shall discuss this point in some detail and try to show how Crane believed that the 'humanities' are best defined in terms of certain arts or disciplines; and a 'discipline,' in turn, is "a body of general principles discoverable in a given subject matter, by means of which that subject matter may be intelligently approached and understood."[12] Thus the Chicago Critics have mainly worked in the field of critical methodology which involves a deep study of the nature and relative worth of general principles used in humanistic study.

Thus, one may say, that in a certain significant sense the Chicago element in the 'Chicago School of criticism' is this very concern for emphasis on the study of principles in our literary study. The sub-title of *Critics and Criticism, in Essays in Method by a Group of the Chicago Critics*. This fact, too, goes in support my argument that the tendency of the Chicago Critics was, to consider humanistic education as a training in the use of principles.

According to Hutchins; "...the best practical education is the most theoretical one.... It is principles, and everlastingly principles not data, not facts, not helpful hints, but principles which the rising generation requires if it is to find its way through the mazes of tomorrow."[13]

Strong echoes of Hutchins can be found in Crane's view regarding the application of "four arts" of the humanities which will be discussed in a detailed manner in Chapter 2. Here it may be mentioned that Crane observed that the "four arts" should be applied to questions raised by the student's experience with the basic materials. He writes: "...that the proper end of training in any of the arts of English Study is not knowledge of principles divorced from the concrete subject matter of particular literary works or linguistic documents but rather a set of trained habits of reflection and inquiry which can be formed only by the constant application to a great variety of specific problems of whatever principles of analysis the student may have learned."[14] Bruce Bashford quotes another passage from a bulletin of the University of Chicago, where Crane observes that "the final justification of training in the methods of English study lies not in the methods themselves but in their intelligent application to the solution of particular problems of philology, criticism, history, or theory raised by English and American writings...."[15] Thus, it may be inferred that the 'Chicago school of criticism' is the by-product of the educational reforms, especially of the methods of teaching literature.

The core of the Chicago School of criticism was formed during the mid-thirties, when late Professor R.S. Crane of the University of Chicago collaborated with Richard Mckeon, W.R. Keast, Norman Maclean, Elder Olson and Bernard Weinberg to give a new orientation to humanist scholarship. What brought them together was a similarity of approach and the unity of outlook and views, which existed among them. But unlike the New Critics they issued no formal manifesto. In reply to my specific query on this point, Bernard Weinberg confirmed by writing a personal letter to me in which he wrote: "I know of no manifesto of the school, but I think that Crane's two prefaces to the two editions of *Critics and Criticism* would be your best sources."[16]

In the Preface to the abridged edition of *Critics and Criticism*, Crane declares: "If there is, then, any 'Chicago Manifesto,' its theme is the desirability of looking at criticism from this 'critical' point of view."[17] He further says that what the Chicago Critics "most needed was a more critical approach to criticism itself, in something like the Kantian sense of 'critical': a consideration of criticism, as a mode of inquiry, that would go behind the doctrines of different schools and try to uncover the basic assumptions about literature and literary study on which they were founded."[18] The best exposition of this critical view of criticism can be found in two essays: one, by Elder Olson and the other by Richard Mckeon,[19] where they show their concern with the "grounds of criticism'—with the conditions that determine the cogency or adequacy of statements and the appropriateness or workability of methods."[20] The central problem of most of the essays of *Critics and Criticism*, says Crane, "is what method of discussion, involving what assumptions, will enable one to deal with this aspect most successfully."[21] Thus, the main aim of the Chicago Critics, says Crane, "has been to explore the possibility of a general critique of criticism (defined as any reasoned and systematic discourse about the poetic arts and their products) such as might yield objective criteria for interpreting the diversities and oppositions among them and for judging the comparative merits of rival critical schools."[22]

The Chicago Critics are popularly known as "Neo-Aristotelians" of the University of Chicago. The name was given to them, says Crane, by their friend Kenneth Burke. This name was found to be appropriate by other critics also. John Crowe Ransom, a leading New Critic also endorsed this nomenclature. He says: I can find no reservations in their commitment to the critical theory of the *Poetics*. They are pure Aristotelians, if we will allow for a little necessary supplementation of the handbook; but perhaps this suggests that we should call them neo-Aristotelians. The 'neo' will cover those extensions of the rules which have to be made if we consider that Aristotle's treatise is occupied with laying down the laws for poetry at large—a thing he does much too easily and then with examining at length the appropriate structure of Greek drama and more briefly the Greek epic; but now they have to look into Shakespeare and modern drama and fiction, where Aristotle through no fault of his own was unacquainted, and into lyric poetry where Aristotle's treatment is missing.[23]

But, the Chicago Critics never accepted this nomenclature as a true description of their efforts in the field of criticism. Crane mentions: "They have never adopted it, but they can recognize that, in Burke's restricted meaning, it does point to one obvious direction of their activities."[24] Let us see what R.S. Crane, the leader of the Chicago group, has to say about the affinities of the Chicago Critics with Aristotle:

> They have been greatly interested, all along, in the particular class of critical problems which Aristotle was the first, possibly the last, to discuss systematically, and for the study of which he evolved an appropriate and workable method. They have thought that these

> are crucial problems for practical critics, literary historians, and teachers of literature, and have deplored the neglect of them by most critics since antiquity. They have accordingly tried to begin where Aristotle left off and to pursue similar lines of study in the poetics of modern literature, using the distinctions he had suggested where these were relevant but attempting to enlarge his analysis in various ways in the light of the new things modern writers have achieved. Aristotle is thus conspicuously behind what they have sought to do in many of their essays in poetic theory and practical criticism. But their relation to Aristotle, as they see it, is not too different from the relation of modern biologists specializing in genetics to the long-neglected founder of that science; and if they are to be called "Neo-Aristotelians," it should be in the same limited sense in which it is accurate to call these biologists "Neo-Mendelians." The kind of poetics they have tried to develop...is one critical method among others, and they have explicitly presented it only as such. It can enable one to do certain things with literary works, and they are persuaded that these are of major importance; but it can be used effectively, as an instrument of practical criticism and literary history, except in conjunction with other modes—linguistic, historical, philosophical, for instance—which rest on principles of a different order. It would make no sense to think of it as an all embracing system of critical philosophy, and the Chicago writers have never done this...if they are interested in Aristotle, they are also interested, strongly and sympathetically, in critics as far removed from him in method as Plato, Longinus, Johnson, and Coleridge.[25]

How far the Chicago Critics are "Neo-Aristotelians" will be examined in detail in Chapter 4 of this book. For the present, it will suffice to say that "they would prefer a somewhat different version of their collective purpose and presuppositions."[26] To quote R.S. Crane again, "the only critical philosophy that underlies them all is contained in the very un-Aristotelian attitude toward criticism, including the criticism of Aristotle, which they have called 'pluralism.'"[27] Their pluralistic approach to criticism found fullest exposition in Crane's book *The Languages of Criticism and Structure of Poetry* (1953). Critical Pluralism, which is the core of their critical position has been discussed in detail in Chapter 4. But the common charge against these pluralist critics, as they describe themselves, is that they are pluralists only in theory and not in practice. In Chapter 6 I have sought to study the practical criticism of the Chicago Critics; I have tried to throw light upon the justifiability or otherwise of this charge. The first and second chapters are devoted to the diagnostic character of the Chicago School of criticism where it has been shown as to how the Chicago Critics, in the beginning attempted to diagnose the maladies of the humanistic scholarship. Chapter 2 shows how R.S. Crane, an early collaborator of the New Critics, reacted against the dominance of the social and historical scholarship. Chapter 3 shows how R.S. Crane, being disgusted with the monistic reduction of the critical theories by the "New Critics" felt called upon to evolve a still "newer" criticism which would be essentially remedial in character.

The remedial aspect of the Chicago Criticism, which has been highlighted here, cannot be properly understood unless their criticism is examined in the light of their concept of the humanities, which has been discussed exhaustively in Crane's *The Idea of the Humanities* (Vol. 1).

Crane points out that the problem of literary criticism, for the Chicago Critics "has been inseparable from the much larger problem of how the humanities in general might be brought to play a more influential role in the culture and action of the contemporary world."[28] "The humanities, as they have assumed," says Crane, are "co-extensive with the arts or methods that enable to isolate (humanistic properties) for our appreciation and use."[29] And, humanistic properties, says he, are "those aspects of man's achievements in sciences, in institutions, and in arts which are most distinctively human in the sense that their causes are not completely reducible either to natural processes common to men and animals or to superpersonal conditions and forces affecting all members of a given society."[30] Thus, we find that the problems that define the humanities are those which arise from the formulation of judgments which are concerned with the appreciation of the 'humanistic properties,' that is, uniqueness of humanistic works.

The Chicago Critics were conscious of the fact that humanist scholarship was endangered by the spirit of scientism which had infected its methodology. Therefore, they were chiefly concerned with the "internal state" of literary criticism as a branch of learning.[31] "If the humanities are to survive, they must defend themselves, as Crane argues, "not primarily against the sciences, as recent controversy would have it, or against the dead hand of the past, or against some one group of humanists like the literary historians, but rather against those twin enemies of intellectual progress, dogmatism and reductionism."[32] These two defects can be easily removed, as Crane says, by adopting a pluralistic approach. Therefore, 'Critical pluralism' is the panacea for ending the verbal wars or the doctrinal conflicts which are constantly going on the critical front.

With a view to fulfilling his remedial aim, as Wayne C. Booth points out, Crane "consistently combated the twin enemies with twin of his own: an aggressively 'differential' method that seeks discriminations adequate to human variety, and a pluralism that assumes the need for many different methods to match that variety."[33]

Richard Mckeon indicates that education in "the humanities" is a process of refining the common man's natural response to the objects of the humanities. Hence, constant refining of the critical tools or methods of understanding and appreciation of a literary work should be the aim of a literary critic. And for this, he must possess the erudition of a historian, the speculative power of a philosopher, the argumentative capacity of a logician, the objectivity of a scientist and the imaginative faculty of a creative artist. Except the last qualification, the Chicago Critics are equipped with all others to a considerable degree. Crane clearly admits that his attitude to literary criticism is scholarly.[34] And what is true of his is true of the other members of this school, as his colleagues were drawn from the Departments of English, Romance Languages and Philosophy.

The Chicago Critics concerned themselves with "the problem of the 'intrinsic' "[35] in criticism. As such, they widely differed from those who emphasized the 'extrinsic' aspect of literature. Considered 'intrinsically,' a given work of art, as Kenneth Burke explains, embodies certain 'principles.' "And these principles," as he says, "are said to reside in the division of the work into its parts, and in the relation of these parts to one another and to the whole."[36] Thus 'intrinsic' criticism approaches a work of literature from within and 'extrinsic' criticism from without. Crane, criticizing the latter mode, says: It is not criticism but psychology when we treat poems or novels as case-books and attempt to discover in them not the art but the personality of their authors. It is not criticism but history or sociology when we read imaginative writings for what they may tell us about the manners or thought or "spirit" of the age which produced them. It is not criticism but ethical culture when we use them primarily as means of enlarging and enriching our experience of life or of inculcating of moral ideals. It is not criticism but autobiography when we content ourselves with stating our personal preferences with regard to them or the adventures of our souls in their presence. Criticism, as we shall understand it, is not any of these things; it is simply the disciplined consideration, at once analytical and evaluative, of literary works as works of art.[37]

The stricture which Crane passes on the 'extrinsic' criticism is based on his assumption that "what a poet does distinctively as a poet is not to express himself or his age or to resolve psychological or moral difficulties or to communicate a vision of the world or to provide entertainment or to use words in such-and-such ways, and so on—though all these may be involved in what he does—but rather, by means of his art, to build materials of language and experience into wholes of various kinds to which, as we experience them, we tend to attribute final rather than merely instrumental value."[38]

According to Crane, the Chicago Critics distinguish literary criticism from literary appreciation by which they mean "direct sensory and imaginative intuition of literary works." Literary appreciation, says Crane, "is certainly a necessary condition of any criticism" but "it is bound to be a once something less than appreciation and something more."[39] Crane adds that literary criticism should be something less because, as we have seen, nobody of statements about a work of art can ever hope to communicate with any adequacy that immediate knowledge of the unity and individuality of the work which is ours as we read it, something more because that immediate knowledge, however, rich and vivid it may be, still falls short of the kind of understanding of literary production which criticism whatever else it may attempt to do, seeks first of all to attain.... The essential thing about the understanding to which the literary critic aspires is that it is understanding of literary works in their character as works of art.[40]

Thus, the criticism of poetry (in the large sense that includes prose fiction and drama), says Crane, is primarily an inquiry into the specific characters and powers, and the necessary constituent elements, of possible kind of poetic wholes, leading to an appreciation, in individual works, of how well their writers have accomplished the particular sorts of poetic tasks which the natures of the wholes they have attempted to construct imposed on them."[41] For such criticism, the Chicago Critics discovered sensitive analytic devices that permitted them to discriminate the various species of wholes that poets or writers have had made; to examine the number, character of their functional constituent units. The method, that the Chicago Critics developed, was a kind of an adaptation of the general method of Aristotle, which he outlined while discussing the problems of productive science or poetics. It is as they claim, capable of doing three things. Firstly, it could examine how "the parts of a work or section thereof contribute to the maximum achievement of its effect...."[42] Secondly, it could "appraise a writer's performance in a given work in relation to the nature and requirement of the particular task he has set himself, the assumed end being the perfection of the work as an artistic whole of the special kind he decided it should be."[43] Thirdly, it could examine "the success and failure of individual work depending upon the analytical isolation of works of art as finished product, from the circumstances and process of their origin."[44] Fourthly, it is "better equipped to explain those effects in a work of whatever date, that was constructed in accordance with the same combination of artistic principles...."[45] In the chapters that follow, an attempt will be made to understand whether the Chicago method is actually capable of doing these things or not.

III

THE CHICAGO CRITICS

After throwing some light on the origin, aims, claims and assumptions of the Chicago School of criticism, I would like to give a brief introduction to the Chicago Critics.

RONALD (ALMON) CRANE

R.S. Crane is the acknowledged leader of the Chicago School of critics. It is through his two prefaces to *Critics and Criticism* (1952, 1957), and the lectures which he delivered at several universities, that he defined the aims and objectives of the "Chicago School of criticism." Between 30's and 40's, he was chiefly pre-occupied with the problem of reforming the University English curriculum. His efforts led to a series of critical essays and studies, designed to critically examine the theory and practice of contemporary criticism. He edited *Critics and Criticism*—a critical symposium, to which he and his colleagues contributed several scholarly essays. His position was most clearly set forth in the *Languages of Criticism and Structure of Poetry* (1953), containing the revised version of his Alexander Lectures for 1951-52 which he delivered at the University of Toronto in March, 1952. The position which he took with respect to critical principles is described as pluralistic. In the Diamond Jubilee Year of the University of Chicago (1967) Crane published his *Idea of the Humanities and Other Essays Critical and Historical* in two volumes, from the University of Chicago Press.

In fact this book sums up the academic career of Crane, as he died soon after its publication. The University of Chicago has been the centre of his activity from 1924 until his retirement as Distinguished Service Professor Emeritus in 1951. He mostly stayed in Chicago, save for a few periods of research abroad. He was, indeed, a splendid professor. The high reputation he enjoyed among the contemporary scholars brought him invitation for teaching from a number of universities. He delivered lectures at Cornell, Carleton, Florida, New York, Oregon, Iowa, Rochester,

North-Western, Indiana, Stanford and in some foreign universities. He continued to hold seminars regularly until 1966. In a memorial to R.S. Crane, William R. Keast, a close associate of the great Chicago Critic, reminisces:

> Crane's career was, in an uncommon measure, a University of Chicago career. The man and the institution were well matched. He typified much that many of us regard as the essential strength of the university: a relentless maintenance of the highest intellectual standards, for himself, his colleagues and students; a habit of experimentation whether with new subject matters, or new institutional forms; a persistent concern with method in teaching or research, as the key to verifiable results and scholarly progress: a desire to seek, in the work of colleagues in other fields, ideas for application in his own; an abiding interest in the students, not for the contribution they could make to his work, but for the help he might give them in discovering and developing scholarly lines of their own.[46]

A revised version of his Pennsylvania doctoral thesis is one of his earliest publications. It was a monograph on the vogue of the medieval chivalric romance during the English Renaissance. Another noteworthy publication of his early period is a brilliant paper on the development of Francis Bacon. R.S. Crane stimulated the interest of contemporary scholars in the eighteenth century studies by publishing New Essays by Oliver Goldsmith, containing some fresh. He mentions: "I have brought Gibbon at this point for two reasons: first, as a concrete example of the type of approach to the humanities I propose to deal with now—the approach which emphasizes particulars and distrusts systems and yet seeks a philosophical basis for its operations."[47] Summing up the salient features of this age, with respect to the position of the humanities, Crane observes: "in short, whether on the side of the literary men or on that of the philosophers, the characteristic effort, in all fields of discussion, aimed at the establishment of some kind of union and harmony—rather than separation—between words and things, the arts of speech and arts of reason, the determination of facts and the formulation of principles and values, the permanently excellent and the immediately useful, the classics of the past and the new knowledge of the present."[48]

Such a description of the eighteenth-century is "misleadingly pacifist"[49] in the context of Crane's methodology. Theoretically he held that all critical methods are valid and equal, but in practice, he always came into conflict with the "New Critics" who adhered to various kinds of reductionist dogmas. Throughout his critical career, he assumed an aggressive posture with regard to the "New Critics." His polemical essays are nothing short of warfare[50] in which he has done a "hatchet job."[51] Eliseo Vivas calls them "commando raids."[52] The military terms used by these critics reflect the belligerent attitude of the Chicago Critics.

Between 1926 and 1932, Crane edited the annual bibliography of eighteenth century studies in the *Philological Quarterly*. These bibliographies and his short reviews in the journal went a long way towards the improvement of the eighteenth century studies during the 40's. His reviews have been re-printed under the title *English Literature, 1660-1800: A Bibliography of Modern Studies*.

Crane succeeded John Matthews Manley as the editor of *Modern Philology* and remained on its editorial-staff for twenty-two years. Under his editorship, the journal maintained not only its distinguished tradition but set new standards in scholarly and critical methods. Wayne C. Booth comments: "Crane has never written an essay...which does not at the same time attempt to solve a particular problem and to illustrate a method for solving a particular problem of that kind, and often he has talked explicitly of "methodological problems."[53] Crane fought lifelong against the twin enemies of criticism: "reductionism and dogmatism" with his twin weapons, differentiation and pluralism.

The essays, contained in *The Idea of the Humanities* (2 Vols.) are so varied that some of them defy classification. The labels, 'literary history,' 'literary criticism' and 'history of ideas' fail to define the nature of some of Crane's essays. Wayne C. Booth attempts to classify the essays under some new categories. He writes, "And we may not be too uncomfortable in calling other parts theory of criticism, literary historiography, or even educational theory. But even if we accept such terms as fitting this or that essay in the collection, there are still a good many pages which are left over. What, for example, is the genre of the history of the humanities and how they were defined, from Vivas to the present, with which the book opens?"[54] No other American scholar of the first-half of the twentieth century has ever attempted this kind of survey of the humanistic studies. Such a survey of the humanities down the ages must have provided a theoretical foundation to his new school of criticism. It is difficult to sum up here Crane's dynamic career as a critic, hence a separate chapter has been devoted to his contribution to criticism.

WILLIAM REA KEAST

William R. Keast became the President of Wayne State University in Detroit, Michigan. He remained a member of the English faculty of the Chicago University from 1933 to 1947.

At Cornell University he was Chairman of the English department and later on he became the Vice President for academic affairs. He spent two years in England working on his edition of Samuel Johnson's *Lives of the Poets*.

One of the main aims of the 'Chicago School of Criticism' was to suggest ways for the future reconstruction of criticism on broader theoretical bases. Keast has done commendable work in this direction. He made a penetrating analysis of Dr. Johnson's critical writings. It is commonly held that Dr. Johnson's criticism had no system and is "the product of sensibility or taste but seldom of reasoned views about the nature of art and criticism."[55] Keast challenges the popular contemporary estimate of Dr. Johnson that the great critical giant had no principles or theory. He examines the validity of such remarks by taking into consideration Johnson's own comments from his critical texts. He believes that Johnson's profound suspicion of abstract speculations might have restrained him from systematic theorizing about literature, as his mind was always preoccupied with concrete questions of evaluation. He holds that although Johnson was not a systematic writer yet he had a systematic mind. Johnson distrusted theory but, as Keast points out, such a distrust has in itself a theoretical commitment. He never expresses his views in explicit terms, in the form of extended statements. They can be discerned in their effects in actual practice. Johnson's repeated stress on the importance of principles and "rational deduction" is easily overlooked by modern critics like C.B. Tinker.

Keast's deep interest in Johnson's critical views and his method has done great reconstructive service to the general body of criticism. He has tried to understand how they could be profitably used by modern critics. Commenting upon Johnson's critical pronouncements, Keast feels that "the chief significance of such particular judgments is in helping us to ascertain the principles of more general import which underlie them and which may be instructive or useful in other contexts."[56]

Johnson subverted a number of critical dogmas namely, the rules of pastoral poetry, comedy, prohibition of tragicomedy, the dramatic unities in order to free literature from the fetters of prescriptive criticism. Keast is interested more in the method than in the content of Johnson's attack on the critical dogmas. Johnson, in attacking the limitations of the critical precepts, says Keast, "is endeavoring to replace what he considers narrow principles with principles more commodious."[57] Johnson's distrust of genres is grounded on the belief that literary works must not be thought of "as specifically identifiable objects, instances of fixed classes of works, and embodying more or less perfectly an ideal form but as human acts to be judged in relation to the agency of their production and appreciation."[58] Johnson assigns important role to "circumstantial accidents in critical judgment"[59] and thus he transfers the focus of principles from art to nature.[60]

Literature, says Keast is "as a natural process, set in the context of other natural processes such as social behaviour, and thus amenable to treatment in relation to its psychological causes and effects, its natural materials, and its circumstantial determinants."[61]

One of the chief characteristics of a Chicago Critic is his pre-occupation with the problems of method. Keast has finally discovered a method in Johnson's criticism, which he calls "circumstantial method." This method will determine the native power of an artist, which is always displayed in some kind of activity. "Since every activity has a circumstantial setting which determines, in important respects, its form and outcome, these circumstances must be isolated and evaluated in order to arrive at the firm estimate of the poet's power."[62] A Chicago Critic attends to the causes of a work of art; and the native power of an author is also one of the causes which is modified by several factors: intention, diligence, time, opportunity, chance, good luck, the availability of suitable materials, education, criticism, models, and a wide range of other forces over which the poet has no control.[63] So a critic who employs "the circumstantial method" has to take into account all these causal factors that influence a work of art, in varying degrees, at the time of production. History and biography are the tools of this method. Johnson's critical method, as pointed out by Keast, might help a critic to answer a particular type of question about a particular aspect of a work of art. Crane calls this type of criticism as "the criticism of qualities or of literary personality."[64]

Like other Chicago Critics, Keast also attacks the *a priori* approach of Heilman in the interpretation of *King Lear*. In the essay, "The 'New Criticism' and '*King Lear*,'" Keast finds flaw with one of the basic assumptions of Heilman that "the proper reading of *King Lear* must be a symbolic reading." Keast points out that such an approach is only justified when there is sufficient textual evidence that a literal interpretation would be incommensurate with the author's intention. Heilman has failed to give any such justification before he attempts a symbolic interpretation of the play. Keast remarks:

> Heilman's error in interpretation are thus the inevitable consequences of his theory. He begins with a determinate structural scheme which, since the work must express meanings, must be embodied in the work if it is to have artistic value. He knows, in all important respects, what he is going to find out before he begins, and it is no wonder that, having begged all the important questions he should find it. His interpretation is, moreover, in the proper sense, materialistic: form and structure are for him derivative form, and therefore strictly dependent on, the matter which the work expresses; the form of the play, indeed, is its total meaning, and this is obviously not the characters, or their actions, or their thoughts, or even the language in which their thoughts are cast, but what all these represent.[65]

RICHARD PETER MCKEON

Richard Mckeon is the chief mentor of the Chicago group of critics. He is essentially a man of philosophy who has been a Distinguished Service Professor of Greek and Philosophy since 1947 at the University of Chicago. He has several books to his credit: *The Philosophy of Spinoza* (1928); *Freedom and History* (1928); *Thought, Act and Passion* (1954), etc.

It is he who provided the theoretical base to the "Chicago School of Criticism." The concept of Critical Pluralism was first of all discussed at length by Mckeon in his essay: "The Philosophical Bases of Art and Criticism."[66] Elder Olson, another important Chicago Critic, acknowledges Mckeon's valuable contribution to the "Chicago School of criticism":

> It was Mckeon whose researches into critical and philosophic methodology both established the basis and determined the direction of critical pluralism...this was more than a triumph of philosophic exegetics, it was a Copernican revolution in philosophy itself, for its radical investigation of the very bases of critical and philosophic method set the principles, methods, and conclusions of the different systems in clear relation, and made unnecessary, for those who grasped its implications, the adoption of dogmatic, skeptical, or eclectic positions.[67]

One of the important limitations of the "New Criticism," according to Mckeon, is that it lacks a theoretical base or critical framework. Mckeon tries to lay down a solid foundation for the "Chicago School of criticism" which came into existence to remedy the defects of the past critical systems and to resolve doctrinal disagreements or methodological confusions of the modern times.

Critical judgments involve conception of philosophy and philosophic method. The subject matter of art is determined by three factors: principles of philosophy, methods and principles of criticism. The essay, "The Philosophic Bases of Art and Criticism" is divided into three sections. In the first section, Mckeon presents a penetrating account of the shifting definitions and evaluations of the nature of art from Plato to Tolstoy. In Plato and Aristotle the nature of art objects is discussed in terms of imitation; in Kant and Bacon, in terms of imagination; and in Horace and Tolstoy, in terms of "operation."

As Mckeon points out "the subject matter of discussions of art is determined by three considerations which depend on three determinants: first, the determination of the kind of things appropriate to the discussion is stated in general philosophic principles; second, the determination of the mode of classifying such things depend on the methodological definition of principles; third, the determination of the characteristics relevant to the evaluation of such things is stated in the principles of criticism."[68]

Although Plato and Aristotle discuss the nature of art in terms of "imitation," yet their conclusions differ. The difference is the result of variations in the three determining factors. For each philosophic doctrine there is a variant interpretation of art or a variant aesthetic.[69] The wide range of philosophic assumptions which control the use of terms gives rise to a large number of aesthetic theories. Mckeon remarks give rise to a large number of aesthetic theories. Mckeon remarks that the words used in criticism are relative to their subject matter, but the subject matter changes with changes of philosophic principles.[70]

Mckeon suggested a pluralistic approach that might successfully resolve the doctrinal differences and methodological confusions. His central thesis is that the disagreements among the critics are often merely apparent, not real. Even when they appear to be talking about a common matter, say, a given poem (using the term in the widest sense), behind the similarity or even the identity of their critical terms are to be found different meanings, because a term is determined by the methods and principles that are employed in the critical discussion. He classifies criticism into six modes: "dialectical," "scientific," "poetic," "scholarly," "technical" and "formal"; and shows that each critical system has its own powers and limitations. He recognizes the relativity of critical approaches and pleads for the use of a variety of methods. His concept of critical pluralism can be best summed up in his own words:

Needless to say, a given critic may successively employ more than one of these modes of criticism and may even combine two or more of them, crudely or effectively, in a single theory or application of criticism. Purity in adherence to a single mode is not necessarily a virtue in criticism since the differentiation of modes is in terms of the purposes envisaged in the criticism, and the identification of the mode employed by a critic is only a step toward the evaluation of his achievement in so far as such identification may indicate the appropriate criterion and thereby contribute to both the understanding and the judgment of his statements.[71]

NORMAN F(itzroy) MACLEAN

Norman Maclean, a close associate of R.S. Crane, has been working at the University of Chicago since 1931, successively as an instructor, an Assistant Professor, an Associate Professor and finally as a Professor. In 1963 he was appointed William Rainey Harper Professor of English at the University of Chicago.

Maclean's importance, as a Chicago Critic, chiefly rests on the fact that he worked for the development of lyric criticism. In his scholarly essay "From Action to Image: Theories of the Lyric in the Eighteenth century" he maintains that it is wrong to say that the neo-classical period was a "non-lyrical" age.

Ironically enough, "the non-lyrical age" regarded the highest form of the lyric—the Great Ode—as one of the supreme expressions of poetry. Here Maclean discusses the eighteenth-century shift from the drama or narrative of action to the lyric of passion and image.

Maclean, as a Chicago Critic, assumes that literary criticism being "a reasoned discourse" is deeply rooted in philosophy. He considers literary criticism to be "a form of medial discourse."[72] He writes:

> The critic furnishes insights, sensitive reactions, and workable distinctions to the speculative aesthetician who clarifies, rationalizes, amplifies, and systematizes; and, in turn, some part of these philosophical clarifications and amplifications seep back and become a part of critical tradition, and somewhat altering the tradition, even if, as is often the case, the rationalization and systematization are blurred by common handling. On the other hand, literary criticism is in good part shaped by particular poems and group of poems; and it, in turn, shapes to some extent subsequent creation.[73]

Thus his explication of the theory of the lyric involves a secondary explication of Longinian aesthetics and some representative odes of the eighteenth century.

Not only in theory but also in practice Maclean suggested a new approach to lyric criticism, the poetics of which was to be developed by the Chicago Critics later on the Aristotelian lines. Maclean attempted a practical criticism of a lyric[74] of Wordsworth (It is a beauteous evening calm and free...). This practical criticism was published along with Olson's " 'Sailing to Byzantium': Prolegomena to a Poetics of the Lyric."[75] In his "Prefatory Note" to these two essays, Crane remarks: "The critical preoccupation and purposes of Messrs Maclean and Olson represent a radical departure from the tradition of poetic analysis which has been largely dominant in our day."[76] Normal Maclean may be regarded as a minor Chicago Critic.

ELDER OLSON

After Crane, Elder Olson is the most prominent practising critic of the Chicago group. Since 1936 he has been on the staff of the English Department of the Chicago University. He went abroad several times as a Visiting Lecturer. He is the only creative critic in the Chicago group. He published several books: *Thing of Sorrow* (1934); *The Cock of Heaven* (1940); (with others) *Critics and Criticism*, 1952; *The Poetry of Dylan Thomas*, 1954; *The Scarecrow Christ*, 1954; *Plays and Poems*, 1958; *Tragedy and the Theory of Drama*, 1961; *American Lyric Poems*, 1963; *Collected Poems*, 1963; *Aristotle's Poetics and English Literature*, 1965; *The Theory of Comedy*, etc.

The Chicago Critics hold that criticism is a philosophic discipline "for the discussion of art must entail assumption which involves more than art...since criticism or the theory of art is a part of philosophy and is determinate or variable according to the same principles."[77] Elder Olson points out that the critical theory of Plato, Aristotle, E. Kant and David Hume, among other philosophers, are not random views but are conditioned by their respective philosophies. They are generated and produced by the "universe of discourse in which their philosophies are concerned."[78] Because criticism is the product of a system of thought, it necessarily involves some sort of formulation, metaphysical or epistemological or possible critical positions. Like Mckeon, he contends that the philosophic positions are determined by two main considerations: "the number of aspects of a subject which can be brought into discussion, as constituting its subject matter; the kinds of basic dialectic which may be exerted upon that subject matter."[79]

In order to elaborate his point, he further distinguishes between art as a subject and its various subject matters: "the subject is what is talked about; the subject matter is that subject in so far as it is represented of or implied in the discussion."[80] He holds that "any discussion of a 'subject' is relative to its formulation."[81]

But any discussion or "discursive reasoning must employ some method of reasoning or inference; and, since there are various possible systems of inference, we may say that a given discussion is a function of its subject matter and of the dialectic, *i.e.*, system of inference, exerted upon the subject matter."[82]

Criticism selects some aspects of art as subject matters for discussion; and there is quite a multitude of subject matters. They are best summed up in Olson's words:

> Thus one aspect of art is its product; another, the instrumentality active or passive, which produced the product; another, the product as relative to or determined by that instrumentality, and hence as a sign of the nature of instrumentality, whether this last be viewed as actual or polemical. Another is the relation of an art to a certain subject or means, as a consequence, and hence as a sign of these; still another aspect is its production of a certain effect; either of activity or of passivity, upon those who are its spectators or auditors; and, lastly there is the art viewed as instrumental to that effect. We may sum up all this by saying that criticism has viewed art variously as a product; as an activity or passivity of the artist; as certain faculties or as a certain character of the audience; as an instrument; or as a sign, either of certain characteristics of the artist or his audience or of something else involved in art *e.g.*, its means, subject etc.[83]

Thus the term 'poem' assumes a number of significance in critical discussions. It appears in different senses in different contexts. Olson further adds:

> In its most obvious meaning it refers to the product of the poetic art; but critics have often used it to refer to what they considered more important aspects of poetic art or have differentiated it by reference to such aspects. Thus those who think that it is characterized by its instrumentality mean by "instrumentality" either the poet or the poetic powers; those who define poetry in terms of the poet see the poet as active craftsman or as the passive instrument of his inspiration or as a mixture of the two; while those who define poetry in terms of poetic powers see the poet as possessed of faculties or qualities either of a certain kind or of a certain degree. With these

differences, both consequently view the poem as a kind of behaviour of the poet; and, for both, the literal poem—the product—becomes a sign: of that behaviour, which is, in turn, a sign of the poetic character or faculties. Others find that the poem properly exists in the audience; the audience is the true poet, for without it, the poem could never come to life; and the audience, like the poet, can be viewed as actualizing certain active or passive potentialities or merely as possessing such potentialities—hence the theories of "audience participation" (the active view) or "art as experience" (the passive view), etc. Finally "poem" may mean the end to which the product is instrumental, *e.g.*, the psychological cure or ethical or political attitude or behaviour.[84]

When two critics are talking about a poem, they may not be talking about the same aspect of the poem in the same sense. Apparently, conflicting views are bound to occur, when critics are dealing with different aspects of the same poem. They do not contradict one another as they have different references. Olson points out that contradictions or inconsistencies occur when the statements have the same reference. Such views of Elder Olson finally crystallized into the concept of "critical pluralism," which is the central thesis of "the Chicago School of Criticism."

BERNARD WEINBERG

Bernard Weinberg is Professor of Romance Languages and Literature at the University of Chicago. Essentially, he is an historical scholar. His brilliant scholarship is simply reflected in the following publications: *French Realism: The Critical Reaction 1830-1870* (1907); ed. *Critical Prefaces of the French Renaissance* (1950); *A History of Literary Criticism in the Italian Renaissance,* 2 vols. (1961); *The Art of Jean Racine* (1963); *The Limits of Symbolism: Studies of Five Modern French Poets* (1966); *Trattati di Poetica e Retorica del Cinquecento*, 3 vols. (1970-71); numerous articles on French and Italian Literature.

The Chicago Critics are commonly described as "Neo-Aristotelians" because they consider the Aristotelian method to be the best among all other systems for structural analysis. But they have reconstructed the Aristotelian system for its modern use. Unlike the Aristotelians of the sixteenth-century Italy and the seventeenth-century French interpreters of Aristotle, the Chicago Critics have accepted Aristotle's method in its original form. Weinberg has pointed out the limitations of the pseudo-Aristotelianism in his essay, "From Aristotle to Pseudo-Aristotle."

> First, they came to the text of Aristotle with habits of textual interpretation, habits of fragmentation and methodological anarchy, which made it impossible for them to understand this closely constructed and tightly argued document. Second, they read the Poetics in the light of a rhetorical tradition, which reduced all aspects of literary documents to considerations stemming from the audience. Third, they could not dissociate from the thinking about poetic matters the numerous details of Horace's *Ars poetica*, which they had long known, and they insisted on reading Aristotle as if he were a kind of Ur-Horace. And finally, they tried to "modernize" Aristotle to adopt him to their own times and their own peoples, in a manner scarcely authorized by the Aristotelian text.[85]

He establishes here that the Aristotelians have made a great departure from the original Aristotelian position, despite their numerous eulogies to Aristotle, citations of his doctrine and appeals to his authority. As they always laboured about isolated pieces or lines or passages of Aristotelian text, they failed to discover any synthesis to correct this fragmentation. They never tried to state the meaning of the text as a whole. Weinberg's analysis separates the chaff from the grain and clarifies the correct Aristotelian approach for the use of the Chicago Critics.

It may be made clear here that the Chicago Critics were not for the revival of the "Aristotelian criticism" but for that of the Aristotelian method.

Bernard Weinberg in his essays on the Aristotelians of the sixteenth century Italy and the seventeenth century France has shown at length as to what happened to Aristotle's theory during the period.

Robertello's system became more a rhetorical system than a poetic system, in the Aristotelian sense. He moved away from the poem towards the demands or expectations of the audience. For him, "credibility" assumes greater importance than—necessity and probability. As a consequence of this shift, the question, "will the audience believe that such an action or character is true? became more important than the question, "How such and such a part integrated into the artistic structure of the poem?" In this way, we find that fundamental conception of the *Poetics* escaped him. The removal of the principal emphasis from the poem to the audience was against the spirit of the *Poetics*.

The "Aristotelians" of the seventeenth century France, Sudery, Chapelain, Corneille, Boileu etc., more or less, maintained the position of the early sixteenth century critics. They were followers of Robertello and Castelvetro and adopted a rhetorician's view of poetry. The neo-classical poetics is basically Horatian and is distinct from the poetics of Aristotle in the conception of poetic form, of the constitutive parts; of their inter-relation and of the unity and whole into which they enter, of the function of poetry etc.

IV

THE CHICAGO SCHOOL OF CRITICISM

A school, as Webster defines, is "a group of people held together by the same teachings, beliefs, opinions and methods" or "formed by the followers or disciples of a particular teacher, leader, or creed" (for example, the Impressionist School), or "a group of artists associated with a specified place" (the Barbizon School).[86] On close examination, we find that this new movement in American criticism, which was started by a group of five Chicago Scholars in middle thirties, fulfils all the conditions of a school, laid down as above.

Let us apply Webster's first criterion. All the Chicago Critics hold the following ideas:

(i) that the problems of literary criticism are inseparable from the larger problem of the humanities.

(ii) that the humanities are distinguishable from the natural and the social sciences.

(iii) that the humanities are concerned with the humanistic properties of man's achievements.

(iv) that the causes of the humanistic properties are not completely reducible either to natural processes common to men and animals or to superpersonal conditions and forces affecting the conditions of society.

(v) that the humanities are co-extensive with arts or methods that enable us to isolate the humanistic properties for our appreciation.

(vi) that the methods of natural and social sciences are inappropriate for appreciating the humanistic properties.

(vii) that in order to save the humanities, humanistic scholars and teachers should be educated on a new line and their efforts be directed "(1) to subjecting the principles currently employed in the various humanistic arts to a systematic critique of their powers and limitations and (2) to investigating the possibilities of particular methods in the different arts which either have not been developed in the past or have been neglected in modern times because the questions to which they are suitable, though as pertinent as ever humanistically, have been allowed to disappear from view."[87]

(viii) that they have tried to explore the possibility of a general critique of literary criticism.

(ix) that they tried to develop on objective criteria for interpreting the diversities and oppositions among critics and for judging the comparative merits of rival critical schools.

(x) that they have taken a pluralist and instrumentalist view of criticism.

(xi) that they have viewed their "Aristotelianism" as strictly pragmatic and non-exclusive commitment.

(xii) that they have employed a *posteriori* inductive method for analysing literary works.

(xiii) that they employ hypothetical regressive reasoning for grasping the artistic reasoning in a literary work.

(xiv) that they were against the monistic reduction of critical concepts.

(xv) that they are opposed to *a priori* approach and adoption of a 'ruling' hypothesis by a critic.

(xvi) that they are in favour of multiple working hypothesis.

(xvii) that they are chiefly concerned with the immediate shaping cause of a literary work.

(xviii) that they view language, the material cause of a literary work, as just one of several factors in its creation, and by no means the most important.

(xix) that they have worked for the "collective development of criticism itself, by providing, in the multiple but compendent differentiations of the specific method, a broad base of ascertained literal knowledge about poetry in the light of which the many discrete and limited insights achieved by contemporary criticism itself, by providing, in the multiple but compendent differentiations of the specific method, a broad base of ascertained literal knowledge about poetry in the light of which the many discrete and limited insights achieved by contemporary critics in the integral, or partly integral, modes might be co-ordinated with one another and developed more fully, to the great advantage of the critical art in all its modes and so ultimately of the humanities in general."[88]

(xx) that, on the whole, their attitude to criticism is remedial.

Now let us apply Webster's second criterion. R.S. Crane forms the nucleus of the Chicago group of critics. His importance can be realised by the very fact that it is he who edited the articles of his colleagues, in *Critics and Criticism*. Again, it is he, who had, for the first time, introduced the practical criticisms of his two Chicago colleagues—Elder Olson and Normal Maclean. Explaining the salient features of the two Chicago Critics, he wrote:

> The critical preoccupation and purposes of Messrs. Maclean and Olson represent a radical departure from the tradition of poetic analysis which has been largely dominant in our day. They are interested in lyrics not as exemplars but as objects; they insist on approaching them as poems of a distinctive kind rather than as receptacles of poetry; the wholes they are concerned with are not the constructed wholes of any dialectic but concrete wholes determined by the poet's choice of such and such parts, in such and such order, in a poem presumably complete only when its final line is reached. In other words, eschewing philosophic generality and the insights which arise from the analogical application to lyrics, or to passages from lyrics, of principles and definitions in no way proper to poems as distinct from other things or to lyrics as distinct from other varieties of poems, they have endeavoured to constitute the criticism of lyrics as a subject-matter by itself and within this subject-matter to orient practical criticism toward as complete a discovery as possible, in individual lyrics, of the internal causes of their peculiar effects. Their end as in any criticism worthy of the name, is appreciation; but the appreciation they wish to make possible is one of which the object is not a universal form or value reflected in the poem itself in its wholeness and particularity as a structure of mutually appropriate parts.[89]

Thus, R.S. Crane being the chief spokesman of the Chicago Critics, is the acknowledged leader of the group. But the stature of Richard Mckeon, is of no less importance. He is also considered to be one of the founders of the Chicago School of Literary Criticism,[90] as it is he who provided its theoretical base: the critical pluralism and the bias for the Aristotelian methods for structural analysis. R.S. Crane acknowledges his debt to Richard Mckeon by dedicating his book, *The Humanities*

(2 Vols.) to him. Again, in the preface *LCSP*, he expresses his gratitude to Richard Mckeon and his Chicago colleagues:

> My most immediate and particular debts, however, are to the friends and colleagues at the University of Chicago with whom I have collaborated last year in a volume called *Critics and Criticism: Ancient and Modern*; the many references to their work in my notes sum up only in the meagrest way what I own to them, and particularly to Richard Mckeon and Elder Olson for guidance and correction during many years.[91]

Elder Olson also pays a similar tribute to Professor Richard Mckeon in the following extract:

> My debt to Professor Mckeon I can hardly assess. After nearly thirty years of friendship and discussion, I cannot be certain what is his and what is mine in my interpretation of the *Poetics*. If I have ever said anything of value about the work, I should gladly see it attributed to him, rather than cheat him one particle of his due.[92]

Finally, let us apply Webster's third criterion to the Chicago Critics. All the Chicago Critics who collaborated with one another were on the staff of the University of Chicago in the middle thirties. Frequent staff meetings must have provided opportunities of cross-fertilization of the minds of the professors. As they were at one place, even in their private talks, they might have influenced one another. Russell Thomas informs that "since 1931 the general courses have been staff-planned and staff-taught. There has been at all times closest co-operation in the deliberations on all matters of policy."[93] Thus we may conclude that it is this sharing of common objectives and free co-operation among scholars at the University of Chicago under the leadership of R.S. Crane that lent the character of a school to the theory and practice of the Chicago Critics, who espouse an approach to critical methodology which quite different from that of the New Critics. The "Chicago School of criticism," is, by and large, homogeneous and monolithic, as all the five critics adhere to one single critical philosophy which is defined as critical pluralism. Like all significant movements, the 'Chicago School of literary criticism,' is too complex a phenomenon to lend itself to any brief, or simple summary. The Chapters that immediately follow are designed to examine the different aspects of the school in a detailed manner.

NOTES

1. Wilbur Scott, *Five Approaches of Literary Criticism* (New York, Collier Books, 1968), p. 179.

2. *Ibid.*, pp. 180-81.
3. "Introduction: *Criticism in America*," *Literary Opinion in America* I (New York, Harper Torchbooks, 1962), p. 22.
4. *Five Approaches of Literary Criticism*, p. 182.
5. *Ibid.*, p. 182.
6. Progressive-conservative reform means reconstruction of university literary studies by "carrying on and reinvigorating the philological and historical tradition, and at the same time,...developing what that tradition had been relatively weak in systematic training in the various modes of critical analysis and judgment." (*The Humanities*, II, 27.)
7. *Ibid.*, p. 26.
8. *Ibid.*, p. 183.
9. First published in the *English Journal* (College Edition), Vol. 24 (1935).
10. *The Higher Learning in America* (New Haven, Connecticut, 1962), p. 107. This book was copyrighted in 1938.
11. *Ibid.*, p. 108.
12. Bruce Bashford, *The Humanistic Criticism of R.S. Crane* (Michigan, University Microfilms, 71-1790), f.n. 37 on p. 25.
13. Richard Mckeon, "Action and the Uses of the Humanities," *Comprendre*, No. 15 (Venice, 1956), p. 194.
14. *The Education We Need* (Chicago, 1947), p. 10.
15. "Requirements for Degrees in English," p. v.
16. Requirements for Degrees in English (Chicago: The pamphletlists no authors). Bruce Bashford mentions in his dissertation (f.n. 3 on p. 4 above) that his source of assigning authorship to Crane is Gwin Kolb, the Chairman of the English Department at the University of Chicago. See Bruce Bashford's dissertation, p. 23.
17. (Chicago, 1945), p. 116. Bashford mentions: "The page preceding this quotation makes it evident that "Criticism" here means practical criticism and "theory" means the analysis of ideas in literary theory. Again my source for assigning authorship to Crane is Gwin Kolb." (*The Humanistic Criticism*, p. 23).
18. An extract of a letter dated March 28, 1969 which Bernard Weinberg wrote to me from Chicago. See appendix, p. 248.
19. *Critics and Criticism* (Chicago, 1957).
20. *Ibid.*, p. v.
21. "An Outline of Poetic Theory" (pp. 3-23) and "The Philosophic Bases of Art and Criticism" (pp. 191-274), both in *Critics and Criticism* (1957).
22. *Ibid.*, p. vi.
23. *Ibid.*, p. vi.
24. *Critics and Criticism*, p. 1.

25. "Humanist at Chicago," *Kenyon Review*, XIV, Autumn, 1952, 651.
26. *Critics and Criticism* (1957), p. iii.
27. *Ibid.*, pp. iii-iv.
28. *Critics and Criticism*, p. 2.
29. *Critics and Criticism* (1957), p. iv.
30. *Critics and Criticism* (1952), p. 2.
31. *Ibid.*, p. 2 (parenthesis mine).
32. *Ibid.*, p. 2.
33. *Ibid.*, p. 5.
34. Wayne C. Booth, Introduction to *The Humanities*, I, xiv (parenthesis mine).
35. *Ibid.*, pp. xiv-xv.
36. LCSP, p. x.
37. Kenneth Burke, *A Grammar of Motives* (Englewood Cliffs, J.N.: Prentice-Hall Inc., 1945), pp. 465-84.
38. *Ibid.*, p. 465.
39. *The Humanities*, II, 12.
40. Crane, *Critics and Criticism*, p. 13.
41. *The Humanities*, II, 12.
42. *Ibid.*, p. 12.
43. *Critics and Criticism*, p. 13.
44. *Ibid.*, p. 645.
45. *Ibid.*, p. 646.
46. *Ibid.*, p. 646.
47. *Ibid.*, p. 646.
48. W.R. Keast, "Ronald S. Crane, 1886-1967," *The University of Chicago Magazine* (November, 1967). p. not mentioned in the xerox copy studies of Goldsmith's sources. The chief merit of this book rests on the fact that a number of anonymously published essays were first attributed to Goldsmith. Again in 1932 he edited a *A Collection of English Poems 1960-1800*, an anthology that did much to arouse the interest of the readers in the eighteenth-century poetry. In those years, he distinguished himself as an eighteenth century scholar. The eighteenth-century assumed importance in the eyes of Crane because it was "an age in which the utility of literary studies was seldom seriously questioned, even by educators interested in diffusing material language; in which the central problems of philosophers were problems of the powers and achievement of man; in which, at the same time that grammarians, critics and historians attempted to be philosophical, philosophers concerned themselves in a humanistic rather than merely scientific spirit with language, criticism and history." It was a period in which the humanities rather than the natural science exercised a

determining influence in the intellectual life of Europe. R.S. Crane's concept of the humanities was shaped by the eighteenth-century humanists.

49. Quoted by Wayne C. Booth in his introduction to Crane's *The Humanities*, I, xix.
50. *The Humanities*, I, 93.
51. Wayne C. Booth's Introduction to Crane's *The Humanities*, I, xix-xx.
52. *Ibid.*, p. xx.
53. Wayne C. Booth, *The Humanities*, I, xx.
54. Quoted on the last cover page of LCSP, an extract of Northrop Frye's review of the book in the University of Toronto Quarterly.
55. R.S. Crane, *The Humanities,* Wayne C. Booth remarks, "Crane's critical pluralism is not the easy eclecticism that generally travels under the name. Until one has seen how a man is able, without inconsistency, to pursue a mode of thought rigorously and even passionately and at the same time to see that mode as only one of the valid modes, one cannot really catch what Crane is about." Crane's pluralism permits a critic to use a number of approaches to answer the problems posed by a work of art. For this a critic must be skilled in "the method of multiple working hypothesis."
56. Wayne C. Booth, *The Humanities*, I, xxi.
57. R.S. Crane, *The Humanities*, I, xii.
58. R.S. Crane, *The Humanities*, I, xiii.
59. Keast, "The Theoretical Foundations of Johnson's Criticism," *Critics and Criticism*, p. 390.
60. *Ibid.*, p. 392.
61. *Ibid.*, p. 395.
62. *Ibid.*, pp. 395-96.
63. *Ibid.*, p. 392.
64. *Ibid.*, p. 398.
65. *Ibid.*, p. 395.
66. *Ibid.*, p. 406.
67. See, *e.g.*, Lives, I, 19, 21, 35, 413, 415-18, 423-24, 443, 447, 458-59, 464-65; II, 145-47, 228; III, 217-20, 337-38, 268.
68. *The Humanities*, II, 185-86.
69. *Keast*, "The 'New Criticism' and 'King Lear,'" *Critics and Criticism*, pp. 117-18.
70. Mckeon, *Critics and Criticism*, pp. 463-45.
71. Aristotles *Poetics and English Literature*, ed. and with an introduction by Elder Olson (Chicago, 1955), p. xxviii.
72. Mckeon, "The Philosophic Bases of Art and Criticism," *Critics and Criticism*, p. 478.
73. *Ibid.*, p. 522.

74. *Ibid.*, p. 492.
75. Mckeon, *Ibid.*, p. 544.
76. *Critics and Criticism*, p. 408.
77. *Ibid.*, p. 411.
78. *Ibid.*, p. 411.
79. *The University Review*, pp. 202-09.
80. *Ibid.*, pp. 209-19.
81. *Ibid.*, p. 201.
82. Olson, "An Outline of Poetic Theory," *Critics and Criticism*, p. 547.
83. Thomas E. Lucas, Elder Olson (New York, Twayne Publishers, 1972), p. 16.
84. Olson, p. 547.
85. *Ibid.*, p. 547.
86. *Ibid.*, p. 547.
87. *Ibid.*, p. 547.
88. *Ibid.*, pp. 547-48.
89. *Ibid.*, p. 548.
90. *Ibid.*, p. 548.
91. Bernard Weinberg, "From Aristotle to Pseudo-Aristotle," *Aristotle's Poetics and English Literature*, p. 200.
92. *New Dictionary* (New Delhi, Amerind, 1972), p. 1274.
93. *Critics and Criticism*, p. 4.

2

The Chicago Criticism as Humanistic Criticism

I

As the Chicago School of Criticism was started by a group of professors of the University of Chicago in middle thirties, it would be worth-while to examine their role in curricular reforms. There were two groups of professors of literature: The first focused its attention on facts of information and, the second was concerned with the analysis and evaluation of the text. Naturally, confrontation was inevitable between them. Howard Mumford Jones, in his essay "Literary Scholarship and Contemporary Criticism" attempted a defence of literary history and argued that the primary purpose of a literary scholar should be "historical, not aesthetic."[1] Another renowned scholar, John Livingston Lowes vigorously argued, that "the ultimate end of our research is criticism, in the fullest sense of an often misused word."[2] The issues raised by these great scholars were hotly debated in the academic circles; and the teachers of literature had to finally decide as to what would be the future policy of the department of English in the universities.

In this battle, the champions of literary history gradually lost their ground. In a way, Howard Mumford Jones accepts his defeat when he says "In offering these essays on literary history I am conscious of the unpopularity into which the form of criticism has fallen. The present cry is for criticism; and a rising generation of English scholars is nothing if not critical...."[3]

The historical approach to the study of literature was based on the blind faith that "a knowledge of the genesis and development of a thing is much the same as a knowledge of the thing itself."[4] It enriched literature in two ways: one, by shedding new lights on certain familiar works and, the other by resurrecting some neglected works. But in course of time, this approach lost sight of its original purpose, namely, illumination of a work of art. A literary text was treated as a linguistic exhibit, having only a documentary value. Drawing our attention to this ominous trend, F.R. White says "that the professors of English have drifted from literature into literary history... ."[5]

Therefore, a group of professors decided to reform the literary studies. In the beginning R.S. Crane and other champions of criticism had a common goal, that is to rescue 'criticism' from the dominance of literary historians. John Crowe Ransom, who later on became an enemy of the Chicago Critics, acknowledges that "If criticism should get a hearing in the universities, the credit would probably belong to Professor Ronald S. Crane, of the University of Chicago, more than to any other man. He is the first of the great professors to have advocated it as a major policy for departments of English."[6] The reformers of the literary studies, who after some time branched off into the Chicago Critics and the New Critics, were in the beginning equally unhappy with the performance of the scholars. The following comments of the contemporary critics raise serious charges against the professors of the English Department:

> The modern English department is notoriously easy to attack; and it is most obviously exposed to attack by the stupid, or trifling, or plainly muddle-headed books, articles, dissertations and these which its machinery commits to turn out. Even random quotations from exhibits allows one to make out a case against.[7]

> The average English professor bears living testimony to this. He has been trained (if he comes from one of our better universities) in linguistics and the history of literature. He possesses a great deal of information, valuable and interesting in its own right, and of incalculable value for a critic. But he himself is not that critic. He has little or no knowledge of the inner structure of a poem or a drama (this is not to say that he does not know the past critical generalizations on it); he is ignorant of its architecture; in short, he often does not know how to read it.[8]

> The vast majority of scholars are devoting their attention to the accumulation of facts about books and authors and taking up for granted the end for which these facts ought to be augmented. They habitually look on the critical activity which concerns itself with that end as at best pleasantly idle and at worst dangerous. Their very considerable ability is being devoted rather to the very ingenious,

> immensely complicated, pseudo-scientific game of scholarship in the conventional sense.[9]
>
> To all of us, furthermore, it is today apparent that we English teachers who have only a pedlar's pack of assorted facts about books and authors, their categories, times and influences, with critics' conflicting appraisals of their sacrosanct and therefore sterilized ideas and a private personality, which is dignified and valued but as little as possible committed in our teaching, must start a new and dangerous composing or we shall presently stand trembling, holding the rifted bag.[10]

All these comments show that the professors of literature were greatly dominated by literary historians.

As I mentioned at the very beginning, the historical scholars mainly pre-occupied themselves with the following questions regarding a work of art; Who wrote the work? When did he write it? Whence? What did he write?—that is, what words in what order? Out of what antecedent materials? For what purpose or audience? With what effects? In order to answer these factual questions, the historical scholars made inquiries into texts, sources, conventions, influences, and the like. Thus they concerned themselves with facts more than the questions of value. But Crane points out that "the matters we study in criticism are intrinsically matters of value—rather than merely matters of fact."[11] The opposition in principle between the two fields is made clear here. But, the questions of "fact" and the questions of "value" are not really separated from, or opposed to, each other. The desire to imitate the objectivity of science, led the literary scholars to rely on facts. The fake scientific methodology of the more elaborate kind, on the one hand, saved criticism from being impressionistic, but on the other hand, it spoiled its normative character. For the literary scholars, dominated by the historical method or the pseudo-scientific method, the question of value-judgment became most important.

It is easier for such a scholar to tell what the 18th century critics thought of a particular poem and why and what the 19th century critics thought and said. On being asked, he will find out the opinion of the 20th century critics by using a questionnaire and comptometer to get the answer; but he would not be able to explain what he himself thinks of that very poem and why? Cleanth Brooks, Jr. felt as early as 1942:

> That English department will have to forgo the pleasures of being "scientific." (This does not mean that it has to divorce itself from intelligence or collapse into impressionistic "moonings.") But it is

> high time for it to give up its search for an easy way out of problems. There is no substitute for imagination (tainted with subjectivity though it may be); and there is no substitute for the inculcation of the discipline of reading (a discipline that involves active critical judgment).
>
> The uncritical pursuit of "facts," the piling up of verified knowledge, the gathering of the historical data—these things however laudable in themselves, are essentially sidelines. If the profession lacks and interest in literature as literature, they may become blind alleys. Some of us feel that is what they have already become.[12]

In a way, the leaders of the New Criticism and the 'Chicago School of Criticism' wanted that historical method should be discarded in the study of literary works. They unanimously held that the defects of this method could be remedied by critical training in the architectonic of literature, rather than by mere training in literary history.

> The location of "mere" is important; for it is hardly possible to have training in criticism without training in vacuum. Literary history we shall scarcely avoid if we are to read literature of the past at all. On the other hand, it is possible to have literary history and no critical discipline; as a matter of fact, that is what we now have.[13]

So, the problem was what to do with literary history in criticism, whether to dispense with it completely or to use it as little as possible. Those who set up "criticism in rather sharp antithesis to be established modes of literary scholarship"[14] are described as "radical reformers" by R.S. Crane. They wanted the reform of the teaching of literature in a "root and branch way." It is they who were later on christened as the New Critics in 1941 by John Crowe Ransom in one of his critical essays. Prominent among them were John Crowe Ransom, R.P. Blackmur, Yvor Winters, and R.P. Warren who frequently wrote in *The Kenyon Review* and *The Sewanee Review* in the 40's. By 1950's, they completely controlled the classrooms of the universities where the practice of close textual analysis came to stay. In the first edition of *Understanding Poetry*, in a "Letter to the Teacher," as Walter Sutton mentions "the editors reject such substitutes for the study of the poem as 'paraphrase of logical and narrative content,' 'study of biographical and historical materials,' and 'inspirational and didactic interpretation.'" This anthology stimulated immense interest in textual criticism, the art of explicating poem on the page, without taking into account the biographical and other social factors that might have influenced the making of the poem.

The close textual analysis, according to R.S. Crane, is indeed an indispensable foundation, for the critics. But, the 'formal analysis of the text as suggested in *Understanding Poetry* is limited in the sense that it attempts only a sensitive grammatical interpretation of texts, deliberately eschewing the non-textual elements. Thus they revolutionized the teaching of literature by boldly reorienting it from the historical to the critical. They almost tried to separate the "critical" from the "historical." As a matter of fact, R.S. Crane himself favoured such a line of reform in his essay "History versus Criticism" as early as 1936, when he along with others had actively campaigned for the revival of criticism in the universities.[15] Such a stand had purely a "political justification two decades ago, but surely no other justification then or since."[16] He felt that the stand taken by the "radical reformers of the literary study" had done great disservice not only to criticism but also to historical scholarship "by continuing to talk in terms of the antithesis between the two."[17]

R.S. Crane, being a "progressive-conservative"[18] reformer of literary studies tried "to reconstruct university literary studies in a spirit of conservative reform: carrying on and reinvigorating the philological and historical tradition, and at the same time, and in this context, developing what that tradition had been relatively weak in—systematic training in the various modes of critical analysis and judgment."[19]

Crane adopted a "middle-of-the-road policy" to preserve the best elements of the two traditions. Therefore, Crane attempting a true description of his own critical programme writes: "The 'critical' is there, assuredly, but so also is 'historical,' and in such a relation to the 'critical,' in intention at least, that neither can be separated from the other."[20] Thus we find that R.S. Crane is dead against the complete rejection of literary history which the New Critics propagated. His views are summed up below in his own words:

> Literary history, I should insist, is a good thing, and it is surely one of our functions to see that its values are safeguarded in the academic world of the culture. As a handmaid to criticism its importance is much less than has sometimes seen thought, but one can easily go too far in contemning the real services, humble as they may be and in many real services, humble as they may be and in many respects chiefly negative, which it is capable of offering to the interpreter of literary works.[21]

Further, Crane points out that the ultimate value of literary history does not lie only in "its value to literary criticism, but the contributions it can make, along with its sister discipline the literary history of ideas, to what everyone will grant is a major concern of any university—the general history of culture."[22] In the second section of this Chapter, it will be shown how 'history of ideas' is one of the four constituent elements of the 'humanities,' essential for the evaluation of the humanistic properties of a literary work. Therefore, literary history should not be discarded altogether by a critic.

What Crane wanted is simply a change in emphasis on the historical scholarship which had occupied too privileged a place in the universities during his time. He was conscious that literary research, instead of becoming original inquiries of all sorts, had become "inquires among documents pursued for strictly historical ends."[23] Pointing out the main defects of the contemporary literary studies, Crane observes:

> We have been accustomed to lecture, to undergraduates as well as to graduates, on details of biography, on the genesis and development of "types," on the social backgrounds and the stylistic and intellectual tendencies characteristic of the "periods" of literary growth. We have allowed ourselves to consider, in suggesting subjects for dissertation, only problems for which the historical method provides the appropriate solution. We have tended, in our examination for higher degrees and in many of our more elementary examinations as well, to subordinate questions about the artistic qualities of texts to questions of a bibliographical or historical nature about writers and the movement of which they were a part. And it is no secret that the scholars in our departments who have attained the highest academic distinctions and who have had the greatest influence in the shaping of our programmes have been with few exceptions men whose competence has been chiefly demonstrated by their contributions to historical learning.[24]

As a result of such a faulty teaching of literature, only "esthetic barbarians,"[25] as R.S. Crane would like to call those students who were trained in the schools and universities of America in the 30's, were produced. R.S. Crane painfully admits:

> That the majority of the freshmen who come to us from the schools are unable to read a page of poetry or a serious play with any comprehension, I will not say of the subtleties of its form, but even of its plainest literal sense. But it is our fault that of the seniors who have had the advantage of majoring in our departments and of taking and passing our courses, and almost equally large proportion show themselves, when put to the test, to be in little better case—more widely read, no doubt, and historically much better informed, but

similarly incapable of intelligently discussing an imaginative work in terms of appropriate to its nature.[26]

According to R.S. Crane, a critic should make only minimal use of the historical data, "subject to the law of diminishing return";[27] because the philological and historical researches can sharpen the critic's observation to some extent, but they would not help him in judging the aesthetic value of a literary work. The genetic and historical investigations help a critic only in an incidental and negative way. Researches in literary history cannot be treated as a 'fundamental requisite' of criticism. A literary work cannot be approached merely as a historical event. They are primarily works of art and the products of imaginative visionary creation. Essays in biography, in source-study, in the development of literary themes, and the like only illuminate the genetic and narrative aspects of a literary work. The "narrative propositions"[27] of literary history inform us about the change in the habits, beliefs, attitudes, tastes and purposes of persons or group of persons or social organizations of a particular period or place. They explain only the "accidental characteristics"[28] of literature and do not tell us anything about the nature of such universal terms as tragedy or lyric poetry as art forms. Owing to this reason, the narrative propositions of literary history remain indifferent to the question of value, which is of prime importance in literary criticism. Crane says that "Criticism is essentially a discipline concerned with the analysis and evaluation of particular literary works in the light of general principles of esthetics...."[29] Crane's new programme of literary studies was to be directed towards criticism and not literary history, with a view to producing "good judges of literature and not merely learned men."[30] The remedial programme which he proposed was to be a thorough-going revision in the policy of the English department of the University of Chicago. At the graduate level, limited provision for seminars in literary history and the history of ideas was to be made, with a view to improving the general historical culture of students. The courses in political history, social history, and the history of thought were to be introduced to improve the background knowledge of students in the light of which they would assess the merit of individual literary works. The new programme was to comprise systematic training in theory, generally of all the fine arts, especially of the art of literature; and it was to be imparted by the department of humanities as a whole. It was to be based on a critical discussion of the principles of esthetic theories to be found in poetry, music and the plastic arts of the Greeks and their own contemporaries. Apart from giving a thorough grounding in esthetic theories, it also included exercises in literary explication of literary texts. Crane's programme of literary studies reflects the new conception of humanistic subject matter and method, which was developed at the College of the University of Chicago in the 30's. The objectives of the curriculum of the College of the University of Chicago were mainly three: (1) "increasing the experience of students with the great products of the arts by the examination of a considerable body of the best works in the fields of literature, the visual arts, and music; (2) training students in the exercise of analytical methods appropriate to humanistic ends; and (3) training students in the use of the arts of criticism which will enable them to recognize some of the differences in values ascribed to works and the kinds of interpretations of the arts which lead to the assertion of these values and, in the light of this recognition, to make responsible and sensitive criticisms." The curriculum of the humanities included three courses. The Humanities[31] was to enlarge the experience of the students with music and visual arts, as well as development of easy analytical skills. The Humanities[32] comprised development of systematic methods of analysis of different literary forms. The Humanities[33] was to focus on the arts of literary criticism, by teaching such literary texts which treat of the philosophic bases of the arts, others which treat of a critical method; and some which apply principles of criticism to particular works, for example, Croce's *Aesthetic,* Aristotle's *Poetics* and Plato's *Phaedrus.*

The origin of the 'Chicago School of criticism' appears to be linked up with the educational reforms of the Chicago University in the 30's and 40's. The scheme of general education was first launched in 1930-31 which remained unaltered until 1942. Between 1942 and 1952 it was subjected to minor changes.[34] Russel Thomas, a professor of the University of Chicago, mentions that "the decision in 1942 to abandon the historical approach to the study of the humanities was not taken lightly, and without appreciation of the place of history in the total programme of general education."[35] R.S. Crane's famous essay "History *Versus* Criticism in the Study of Literature"[36] (1935) shows the impact of the decision of the academicians of Chicago University. Crane's approach to literary studies seems to have been influenced by the content and aim of the "three courses" which were introduced in the Department of the Humanities at the University of Chicago in 1942.

According to Russell Thomas the "three courses" were as follows:

> The first of the three courses was planned as an introduction to the arts: music, visual arts, and the poetic or, as they are sometimes called, the imaginative forms of literature. The second course, though restricted entirely to literature, is concerned with major modes of

> literary expression and interpretation. I extend the study of the poetic forms begun in the first course, and enlarges the scope of the students' experience through the study of historical, philosophical, and rhetoric works. The third course is an introduction to the principles and practice of criticism of the arts; it has been developed and taught co-operatively by the humanities staff, the English staff, and the foreign language staff of the college (1942-48).

Russell Thomas writes: "We agreed, too, that in each course and at all times the particular work of art ought to be the principal object of study. Each work of any kind should therefore be chosen not merely because it was representative of a type, of historical period, or of any of the great ideas that have stirred the minds and emotions of men, but because it possessed values which were its own unique achievement."[37]

R.S. Crane, the founder of the 'Chicago School of criticism' joined the University of Chicago in 1924. Only a year before, Ernest Dewitt Burton had joined this University as President and initiated a faculty study on reorganizing the University's departmental structure and curriculum. This programme of general education was also actively pursued by President Max Mason but was fully implemented in the tenure of President Hutchins who took office in 1929. Naturally, R.S. Crane would have been fully exposed to the deliberations of these academicians who attempted to bring about a renaissance in higher education. Crane's attitude towards the use of historical scholarship appears to be the result of his view of the nature of the humanities and literary study.

II

In the preceding section, it has been shown how Crane attempted to minimize the importance of historical scholarship in order to preserve the normative character of contemporary criticism. In this section, I would like to place R.S. Crane's idea of literary criticism in the context of his concept of the humanities and show how he attempted to play down the dominance of the scientific methods in literary studies.

Again, in this very remedial venture, R.S. Crane and Cleanth Brooks, have a striking similarity. Both of them were deeply concerned with question of the survival of the humanities in a scientific age. Brooks observed that the survival of literary study as such is part of the general problem of reviving the humanities in our day and that the humanities can survive only by making normative judgments.[38] In 1935, the birth-year of the Chicago School of criticism, R.S. Crane was also deeply worried about the fate of literary criticism, which he considered to be a humanistic art in the universities dominated by science and history.[39] For Crane the 'factual sciences' include not only the natural and social sciences but also all the methods used in the humanities to provide the factual information which is essential to understand and judge the objects of the humanities.

R.S. Crane maintains that scientific methods are inappropriate for the study of humanistic works. What disturbed R.S. Crane most in the thirties was that a good many leading scholars of his time relied upon the methods of natural and social sciences.

Howard Mumford Jones went to the extent of saying "that the superiority of modern humanistic scholarship over that of the past is due 'to the adoption [in the last fifty years] of scientific methodology in the appreciation of literary history and philosophy.' "[40] I.A. Richards declared that rhetoric or interpretation, as he calls it, is "essentially a branch of biology."[41] Thomas Pollock, in 'The Nature of Literature,' observed that literary criticism should be reconstituted "in terms which are consonant with our contemporary knowledge of language and with the development of modern science."[42] The unhumanistic approach to humanistic studies was a matter of great concern to R.S. Crane. This is clear from his following statement:

> I have met many humanists (in the sense of professors of the so-called humanistic subjects), or have read their works, who have seemed to me much less humanistic, in their essential ways of thinking, than these scientific friends. They are the students of language who refuse to entertain any questions of better or worse in speech; they are the philosophers who want to make philosophy a branch of mathematics; the historians who insist on explaining all human events in terms of impersonal social or natural forces; the professors of literature and the critics who would resolve the appreciation of literature into a play of the unconscious mind and the literary texts themselves into vestiges of primitive ritual and myth. I don't mean to say that in doing any or all of these things the humanists I have in mind have not given us valuable insights into the subjects they deal with. The point is not that. The point is merely that if we wish to be clear about what the humanities are, as distinguished from the sciences of nature and society, we won't get very far if we are content to identify the humanities merely with a certain list of subjects in the curriculum and let it go at that, you can study Greek or philosophy all your life and not be a humanist....[43]

Therefore Crane suggested certain reforms of the humanistic studies which were dominated by science. Science, as he observed at several places, in its effort to form general laws ignore the richness of the objects that it studies, while it is the objective of the humanities to accentuate 'uniqueness' and 'richness.'

Now, let us see how Crane's idea of the humanities gave a new orientation to literary studies by discrediting the use of scientific methods. A scientist is always after something that is reducible to a common denominator.[44] "The sciences," says Crane, "seek to move from the diversity and particularity of their observations towards as high a degree of unity, uniformity, simplicity, and necessity as their materials permit."[45] Pointing out the limitations of a scientist Wayne C. Booth, a disciple of Crane, observes that "the scientific student of man will want to discover precisely what men in general must do or tend generally to do. But in general, even playwrights in general, do not tend to write plays like *King Lear*."[46] Elder Olson, another leading Chicago Critic, almost echoes Crane's views when he says:

> All sciences...depend upon the suppositions of constancy...what possible constancy can be found in art? Hydrogen explodes under certain conditions, anyone who fulfils those conditions, animal or man, willingly or unwillingly, will explode it; but whether a tragedy at all, is entirely dependent on the skill and genius of the poet; the forms of the individual works of art are never predictable from an inspection of their medium; the very painter who produced good painting last month now produces one which is bad; and so on. On the contrary, art is always individual; an individual work is produced by an individual artist, and of the individual there is no science.[47]

But a literary work, being a human production, possesses uniqueness, unexpectedness, complexity and originality that cannot be discovered through scientific methods. These elements can only be appreciated by humanistic approach, as Crane conceived. "Surely one of the tasks of the humanities" says Wayne C. Booth "is to come to terms with such wondrously uncommon creation as escape the generalizing mind because they are not, as the scientists say of their experiments, replicable."[48]

But before the remedial character of the humanities is discussed, Crane's idea of the humanities is explained here.

Since the Renaissance several attempts have been made by the humanists to define the humanities. In his long essay, "Shifting Definitions and Evaluations,"[49] R.S. Crane has surveyed at length what the humanities have been taken to be in the past by great humanists like Cicero, Quintillian, Juan Luis Vives, Sir Philip Sidney, John Milton,

Cardinal Newman, Matthew Arnold, Sir Thomas Elyot, John Stuart Mill, Walter Lippman and others and examines the adequacy of their definitions. Some of the humanists have identified the humanities with certain subject-matters or departments and some have equated them with certain purposes to be served by their study.[50]

To R.S. Crane their definitions appear to be defective on the following grounds: firstly, certain subject-matters, officially or conventionally considered to be the humanities, can be studied in ways that we would not consider as humanistic, and second, because the ends ascribed to the humanities are always stated in such general terms and are capable of being achieved by so many means that they cannot be used to create specific programmes of study. Analysing their defects, Crane writes:

> The great defect of all these attempts to define the humanities in terms of the useful or lofty ends they may be made to serve if their persistent vagueness about the means by which these ends are to be accomplished in the everyday affairs of education. We get from the writers who approach our question in this way a great deal of eloquent writing about what the humanities, or only the humanities, can do for us, but very little specific discussion of how they can be expected to do this—very little beyond the dogmatic statement that some subject-matters are more humanistic than others and hence ought to be studied.[51]

After rejecting the two most common ways of defining the humanities, Crane suggests a third way. His idea of the humanities is clearly based on a passage that occurs in *Attic Nights* by Aulus Gellius who was a minor Latin grammarian of the second century. He refers to the passage in this book[52] where the term "humanities" was used in a special sense, meaning *eruditionem institutionemque in bonas artes* (education and training in the good arts).

Cf. "Those who have spoken Latin and have used the language correctly do not give the word humanities the meaning which it is commonly thought to have, namely, what the Greek called philanthropia, signifying a kind of friendly spirit and good-feeling towards all men without distinction; but they gave to humanities about the force of the Greek paideia; that is, what we call, *eruditionem institutionemque in bonas artes*, or "education and training in the good arts." Those who earnestly desire and seek after these are most highly humanized (*maximi humanissimi*). For the pursuit of that kind of knowledge and the training given by it, have been granted to man alone of all the animals and for that reason it is termed humanitas or "humanity" (Quoted on p. 23, *The Humanities*, I, 23).

The concept of the humanities, as suggested by Gellius describes 'humanities' simply as "education and training in the good arts or disciplines."[53] Crane's idea of the humanities is summed up below in his own words:

> It is a view that identifies the humanities, not with certain subjects of study merely, or with the pursuit of certain abstract ends, but with the proper cultivation of certain arts or disciplines, that is, of certain means; and it makes the humanistic character of such arts or methods to consist in their peculiar capacity to deal with those aspects of human experience that differentiate men most completely from the animals, to the end that individual men may actualize as fully as possible their potentialities as men. But what are the aspects of human experience that distinguish men most completely, now and in the past, from the animals? I think the answer is not hard to give. They consist, generally, in all those things which, because no all men or all groups or men can, or do, do them, are therefore not amenable to adequate explanation in terms of general laws of natural process, physical or biological, or in terms of collective social conditions or forces. They are the things which we cannot predict, in any scientific way, that men individually or in groups will do, but which, when they are done, we recognize as signs, not of any natural or social necessities, but of possibilities inherent in man's peculiar nature. They are, in short, what we commonly speak of as human achievements—whether in sciences, in institutions, or in the arts. And, more especially, they are those human achievements, like Newtonian or modern physics, the American Constitution, or Shakespearean tragedy, to which we agree in attributing that kind of unprecedented excellence that calls forth wonder as well as admiration.[54]

III

In brief, "the humanities," writes Crane, "are...co-extensive with the arts or methods that enable us to isolate these aspects (humanistic properties of human achievements) for our appreciation and use."[55] The four humanistic methods or "good arts" are mutually supplementary.[56] It is convergence of all of them upon any subject-matter that makes it, in the complete degree humanistic.[57]

Crane discusses the nature and the scope of the 'four arts' as given below:

> There are the arts, first of all, of language, comprising the many varied techniques we have for dealing with the symbolic media in which

the achievements of men are embodied or through which they reach us, from grammar in the ordinary sense, through prosody, rhetoric, the simpler parts of logic, and textual criticism, to the refinements of modern linguistics. There are the arts, in the second place, of which the special province is the analysis and appreciation of ideas—of the conceptions and reasons, of all kinds, which men have expressed either in the elaborate forms of philosophic, scientific, and religious systems or more informally in works of literature and fine art. In the third place, there are the arts of literary and artistic criticism—the numerous devices at our disposal for grasping and appreciating the esthetic structures which men have made. And, finally, there are the arts that give us knowledge and understanding of the particular historical situations and causes in the midst of which the objects of humanistic study have emerged.[58]

The four humanistic arts: linguistics (in the broad sense of the word); the analysis of ideas (those which explore ideas and relations); literary and artistic criticism (those which help appreciation of artistic structures); and historiography are to be developed and applied simultaneously, as analytical tools. "Wherever any of them," says Crane, "...is exalted over the others the humanities are threatened." Commenting upon the usefulness of them, Crane writes, "The various different arts of the humanities all have a distinctive work to do, which no one of them can do alone; the ideal is one of free co-operation among them upon the concrete objects of the humanistic study; and this ideal is always in peril when philologists fight for their supremacy with philosophers, historians with critics or critics with historians."[59]

Thus we find that Crane's concept of the humanities was essentially remedial in nature as it aimed at correcting the errors of the methods which were applied in literary studies during the 30's. On the one hand, it exposes the inappropriateness of the scientific methods as applied in literary studies and, on the other hand, it points out that criticism should not be completely divorced from literary history.

NOTES

1. *The Humanities* I, 7-8.
2. See Anlus Gellius, *The Attic Nights*, trans. Tohm C. Rolfe II.
3. Quoted in Crane's "History *versus* Criticism in the Study of Literature," *The Humanities*, II, 3.
4. *Ibid.*, p. 3.
5. Howard Mumford Jones, "The Literary Spirit of Each Age," *The Theory of American Literature*, Cornell Univ. Press, 1965, p. 1.

6. See Frederic R. White, "Historical Studies and the Humanist," *College English*, II, (February, 1941), 571.
7. *Ibid*., p. 571.
8. John Crowe Ransom, "Criticism Inc.," *American Literary Criticism*, ed. by Clicksberg (New York, 1951), p. 456.
9. Cleanth Brooks, Jr., "Literature and the Professors," *Kenyon Review*, Vol. II, No. 4 (1940), 403.
10. *Ibid*., p. 405.
11. Arthur Mizener, "Literature and the Professors: II Scholars as Critics," *Kenyon Review*, II (Autumn, 1940), 422.
12. Sidney Cox, "Literature and the Professors: III, "If We Care *Enough*," *Kenyon Review*, II (Autumn, 1940), 428.
13. *The Humanities*, II, 28.
14. Cleanth Brooks, Jr., *Kenyon Review*, Winter (1942), 412-13.
15. Cleanth Brooks, Jr., "*Literature and the Professors*," *Kenyon Review*, Vol. II, No. 4 (1940), 406.
16. *The Humanities*, p. 26.
17. *Modern American Criticism*, New Jersey, Prentice-Hall, Inc., 1963, p. 116.
18. Cf. It was probably inevitable that the early enthusiasts for this revolution in the academic study of literature should tend to set criticism in rather sharp antithesis to the established modes of literary scholarship. I did it myself, in 1935, in the essay [History *versus* Criticism] [...] I should not want, even twenty years later, to repudiate all I said in that paper, certainly not its central thesis of the importance of criticism or the whole of the analysis of which I distinguished criticism from literary history. *The Humanities*, II, 25-26.
13. *Ibid*., p. 27.
14. *Ibid*., p. 27.
15. *Ibid*., p. 26.
16. *Ibid*., p. 27.
17. *Ibid*., p. 27.
18. *Ibid*., p. 19.
19. *Ibid*., pp. 19-20.
20. *Ibid*., p. 21.
21. *Ibid*., p. 21.
22. *Ibid*., p. 22.
23. *Ibid*., p. 21.
24. *Ibid*., p. 16.
25. *Ibid*., p. 6.
26. *Ibid*., p. 7.
27. *Ibid*., p. 16.
28. *Ibid*., p. 19.

29. Russell Thomas, "The Humanities," *The Idea and Practice of General Education* (Chicago: The University of Chicago, 1950), p. 103.
30. *Ibid.*, p. 103.
31. *Ibid.*, pp. 105-06.
32. See Russell Thomas, *The Search for a Common Learning: General Education, 1800-1960* (New York, 1962), pp. 82-84.
33. Russell Thomas, "Humanities in the University of Chicago" *The Humanities in General Education*, ed. James A. Fischer (Wm. C. Brown Company Publishers, Iowa, 1960), p. 27.
34. First published in the *English Journal* (College Edition), Vol. 24 (1935), reprinted in *The Humanities*, I, 3.
35. Russell Thomas, "Humanities in the University of Chicago," *The Humanities in General Education*, ed. James A. Fischer (Wm. C. Brown Company Publishers, Iowa, 1960), p. 127.
36. *Ibid.*, p. 127.
37. "History Versus Criticism in the Study of Literature," *The Humanities*, II.
38. *The Humanities*, I, 20.
39. *Ibid.*, p. 21.
40. *Ibid.*, p. 21
41. *Ibid.*, pp. 4-5.
42. Wayne C. Booth, Introduction to *The Humanities*, I, XV-XVI.
43. Ibid., p. xv.
44. Ibid., p. xvi.
45. Elder Olson, "Education and the Humanities," I, *Pedagogia*, 1953, p. xvi.
46. *The Humanities*, I.
47. *Ibid.*, pp. 169-70.
48. *Ibid.*, pp. 4-6.
49. *The Humanities*, I, 7-8.
50. See Aulus Gellius, *The Attic Nights*, trans. John C. Rolfe, II (London, 1927), 457.
51. *The Humanities*, I.
52. *Ibid.*, p. 7.
53. *The Humanities*, I, 13-14 (parenthesis mine).
54. *Ibid.*, p. 13.
55. *Ibid.*, p. 13.
56. *Ibid.*, p. 10.
57. *The Humanities*, I, 12.
58. *Ibid.*, p. 13.
59. *Ibid.*, p. 23.

3

Quest for Remedial Criticism

I

The "radical reformers" of literary studies, says Crane, "were in revolt not merely against the limitations of the older learning but...against the very conception of the intellectual method."[1] The first aspect of the critical revolt was merely concerned with setting up antithesis between criticism and historical scholarship; but the second, with "a sharp and irreconcilable opposition in principle between the two fields."[2] In the field of historical scholarship, *a priori* reasoning was always distrusted by scholars. But, to Crane's great annoyance, in contemporary criticism, this mode of reasoning has been frequently used by the critics. He writes: "I am much more disturbed when I see confidence in *a priori* reasoning and 'ruling hypothesis' being erected into a principle of method, or at least an accepted habit of procedure, in studies of particular critical fact."[3] In his essay "Criticism as Inquiry;" or "The Perils of the 'High Priori Road,'" Crane explains at length the limitations of the *a priori* approach. The "high priori road," in the words of Crane, refers to too "high" a way which the contemporary critics often pursue. The expression suggests the imposition of aesthetics or critical theories from above. The ready-made approaches of the contemporary critics are "ways of arriving at particular conclusions which assume the relevance and authority, prior to concrete evidence, of theoretical doctrines or other general propositions concerning the subject-matters in question.[3]

In Crane's analysis the New Critics "do not need to creep up *a posteriori* to a little general knowledge. They can at once seize upon first principles, purporting to have a universal or approximately universal scope of application, and descend from these, armed with systems and arguments *a priori* "to the more particular problems that interest them, such as the special use of languages in poetry or the distinctive nature of the "meanings" which poetry conveys."[4]

There are two principal ways in which these New Critics acquire their "first principles." The first way is to derive the "primary concepts from other contemporary sciences"[5] and the second is to get them from dialectical reasoning. The psychological critics, both Freudian and Jungian, derive their critical concepts from recent developments in the field of psychology, myth and anthropology and the New Critics from the method of dialectical analysis. Both the ways of acquiring "first principles" in literary criticism are regarded as *a priori* approaches by Crane. The purpose of this Chapter will be to examine Crane's charges against the methodological limitations of the contemporary critics.

II

I shall first examine the limitation of the first type of *a priori* approach. The Freudian critics, Crane writes "tend to subsume literary works under (say) the theory of dreams, and thus get a ready-made system of symbolic interpretation in dreams of manifest and latent content in spite of the warnings of Freud himself, in his more scientific moments, against just this sort of thing."[6]

Let us briefly analyse this remark and note the points that matter. Can literary works be completely subsumed under the theory of dreams? Art, as the psycho-analysts tell us, is a kind of phantasy. And phantasy, Freud tells us, "is sanctioned by general human consent, and every hungry soul looks to it for comfort and consolation."[7] Phantasy provides an opportunity for our wish-fulfilment.

Day-dreams, being a form of phantasy, gratify our egotistic cravings and erotic desires. It is these day-dreams which, according to Freud, "form the raw material of poetic production for the writer by transforming, disguising, or curtailing them creates out of his day-dreams the situations which he embodies in his stories, novels and dreams."[8] Psycho-analysis, which is based on the theory of dreams, cannot be a useful tool in the hands of a literary critic. The provinces of psycho-analysis and literary criticism are not the same, as the subject-matters of the two are different. Herbert Read also observes:

> Psychology is concerned with the processes of mental activity, literary criticism with the product. The psychologists only analyses the product to arrive at the process; art is, from this point of view, as significant as any other expression of mentality. But of no more significance: its significance does not correspond to its values as

> literature. The psychologist is indifferent to literary values (too often, alas, even in his own work), and many even definitely deplore them, especially when they represent the trimmings of subjective phantasis under the influence of some objective standard or tradition.[9]

In fact, the essential nature of literary criticism always lies outside the province of psycho-analysis. Psycho-analysis does not throw light on the artistic gift. It simply supplies information about the artistic technique, which may not be always relevant from the point of view of literary criticism: A psycho-analyst is primarily interested in mental process of the artist as psychic being and not in the literary values of his creation. As such, for him, a bad work of art and a good work of art, are equally significant. But a literary critic has to judge the success or failure of the work he analyses. He is primarily interested in evaluation. Psycho-analysis is a science. Hence its methods lack the normative character which is essential for literary criticism. The business of criticism, as it is commonly held, is to compare and evaluate experiences and not to merely explain them with scientific precision, as the psycho-analysts do in the light of their sophisticated theories. Thus the psycho-analytical methods cannot always help the critic in his main business. They help him only indirectly and incidentally, if at all. Crane rightly observes:

> No literary work is other than what it is or better or worse than it is because of any circumstances of its origin or of any personal peculiarities of its author.... If information about any of these matters helps the critic to approach his author more sympathetically or with fewer prejudices, well and good; it has thereby justified itself in a humble and negative way.[10]

A literary work may contain symbols and a symbolic interpretation may be useful in specific cases, but not always. Crane writes: "Our theory may tell us, for instance, that poetry is or tends to be symbolic; but there is nothing in this proposition, whatever its dialectical guarantees, that warrants us, as scholars, in saying more than that there may perhaps be symbols in the poem before us."[11] Again, he clearly states that "If a non-symbolic interpretation makes adequate sense of the text and, all other things considered, is relatively more probable, then anything we may believe about symbolism and poetry in general is beside the point. And the same would be true of a symbolic interpretation that satisfied the same requirements." I quite agree with Crane that to keep faith in the universal applicability of the method, of symbolic interpretation, as most of the psychological critics do, is an absurdity. It is sometimes rightly suggested by some critics that Keats's *The Eve of St. Agnes* and *La belle dame sans merci* manifest the longings and disillusionment of the poet. But, when it is said that all his poems have the same sort of things, it sounds quite absurd. It is one thing to say that it always consciously or unconsciously expresses his repressed desires and feelings is something that sounds preposterous. To apply ready-made formulas like 'Oedipus Complex,' 'Electra Complex' etc. to all kinds of literary works is an *a priori* approach, which Crane severely criticizes.

The literary critics, who are influenced by Jung, also go the Freudian critics' way. Their assumptions are based on the Jungian principles and the findings of anthropology. As such, according to Crane, they hold that the structure and the emotional appeal of great literary works are functions primarily of the psychological and ritualistic 'archetypes' which they necessarily embody and of which the detection in individual works is a simple matter of applying tables of symbolic meaning known in advance: this, again, in spite of repeated statements by Jung that "that which constitutes the essential nature of art must always lie outside the province of analytical psychology."[12]

Maud Bodkin, who accepts Jung as her guide, wrote a book *Archetypal Patterns in Poetry* (1934), under his direct influence. In this book, she applies the theory of "Primordial images" or archetypes—"the psychic residua of numberless experiences of the same type" set forth in Jung's famous essay "On the Relation of Analytical Psychology to Poetic Art," in *Contributions to Analytical Psychology* (1928). She searches out archetypal patterns in Woolf's *Orlando*, Eliot's *The Waste Land*, Coleridge's *The Rime of the Ancient Mariner* etc. The "rebirth archetype" is commonly applied by other myth critics as a ready-made formula of literary criticism. For the myth critics in general, literary critics in general, literary criticism becomes merely a search for archetypes. Joseph Campbell reduces all mythic patterns to a mono-myth in his book *The Hero with a Thousand Faces* (1949). Kenneth Burke attempts an archetypal interpretation in his essay "Symbolic Action in a Poem by Keats" which is incorporated in his book *A Grammar of Motives* (1945).

The vogue of symbolic interpretation of literary works has been wrongly applied, out of sheer enthusiasm, to certain works which do not require it. Certainly many such critics have been interested more in their critical theories than in literary works before them and have fashioned procrustean beds, each to his own measurement, instead of doing the more open and empirical job that is demanded of criticism. "In such cases the primary concern with the *a priori* to the neglect of thing itself does construct too 'high' a way for criticism and still remain literary criticism."[13]

Elder Olson, reviewing an article by Robert Penn Warren, a leading New Critic, exposes the limitation of an unwarranted symbolic interpretation of Coleridge's *The Rime of Ancient Mariner*. He argues in his essay "A Symbolic Reading of the Ancient Mariner" that if by "symbolic" we mean merely the more particular as revealing the more universal, which is all that Coleridge seems to intend, we need not quarrel. But if by any interpretation of the term we commit ourselves, as does Warren to an exegesis of how one thing in Coleridge must always mean something else, we are exceeding our evidence."[14] Olson points out that nowhere in Coleridge's critical writings there is any discussion of 'symbol,' as Warren develops for the discussion of this poem. Warren says that for Coleridge a symbol is "focal, massive, and not arbitrary."[15] But Warren, according to Olson, fails to follow his own line of argument.

Warren should have shown, as Olson remarks "that the moon is the symbol of the imagination; but he does not—and, in fact, it is not. All such interpretation is really uncontrolled analogy; the double themes, their fusions, and the multivalent symbols permit anyone to make of the poem whatever he may choose."[16]

III

As I have already pointed out, the second way of deriving "first principles" is based on dialectical reasoning, so an analysis of the dialectical method is essential to find out its chief defects.

The dialectical reasoning proceeds typically by devices of division and composition. It begins by laying down some general postulates, such as, poetry is the polar opposite of science, and, then, it proceeds to work out logically all the implications of this major premise. Crane calls it the "other scientific method"[17] in the Humeian sense. In the dialectical method, a general abstract principle is first established which is then branched out into a variety of inferences and conclusions. Finally, such conclusions are applied to the work that a literary critic examines. Cleanth Brooks concludes that the language of poetry is the language of "paradox."[18] In *The Well Wrought Urn*, he applies this test to several poems.

The dialectical analysis is a method of dichotomous division in which "one thing is paired against another at different levels of generality throughout... ."[19] The New Critics begin by fixing upon some familiar type of verbal expression which is admittedly "not-poetry." According to them, non-poetic verbal matter includes plain prose, prose, discursive prose, "rational" prose, and scientific prose. They define poetry negatively.

In contrast to the words of prose, the words of poetry are emotive, or evocative of attitudes and feelings, rather than directly referential.[20]

The New Critics have employed the dialectical mode in literary criticism in two principal ways: either, constructively or negatively. The critics who tend to give a "constructive" account of poetry, first reduce poetry to its common properties, for instance, "paradox" or "ambiguity." The critics who give a "reductive" account of poetry, interpret poetry 'reductively,' in terms of something assumed to be far more primitive and basic in human experience, for example, archetypes and rituals. In the first mode, the critic employs the method constructively, "by retaining the basic oppositions afforded by the model but showing that they are inevitably particularized and qualified as they manifest themselves in more differentiated forms... ."[21] In the second mode, the critic employs it "by arguing that the literary object he is concerned with is 'nothing' but the more simple or general model to which it is referred (as in much contemporary psychoanalytic and 'archetypal' criticism)... ."[22] The first mode is based on negative analogy, the second is based on positive analogy.

For the first group of critics, the meaning of words in poetry is born out of a paradoxical "tension" in poems between the logical and counter-logical possibilities of speech and rhythm; and, for the second group, it is determined by "archetypes," the extralogical or pre-logical types of language.[23]

Thus, we may state that the first stage of this method is the assumption of a general abstract principle by a critic which serves as a postulate. Invariably, it is the distinction between two kinds of discourse, poetic and scientific, that I.A. Richards distinguished in his book[24] *Principles of Literary Criticism* as early as 1924. Since then, critics, in the line of I.A. Richards, have been expressing their exclusive concern with those aspects of poetry, considered as a homogeneous kind of thing, that are isolated when we make poetry a mode of discourse sharply opposed in its materials and methods to science.

Therefore, the initial problem of New Critics in theorizing is always a negative one, that is of distinguishing poetic language from scientific language. They proceed by fixing upon some familiar type of verbal expression which is admittedly not poetry and then derive the distinctive attributes (for example paradox) and structural patterns of poetry (symbol etc.) by dialectical comparison. After stating that 'poetry' is 'not-science' or 'poetic language' is 'not-scientific' language, they look for other significant extremes of differences. As a result of that they get a series of contraries, which yield differentiae of poetry. "In the table of contraries thus established," Crane points out that "one column will be headed 'poetry' and the other column 'not-poetry' or something else more specific such as 'science' or 'logical discourse,' and in this way a definition of poetry with a differentia signifying what is special to its language or content or both will be set up as a means of selecting the referents of the critic's propositions."[25]

Mr. Ransom employed this sort of dialectical reasoning in arriving at a definition of poetry in his book *The World's Body*. If we analyse the essays of this book, we find that the foundation of his poetic theory is laid on dialectical reasoning.[26]

First, a general hypothesis or supposition concerning man and his possible relations to the world of concrete things is made. Now, according to this hypothesis the fundamental opposition in human life is found to be between "the impulse to use, take and 'devour' things in the interest of conceptual knowledge and practical or 'economic' action and the impulse to contemplate and love things in all their 'wild' particularity for their own sake."[27] From this inherent opposition in man's life, proceed, "by strictly logical disjunction and equation, a whole series of more particular oppositions—between 'idea' and 'image' ('An idea is derivative and tamed. The image is in the natural or wild state, and it has to be discovered there, not put there, obeying its own law and none of ours'); between science, as one extreme, and religion, manners, and art, as the others; between poetry 'of feelings,' (in which, 'the subject does not really, propose to lose himself into the object') and 'metaphysical poetry' (which, starting with feelings, tends to 'objectify these imaginatively into external action') and so on."[28] Thus, the process of dichotomous division goes on in a dialectical analysis and pairs of contraries come out of it. The starting-point of all such speculations is the dialectical opposition between the two human: impulses. In the pairs of contraries, the derivatives of the two opposing impulses, continue throughout the analysis. "Science and art are thus necessarily contraries but not wholly exclusive of one another: Science gratifies a rational or practical impulse and exhibits the minimum of perception. Art gratifies a perceptual impulse and exhibits the minimum of reason.' And so with poetry 'The poetic impulse is not free'...there must be some element of 'science' in it if only in its metre—'yet it holds out stubbornly against science for the enjoyment of its images.' "[29] The necessary inference of this sort of dialectical reasoning yields a differentia of poetry that is "a composite of 'logical structure' (science we must have some concepts if we are to grasp anything) and of 'irrelevant texture' (science the differentia of poetry is that it gives us, in opposition to science, the 'world's body' rather than merely ideas about)."[30] Thus, on the basis of Crane's analysis, a brief-sketch of Mr. Ransom's procedure has been given here. Mr. Ransom's well-known contention that any good poem is a composite of a 'logical texture' and an 'irrelevant local texture' and is based upon a kind of dialectical reasoning.

"Logical structure" (prose) is the prerequisite of the "irrelevant local texture" (poetry) in some degree. Mr. Ransom considers the opposition between "logical structure" and "irrelevant local texture" as a necessary formulation of the nature of all poems. He employs this particular pair of contrary terms in the analysis of Marvell's "To his Coy Mistress" and believes that it can be universally employed in practical criticism.

Other good examples of dialectical analysis may be found in Cleanth Brooks's [statement) in *The Well Wrought Urn* that the language of poetry is 'the language of paradox,' in Charles Feidelson's argument in *Symbolism and American Literature* that metaphor in poetry is something quite distinct from metaphor in prose, and, most recently, in Philip Wheelwright's discussion of 'plurisignation' (or multiple verbal meaning) as an essential principle of poetry or "depth language" in *The Burning Fountain*.[31]

The method employed by Feidelson in his treatment of metaphor is a typical example of dialectical analysis in modern criticism. The initial argument is that the symbolic language of poetry must necessarily possess the contraries of all qualities commonly asserted of logical discourse. And the conclusion is that, whereas metaphor in prose undoubtedly consists in using words in such a way as to analogize one thing to another, metaphor in poetry, despite most earlier writers on the subject, obeys a wholly different principle, which he calls the principle of 'creative interaction.' The chain of argument by which he arrives at this conclusion is purely *a priori* and dialectical. This becomes evident in Feidelson's analysis of Andrew Marvell's poem 'To His Coy Mistress,' especially in his analysis of the metaphor "the iron gate of life."[31] Crane objects to the conclusion arrived at by Feidelson and points out that the principle of "creative interaction" which works in metaphor "the iron gates of life" "is at once the special kind of life that we can entertain under the aspect of iron gates, and the special kind of iron gates that are capable of being thought under the aspect of life."[32]

The critical procedure, which is based on "an old method of bipartite division,"[33] is commonly employed by the New Critics in their practical criticism. The method explores a subject matter by "applying to it a more or less elaborate pattern of logically contrary terms unified by a single principle of classification."[34] The practitioner of this method begins with a very large concept such as "language" or "discourse" in general and then he moves down from this plane by setting up dialectical oppositions between the major concept and its subordinate concepts, for example, between poetic discourse and logical discourse or between the symbolic discourse and the simple discourse. He goes on narrowing down until he stops at a particular attribute of discourse. Thus he determines the characteristic of poetry through a scheme of antithetical distinctions, which may be called "dialectical method." The "dialectical" reasoning aims at uniting contrary concepts of thought which are logically separated. The "dialectic" works backward by finding the more inclusive term in which the opposing concepts may be reconciled.

After describing the dialectical method, as employed in contemporary criticism, Crane pointed out its shortcomings. Firstly, the method is inappropriate to literary criticism and, secondly, it is incompatible with the spirit of inquiry. A piece of literature is not a natural phenomenon but a product of human inventiveness; therefore, it is shaped and conditioned, however remotely, by historical factors too. Its real nature, as Crane points out, can be found out *a posteriori*, that is, by investigating the effects in order to understand their causes. The dialectical method is always based on pre-conceived notions. Therefore, it proves unsuitable for the literary criticism of a particular literary work whose nature can only be defined after its investigation. A critic can understand the principle of construction only through "*ex post facto* means."[35]

A literary critic is not a scientist. A scientist tries to study the element of predictability or the determinate aspects of human productions. But, a literary critic has very little scope of dealing with the element of predictability or necessity. There is a little scope for the element or necessity in literature, because literature is an art, and hence partakes of reason. The necessities of a literary work, says Crane "are always relative to the specific tasks which writers set themselves in writing individual works, and they vary according to the variant character of these tasks."[36] For instance, a poet who writes an elegy is faced with the artistic necessity of showing humanly significant cause, for his despondent mood in the poem. Only in this restricted sense, "literature may be said to involve an element of predictability... ."[37]

The dialectical method appears inappropriate to literary criticism when we consider what it does to the concrete nature of a particular literary work. It is based on the basic antithesis that the language of poetry is different from the language of science. Therefore the New Critics reduce the relation between a literary work and a scientific work "to an abstract contrariety between something called 'poetry' and something called 'science' or 'logic.'"[38] Such a view of science and poetry merely turns them into "hypostatized qualities."[39] But we know from our experience that the nature of poetry is determined not by the logic of the critic's divisions and definitions but by variable human choices and actions of the poet. Each poem, which is an individual production, is what it is as a result of various decisions of the poet; and such decisions can be understand sufficiently only by examining the principles of construction of a particular work. Crane rightly observes: "Literature is just not suited to such a quasi-mathematical treatment."[40]

A critic need not prove but discover the nature of a particular work of literature that he examines in practical criticism. If he reduces the critical activity to proving a geometrical theorem, then, as Crane says, he will bring "inquiry in practical criticism to a stop before it is well begun, or at least...reduce it to a mere application of a pre-established dogma."[41] Cleanth Brooks and William Empson, know from their critical theories, in a determinate sense, that poetry is either "paradox" or "ambiguity." They merely identify certain structures, which they have known already by dialectical analysis in poems they examine. Their critical activity in the hands of the New Critics is just like putting "money into the dialectical machine"[42] and collecting the same money back. Therefore, dialectical analysis is incompatible with the spirit of inquiry.[43]

Here Crane sums up his main objections to dialectical reasoning on which some of the modern critical theorists have based their criticism. Special notice has got to be taken of Crane's use of such adjectives as 'inappropriate,' 'absurd' and 'futile,' for this method. They are indicative of Crane's strong disapproval of the method of the New Critics.

Crane considered criticism to be a form of inquiry. But the method, as he points out, stops inquiry before it is well begun. The New Critics, instead of exploring the uniqueness of the poems, merely demonstrate their own theoretical conclusions, already inferred through dialectical reasoning. Such a 'quasi mathematical approach' is certainly, inappropriate to human productions. It does not take into account the principles of construction that vary from work to work. What is really wrong is that the conclusions derived through dialectical reasoning, initially based on the opposition to be a universally applicable principle—true of all poems or literary works of imagination. It is a kind of fallacious argument which is termed as 'dialectical fallacy' by R.S. Crane. He writes:

> The "dialectical fallacy," then, is simply the tacit assumption that what is true in your theory as a dialectical consequence must also be or tend to be true in actually—that if you can so read a literary work as to reveal in it the particular kind of meaning or structure that is entailed by your definition of literature, poetry, poetic language, or the like, or by your formula for the author or his age, you have sufficiently demonstrated that it has that kind of meaning or structure. The fallacy lies in the circumstances that, with a little interpretative ingenuity, these conditions can almost always be fulfilled. I have said before how incompatible all this is with the spirit of inquiry. Our theory may tell us, for instance, that poetry is or tends to be symbolic; but there is nothing in this proposition, whatever its dialectical guarantees, that warrants us, as scholars, in saying more than that there may perhaps be symbols in the poem before us. But, by the some token, there also may not be; and so we have no business to conclude that there are unless we are forced so to conclude by the poem itself when we look at, independent of theory, as the work of a given poet at a given time, and examine it with the other possibility actively in mind. If a non-symbolic interpretation makes adequate sense of the text and, all other things considered, is relatively more probable, than anything we may believe about symbolism and poetry in general is beside the point. And the same would be true of symbolic interpretation that satisfied the same requirements.[44]

At the very outset of this Chapter it was pointed out that there is an inherent defect in dialectical reasoning, as it involves the possibility of simultaneous emergence of conflicting theories regarding the definition of poetry. When dialectical reasoning establishes a theory it implies that it will have its practical application in all cases comprehended by it. Through a similar process of dialectical reasoning another—almost a different—theory can be established and even that will make a similar claim about its practical application. In this way, there arises the possibility of the emergence of a paradoxical situation in which conflicting claims will individually claim to be true. For example, let us suppose that reasoning dialectically, one is able to construct a theory that 'poetry is ambiguity.' Now one will try to demonstrate successfully that in every poem there is nothing but ambiguity. Here, by a similar process of reasoning another theory can be constructed asserting that 'poetry is paradox.' Now, this is a paradoxical situation as this implies the possibility of opposing claims being true at the same time. Such an absurd possibility implies that the reasoning as employed in modern criticism is inherently defective.

IV

Another serious methodological defect of New Criticism, as Crane points out, is that it is still in the stage of "ruling hypothesis"—an intellectual stage which historical scholarship and the empirical sciences have long since passed through.[45]

The method of the New Critics, as pointed out earlier, is based on *a priori* reasoning. And, the *a priori* critical approach, encourages a critic to analyze a literary work in the light of 'ruling hypotheses.'

One of the most common 'ruling hypotheses' of the New Critics is that poetry is a special kind of language. But, this hypothesis is inadequate "when the differentia of poetic language the critic chooses concentrates attention on devices which are demonstrably not peculiar to the particular body of works he has agreed to call 'poetry,' or when the inherence in all poems or all good poems of the characteristic he has selected—whether it be 'ambiguity,' 'paradox,' 'irony' or something else of the same sort—depends largely or solely upon his having applied to them a technique of reading determined by the very hypothesis he is attempting to establish."[46] The linguistic hypothesis may serve some useful purpose; but, it cannot be universally applied. No hypothesis can serve as a golden key. Excessive reliance on the ruling hypothesis has given rise to the worst kind of 'critical monism' in contemporary criticism.

Crane rightly argues that language is one of the several internal causes of a literary work. According to him Cleanth Brooks's critical theory is narrow, because, he begins and ends with the analysis of language only, as if there are no other causes to be analyzed. Crane comments that "The choice is regrettable since it prevents him [Brooks] from dealing adequately with poetic works in terms of the sufficient or distinguishing causes of their production and nature; but it would be unfair to blame him unduly for making it, inasmuch as it has been a characteristic methodological choice...in the school of 'New Critics' to which he belongs."[47] Irony, in Brooks's sense of the term may be discovered in all good poems, but it cannot be made a basis of all good poems.[48] Crane complains: "What troubles me is that, for Brooks, there are no other points."[49] In Brooks's critical theory 'irony' becomes the single source of all critical predicates, "the unique cause from which he generates all effects."[50] But Cleanth Brooks is not the only modern critic whose critical theory suffers from 'monism.' Crane writes: "The terms may differ, but the same tendency toward monistic reduction of critical concepts is manifest in Allen Tate's doctrine of 'tension,' in John Crowe Ransom's principle of 'texture,' in Robert Penn Warren's obsession with symbols and, above all, in I.A. Richard's pavlovian mythology concerning the 'behavior of words.' "[51]

Olson points out that I.A. Richards's disciple William Empson is obsessed with his favourite term 'ambiguity.' He writes: "The theories of Richards and Empson illustrate a tendency, very prevalent among critics who rate diction as important, to rate it as entirely too important."[52] Thus, the Chicago Critics hold that the New Critics, by reducing critical concepts to a single formula, have done great harm to criticism.

Myth critics have also gone the way of the New Critics by penetrating "beneath the surface of what men say or do to the underlying nature of the experiences which their symbols serve to express."[53] Whereas the New Critics deal with language "as quite distinct in its grammar and logic from any of the conventional language we use in science or everyday intercourse, the myth critics deal with "the one natural and universal language of the human race, common alike to civilized men and savages"[54] whereas the New Critics look for 'irony' or 'ambiguity' or the like, the Myth Critics look for archetypal patterns. Therefore, we find that Crane rightly points out that the New Critics and the Myth Critics are chiefly preoccupied with language in one way or the other as "the centre of interest in their theories has shifted from a pre-occupation with the negative analogies between poetry, in its verbal aspects, and science, to a pre-occupation with the positive analogies between poetry, viewed in terms of its content of meanings, and the various other modes...."[55] The Myth Critics deal with the "pre-logical or extra-logical types of 'language.' "[56] Hence, the chief pre-occupation of the modern critics is with language. Their morbid obsession with language—"the material cause of poetry," reminds the Chicago Critics of the early Greek physiologers who had tried to explain the phenomenal universe in terms of its material cause, the principle of water.[57] Crane quotes Aristotle who held: "that with which the ancient writers, who first philosophized about Nature, busied themselves, was the material principle and the material cause. They inquired what this is, and what its character; how the universe is generated out of it, and by what motor influence whether, for instance, by antagonism or friendship..., the substratum of matter being assumed to have certain inseparable properties... ."[58] Crane argues that "in the arguments of most of these critics a moving principle of explanation that has startling affinities with the contrariety of antagonism and friendship ascribed by Aristotle to the early natural philosophers."[59]

Olson tells that the New Critics fail to explain "the distinctive forms which water assumes as rain, cloud, ice, or snow, nor the motive forces which cause water to assume such forms, nor the functional organization of animate things; it offers only one principle of explanation where several are required."[60] He rightly sums up that "Modern criticism is very much in the condition of Thales."[61]

Thus we find that the Chicago Critics got the idea of remedying the defects of contemporary criticism directly from Aristotle, as they also hold that language is just one of several internal causes of a literary work. How far the Chicago Critics succeeded in offering the Aristotelian remedy to the main shortcomings of the modern critics will be examined in Chapter 4 in a detailed manner.

After examining the bad consequences of the 'ruling hypotheses,' we shall examine the definitions and hypotheses of modern criticism, which are also defective according to the Chicago Critics. Olson argues that "we have a right to hold [a critic] to the accepted canons of reasoning and hypothesis-making, as well as of common-sense, that apply in any branch of inquiry dealing with particular things."[62] Neither the definitions nor the hypotheses of modern criticism are what they should be, according to the accepted canons of logic.

Poetry is defined as a particular attribute of language, say, 'ambiguity.' Such a definition is based on "accidental likenesses."[63] As Olson points out, Empson does not show how it is related to the nature or essence of poetry. And, as the definitions of poetry given by modern critics, do not state the nature of poetry, they are not, strictly speaking, definitions. The definition, based on the accidental characteristics of things, "has a minimum reference to the object defined, or it touches only a certain attribute which is itself not shown to be essential to the object."[64] His second objection is that, as the definitions are based on accidental characteristics, an definitions are based on accidental characteristics, an infinite number of definitions of the same thing can be framed. The third objection is that the definitions of modern criticism do not function heuristically. Olson says that definitions should serve "as matter for inquiry, and not as the basis of inquiry."[65] He however, function thus heuristically; instead, they operate as a basis for proof, as principles of demonstration; and as such they are sources of misreasoning and error, and hinder rather than foster further discussion.[66] Such definitions no doubt permit the discussion of a subject the nature of which is unknown, and, they, at best, are lights in which the object 'poetry' is viewed. Olson's objection can be best summed up in his own words:

> It is one thing to suppose tentatively that poetry is language characterized by ambiguity, and then to inquire whether this

> characteristic is common to all poetry, whether it is peculiar to poetry, whether it accounts for all that poetry is and does; it is quite another thing to employ it to insist that any interpretation of poetry must turn upon ambiguities, and to twist the language of *Macbeth* into a meaningless and tasteless muddle, merely because, according to the definition, poetry must be ambiguous. It is the reverse, not merely of science, but also of sense, to erect a hasty guess into a principle of method, so that, far from being tested by the data, it tests the data by itself, silencing all adverse testimony, and forcing assent where it should itself yield to correction.[67]

Olson further maintains that the hypotheses of modern criticism which are framed to support or supplement such pseudo-definitions are also not hypotheses.[68] His first argument in this regard is that the hypotheses of modern criticism are mere rationalizations of critics' opinions and not any kind of poetic principles. He explains:

> in Empson's case, for instance, the definitive property of poetry, ambiguity, rests upon the hypothesis that there is a connection between ambiguity and interesting or valuable situations; that is, if poetry deals with valuable interesting and valuable situations, and these tend to involve ambiguity, poetry must involve ambiguity. Such a hypothesis does not really give the cause, for it does not state why the thing is such-and-such; it is merely a reason, a ground of belief, stating why the theorist thinks the thing is so. It is not a poetic principle; it is the rationalization of an opinion. Even if the opinion and its ground were not false, however, both would still be inappropriate, for the terms in which they are couched are much too general: neither ambiguity nor a concern with interesting and valuable situations is peculiar to poetry. Moreover, even if they were appropriate, they would be falsely reductive; ambiguity, when it is present in poetry, is present through a variety of causes, and not simply through the fact that a certain kind of situation tends to involve it.

Olson's second objection is that the hypotheses of modern criticism are, logically speaking, postulates and not hypotheses, as they neither imply facts nor are implied by them. In order to build up his point, he divides hypotheses into three: "the heuristic, the demonstrative, and the nameless kind that serves both functions,"[69] and indicates that hypotheses of modern criticism do not satisfy the condition of any one of them. He finally argues that "First, they are inadequate; second, they are preclusive of supplementary hypotheses which might compensate for their inadequacies."[70]

The arguments of the Chicago Critics are viable, as they are based on sound logic. Unlike other critics of New Critics they do not indulge in surface criticism, rather they go deeper to point out what is really wrong with the fundamentals of the New Critics. According to them, New Criticism is deficient as it has "terms for dealing with only one or a few of the many causes of poems… ."[71] Olson rightly argues: that "All poetic theory is a formal causal explanation; and such explanation must comprise all the causes requisite to make a thing what it is. Unless the causal account is complete, the explanation is inadequate; if it is insisted upon as adequate, if it is claimed to account for the whole and not merely for the part, it is also preclusive.

One of the serious drawbacks of the New Critics who employ ruling hypothesis, which treats poetry as language or language of a certain kind, is that they have paid exclusive attention to basic constituent elements of the language of literary works: words, lines, sentences, paragraphs, speeches, and so on. Anyone, who is conversant with the textual analysis of the New Critics is aware of the fact that they dissect language of a literary work into different units, and analyze them at various lexicographical, prosodical, and syntactical levels in order to find out semantic and symbolic structures. But, they have unfortunately missed the point that, "The elements and devices of literary works, however, are never there for their own sake merely but ultimately for the sake of what is done with them in the making of concrete literary wholes."[72] Since words function in literary works, they must be subordinate to their functions. The New Critics, according to the Chicago Critics, do not take into consideration the function of words. Thus any textual analysis which examines a literary work "in abstraction from the peculiar formal ends and effects at which different poems aim"[73] will always remain incomplete.

The Chicago Critics were not the first to voice their deep concern over this kind of perversity of the textual criticism of the New Critics. As Crane was critically aware of the limitations of the method employed in the analysis of poems in *Understanding Poetry*.[74] T.S. Eliot was also aware of the abuses of the method as employed in *Interpretations*.[75] Eliot brands New Criticism as "Lemon squeezer" school of criticism. He sums up their method in the following words: "The method is to take a well-known poem—each of the poems analysed in this book is a good one of its kind—without reference to the author or to his author or to his other work, analyse it stanza by stanza and line by line, and extract, squeeze, tease, press every drop of meaning out of it that one can."[76] In this way, the New Critics dehumanized literary criticism. I think Crane rightly points out that New Criticism, "which rests upon such a general or simple hypothesis that they invariably tend to reduce the particularities and developed structures of poetry to a common denominator of universal and hence aesthetically insignificant human traits."[77]

The other main defect of New Criticism is based on the hypothesis that poetry is one homogeneous kind of things. In their search for common poetic qualities, the New Critics, as the Chicago Critics tell, completely ignored the theory of poetic genres. Which "may still be useful to discriminate the different possible patterns—such as the logical, the narrative, the descriptive, the repetitive, etc.—that may predominate in the arrangement of their parts."[78] Olson does not advocate the revival of genre criticism in its original form; but, certainly he holds the view that it is still capable of warding off one of the dangerous tendencies of modern criticism, which, by focusing our attention on the common poetic quality, blinds us to "great variousness of poetry."[79] He rightly observes:

> The theory of genres has been demolished; but what was true and useful in it perished along with what was false and dangerous. Criticism has been either wholly general or wholly particular ever since; and its present plight, indeed, is in great part due to its lack of such specific principles as might have eventually developed out of theory of genres.[80]

As no poetic principle can assume universality in literary criticism, the Chicagoan charge against the New Critics appears to be valid. Truth is always relative and it cannot be divorced from its context. Therefore, a literay critic must not emphasize that a particular poetic principle is absolutely true. If he does so, he will completely ignore the infinite variety of poetic works.

Crane's objections to their view that the poems have a common structure, seem to be quite convincing, as it is absurd to argue that all good poems are constructed on identical principles.

Thus, we find that the Chicago critics chiefly concerned themselves with the shortcomings of the contemporary criticism. Naturally, they had to search out a number of remedies that could supplement the deficiencies of contemporary criticism. The Aristotelian solutions to the problems created by the New Critics will be examined in the next chapter. It will be also discussed as to how far the Chicago Critics succeeded in getting suitable remedies for various critical vices: 'critical monism,' *a priori* approach, ruling hypotheses, erroneous definitions, pseudo-hypotheses (postulates), dialectical fallacy, dehumanising effect of 'lemon-squeezing' in textual analyses etc.

So far we have discussed the prognosis and diagnosis of the Chicago Critics of the pathological state of contemporary criticism as they viewed but, from now onwards, we shall examine the remedies suggested by them.

NOTES

1. *The Humanities*, 11, 26.
2. *Ibid.*, p. 27.
3. *Ibid.*, p. 31.
4. A statement may be used for the sake of the reference, true or false, which it causes. This is the scientific use of language. But it may also be used for the sake of the effects in emotion and attitude produced by the reference it occasions. This is the emotive use of language. The distinction once clearly grasped is simple. We may either use words for the sake of the references they promote, or we may use them for the sake of the attitudes and emotions which ensue. Many arrangements of words evoke attitudes without any reference being required *en route*. They operate like musical phrases. But usually references are involved as conditions for, or stages in, the ensuing development of attitudes, yet it is still the attitudes not the references which are important. (I.A. Richards, "The Two Uses of Language," *Principles of Literary Criticism* [Routledge & Kegan Paul Ltd., London, 1955], p. 266).
5. *The Humanities*, II, 29.
6. *Ibid.*, p. 32.
7. *Ibid.*, p. 33.
8. *The Humanities*, II, 32.
9. K. Ahmad, *Psycho-analysis and Literary Criticism* (Patna, Shri Ajanta Press), quoted on p. 24.
10. *Ibid.*, p. 25.
11. Herbert Read, *Collected Essays in Literary Criticism* (London, Faber & Faber), p. 126.
12. *The Humanities*, II, 16.
13. *Ibid.*, p. 40.
14. *Ibid.*, p. 40.
15. *Ibid.*, pp. 32-33.
16. Murray Krieger, *The Play and Place of Criticism* (Baltimore, The John Hopkins Press, 1967).
17. *Critics and Criticism*, p. 142.
18. *Ibid.*, p. 138.
19. *Ibid.*, p. 144.
20. LCSP, p. 123.

21. Cleanth Brooks, "*The Language of Paradox*," *The Well Wrought Urn* (London: Demms Dobson, 1949), p. 3.
22. "Criticism as Inquiry," *The Humanities*, II, 37.
23. I.A. Richards, *Principles of Literary Criticism*, pp. 261 -71.
24. LCSP, p. 24.
25. *Ibid.*, p. 24.
26. *Ibid.*, p. 109.
27. *LCSP*, pp. 23-25.
28. LCSP, p. B7.
29. See *The World's Body* (New York, 1938), especially pp. 36-38; 41-46; 181-83; 195-211; 278-95.
30. LCSP, p. 22.
31. *Ibid.*, p. 22.
32. *Ibid.*, p. 22.
33. *Ibid.*, p. 22.
34. "Criticism as Inquiry," *The Humanities*, II, 33.
35. See *Symbolism and American Literature* (Chicago: The University of Chicago Press, 1953, Third Impression, 1960), p. 60.
36. "Criticism as Inquiry," p. 33.
37. Crane, "Criticism as Inquiry," *The Humanities*, II, 34.
38. *Ibid.*, p. 34.
39. LCSP, p. 155.
40. "Criticism as Inquiry," p. 35.
41. *Ibid.*, p. 35.
42. *Ibid.*, p. 35.
43. *Ibid.*, p. 36.
44. The great virtue of a textbook like *Understanding Poetry* is the exercise it gives in the sensitive grammatical, interpretation of texts; its shortcoming is that it superimposes on this a partial and one-sided theory of poetic form, with the result that the student is in sensibly conditioned to see only those meanings and stylistic devices in poems which the theory selects as important. Interpretation is one thing, and formal analysis another; it is well, I think, not to allow the first to be controlled by the second, so that our students become adept in finding instances of "ambiguity," "irony," "paradox," "symbol," or "myth" before they are able to say, independently of such notions what the words and sentences actually mean, what the actions or the arguments are as stated or implied, and how such distinction as the language has is brought about Crane "The Teaching of Literary Texts," *The Humanities*, II, 183.
45. *Ibid.*, p. 37.

46. *Ibid.*, p. 37.
47. *Ibid.*, p. 37.
48. *The Pattern of Inquiry, Logic: The Theory of Inquiry* (Chicago: Holt, 1966), pp. 104-05.
49. *Ibid.*, p. 40. [Crane, "The Teaching of Literary Texts," The Humanities, II, 183].
50. *Ibid.*, p. 43.
51. LCSP, p. 33; Cf. *Critics and Criticism*, pp. 100-05.
52. *Critics and Criticism*, p. 105.
53. *Ibid.*, p. 105.
54. *Ibid.*, p. 105.
55. *Ibid.*, p. 105.
56. *Ibid.*, p. 105.
57. *Ibid.*, p. 105.
58. LCSP, p. 111.
59. *Ibid.*, p. 111.
60. *Ibid.*, p. 109.
61. *Ibid.*, p. 109.
62. *Critics and Criticism*, p. 61.
63. *On the Parts of Animals*: 1 641^{a} 15-17.
64. LCSP, p. 106.
65. *Critics and Criticism*, p. 61.
66. *Ibid.*; and also see *Ibid.*, p. 29; pp. 84ff.
67. LCSP, pp. 32-33.
68. *Critics and Criticism*, p. 58.
69. *Ibid.*, p. 58.
70. *Ibid.*, p. 58.
71. *Ibid.*, p. 58.
72. *Ibid.*, p. 58.
73. *Ibid.*, pp. 59-60.
74. *Ibid.*, p. 60.
75. *Ibid.*, p. 60.
76. LCSP, p. 36.
77. *The Humanities*, II, 183.
78. LCSP, p. 117.
79. *The Humanities*, II, 183.
80. "The Frontiers of Criticism," *On Poetry and Poets*, London, Faber & Faber, p. 113.

4

The Aristotelian Bias

In the preceding chapter, it was shown how the Chicago Critics found the method of the contemporary critics, especially the New Critics, deficient in many ways. In the present chapter an analysis will be made of the factors that led the Chicago Critics to embrace the general method of Aristotle with a view to remedying the crucial shortcomings of the theory and practice of the contemporary criticism. Such an analysis will naturally involve an examination of the relationship between Aristotle and the Chicago Critics, as the latter are popularly known as the "Neo-Aristotelians." Many threads lead from the basic philosophy and poetic reasoning of Aristotle to the texture of the central assumptions and the methods of the Chicago Critics. But the threads can be clearly visible only when the main threads of the texture of Aristotle's thought and methodology are presented here. Therefore a brief introduction to the basic critical and aesthetic concepts of Aristotle may help us explain the nature of the subtle and complex relationship of Aristotle and the Chicago Critics.

Crane's claim, that the Chicago Critics adopted only Aristotle's general method "without committing themselves to the total philosophy in which it was evolved,"[1] does not give a true picture of Chicagoan indebtedness to the great philosopher. The principles and method, that the Chicago Critics have developed, are rooted in the fundamental concepts of Aristotle which they gathered from their intensive readings of Aristotle's major Treatises: *Poetics, Rhetoric, Metaphysics, Politics, Physics, Posterior Analytics, Niomachean Ethics, on the Parts of Animals, De Anima, Meteorology* etc. Hence a summary of the fundamental concepts of Aristotle is given below to show their impact on Chicago criticism.

FUNDAMENTAL CONCEPTS OF ARISTOTLE
CONCEPT OF "CONCRETUM"

According to Aristotle a 'concretum' or a *synolon* or a 'whole' is an artistic composite of form and matter. This concept is based on his doctrine of 'interactionist ontology,' *i.e.*, a dynamic interaction of form and matter. Therefore, it is inadequate to define any object either in terms of its material character or formal character alone. For him, a term like snub, involves not merely nose or concavity, but both—a nose (matter) which is concave (form).[2] A coach, as he says, "is such and such a form embodied in this or that matter, or such and such a matter with this or that form; so that its shape and structure must be included in our description."[3]

It must be mentioned here that, by matter, he did not exactly mean the same as we do, namely physical substance, such as brass or steel; and by form, simply shape of an object. Our conception of matter, as a physical substance, is absolute because an object which we call matter is absolutely, one and for all, matter. It never ceases to be matter in process of time and is never immaterial, from any point of view at any moment. Aristotle believed in the relativity of form and matter. For him matter and form are relative terms, as the two flow into each other. The same thing may be viewed as matter from one angle, and form from another angle. In all creations, or productions matter is that which becomes something. It is that in which the principle of change operates; and, the form is that, toward which the change operates. For example a piece of marble, out of which a status is carved out, is quarried from a mass of stone; hence it is both matter and form. It is matter when it realizes its form in a status; but the same is form, when it is excavated from a quarry. Take another example. Acorn grows into oak. Here the oak is the form of acorn, but the same becomes matter of the oak furniture.

Aristotle's doctrine of the immanence of form and matter takes into account on the two aspects of nature which are manifested in the process of existence: potentiality and actuality or realization. According to him every artistic production is realization of potentiality.

Matter, in itself, is nothing unless it assumes some form, by a process of change. Thus, logically speaking, in order of time, matter exists prior to form; but, in order of thought, its form exists earlier. For when it is argued that matter is the potentiality of what it is to become, it is implied that what is to become is already present in it ideally and potentially, though not actually. Though paradoxical, it may be argued that this sort of Aristotle's line of thinking will imply that the end is already present in the beginning. Therefore, it may be said that oak is in the acorn ideally, otherwise the oak would not have sprouted forth. The principle of form, as Aristotle says, is logically prior to its end. For him it is the ultimate reality—the 'first principle,' from which the entire universe flows out.

It will not be out of place here to point out that the Aristotelian doctrine of form-in-matter influenced the Chicago critics immensely as one of their basic assumptions is that a literary work is a union of a certain material with a certain form. Of all the conceptual borrowings that they made from Aristotle's philosophy, the conception of poetic works as concrete whole's[4] is of utmost importance. Crane illustrates this doctrine with the help of a common experience of clay modelling. He writes:

> I take for instance, a piece of modelling clay. There are many things which I cannot do with it—of which, as Aristotle would say, it cannot be the matter; but on the other hand the potentialities it does hold out, within these limits, are indefinite in number: I can make of it, if I wish, a geographical globe, with all its continents indicated, or the model of a house, or the bust of a sinister-looking man and so on through a vast range of similar possibilities that is bounded only by my invention and skill. In any of these realizations the thing I make remains a thing of clay, having all the permanent characteristics of such a thing; but it remains this only in a partial sense; in itself as a particular object to which we may respond practically or aesthetically, it is at the same time something else—a globe, a house, a sinister-looking man; of it, though it must obviously specify its clayness—that is, its material nature—would be of no use to anybody unless it also specified the definite kind of thing into which the clay has been shaped—that is, its formal nature. And the latter is clearly more important than the former since it is what accounts, in any particular case, for the clay being handled thus and not otherwise and of our response being of such and such a quality rather than any other. It is not difficult to see how the conception fits the work of the poet or of any other writer.[5]

This last sentence of Crane amply shows that the Chicago Critics shared Aristotle's concept of "concretum." Crane also demonstrates how the same can be applied in practical criticism by analyzing a prose extract from Emma and a poem entitled "The Duke of Benevento," by Sir John Henry Moore.[6]

THE CONCEPT OF FOUR CAUSES

Aristotle discovered four explanatory causes to know a thing: '*material cause*,' '*formal cause*,' '*efficient cause*' and '*final cause*.' His concept can be explained with the help of a common object. Take the example of a desk. It is made of wood, pegs, glue and varnish which constitute its *material cause*. All these material components are integrated into the shape of a desk to form a piece of furniture. Therefore, that into which the materials are shaped is the formal cause. The process by which materials are shaped into desk comprise of other subsidiary activities—sawing, planning, joining, and finishing. All these specific operations are *the efficient cause* of the desk. But, a desk is made to serve certain type of purpose or end for the sake of which it is made. This is the *final cause* of the desk.

The other most important observation which he makes is that *the formal cause, efficient cause* and *the final cause* all melt into the single conception of 'form.' As the conceptual form exists logically prior to its expression into a definite form, the principle of form contains the formal, the final and the efficient causes. Aristotle reduces the four causes to two only, which he calls matter and form. He views the formal cause and the final cause as the same. The formal cause, according to him, is the essence or the concept or the idea of a thing. And the idea of a thing aims at its form.

Therefore, the end of a thing—its final cause, is the same as its formal cause. Again, the efficient cause is the cause of becoming; and what causes the becoming is just that it aims at the end. According to Aristotle, the striving of all things is towards the end, therefore, the end is thus itself the cause of becoming or motion or, in other words, the final cause is the real efficient cause.

In case of artistic production, this reduction of the two causes to final cause can be explained as follows; Take the example of a statue. It is the sculptor that moves the material— say, brass, bronze, marble or stone. But what moves him imperceptibly is the idea of the completed status in his mind. Thus, the idea of the end—the final cause, generates the movement or the artistic process—the efficient cause. The material cause cannot be reduced to any other cause. Thus, matter and form are the two fundamental categories of Aristotle's philosophy.

In Chapter 3, I have already discussed how the New critics try to understand the structure of poems by analyzing their language only. Language, as the Chicago Critics say, is the material cause of poetry. Therefore, the New Critics, according to the Chicago Critics, are materialistic monists.[7] Aristotle's emphasis of a literary work which he considered as a 'concretum' of form and matter. He did not permit the analysis of matter in abstraction from 'form' which includes function also. But he attaches greater significance to 'final cause.'

The New Critics, in their formal analysis, generally focus their attention on language or the 'material cause' of a literary work, but the Chicago Critics concentrate on its the 'intended effect,' *i.e.*, the 'final cause.' Crane and Olson have explained how "form" is the most important factor and language the least important in practical criticism. They hold that language is the material of thought or what is to be expressed with respect to "form." They explain their views with the help of those very illustrations which Aristotle used in his treatises. Passages dealing with the importance of language from Aristotle and the Chicago Critics are compared below to determine the area of agreement between them. Let us first see what Aristotle says with regard to form:

> ...a thing is not said to be that from which it comes, here the statue is not said to be wood but is said by a verbal change to be wooden, not brass but brazen, not gold but golden, and the house is said to be not bricks but bricken (though we should not say without qualification, if we looked at the matter carefully, even that a statue is produced from wood or a house from bricks, because coming to be implies change in that form which a thing comes to be, and not permanence).[8]

An almost similar view is expressed by Elder Olson in the passage quoted below:

> Now-a-days when the nature of poetry has become so uncertain that everyone is trying to define it, definitions usually begin: 'poetry is words which, or, language which, or discourse which, and so forth.' As a matter of fact, it is nothing of the kind. Just as we should not define a chair as wood, which has such and such characteristics—for a chair is not a kind of wood but furniture—so we ought not to define poetry as a kind of language. The chair is not wood but wooden; poetry is not words but verbal. In other sense, of course, the words are of the utmost importance; if they are not the right words or if we do not grasp them, we do not grasp the poem. In another sense, they are the least important elements in the poem, for they do not determine the character of anything else in the poem; on the contrary, they are determined by everything else. They are the only things we see or hear; yet they are governed by imperceptible things which are inferred from them. And when we are moved by poetry, we are not moved by the words, except in so far as sounds

and rhythms move us; we are moved by the things that the words stand for.[9]

In this way, we find that 'form' is the most important factor. It conditions the nature of language—the 'matter' of a literary work. Crane quotes Aristotle's standard example of a saw which explains this fact. Aristotle says that "if a piece of wood is to be split with an axe, the axe must of necessity be made of bronze or iron."[10] Thus, an axe exists because it has a definite function, namely, sawing and not because it is made of a certain metal. It is the function of the saw that determines the nature of the metal. In the case of a literary work, it is the 'emotional form' or the 'intended effect' which governs the handling of words and also other constituent that form the matter of a work. Directly drawing upon Aristotle, Crane says that "we may...speak of the words of a poem as the material basis of the thought they express, although the words also have form as being ordered in sentences and rhythms; and similarly we may speak of thought as the matter of character, of character and thought in words as the matter of action or emotion so on up to but not including the 'overall form' which synthesises all those subordinate elements, into a continuous poetic whole."[11] Crane's remark immediately reminds one of Aristotle's concept of relativity of form and matter.

According to Aristotle, the end or the final effect of which the material elements of a literary work is synthesized into a 'concrete whole' is the *dynamis* or the 'power' of the work.

Therefore, according to him catharsis is the *dynamis* of a well-made tragedy, in the same sense as the capacity to chop off trees or split wood, is the *dynamis* of an axe. The peculiar *dynamis* or 'power' expresses the form or the synthesizing principle of any specific whole or a literary work. Therefore, in order to grasp this form, a critic will have to reason back "from the nature of an achieved result to its necessary or desirable conditions."[12] He will try to analyze the hypothetical necessities the writer might have felt at the time of writing a poem, for Aristotle says "if a house or other such final object is to be realized, it is necessary that such and such material shall exist; and it is necessary that first this and then that shall be produced, and first this and then that set in motion, and so on in continuous succession, until the end and final result is reached, for which each prior thing is produced and exists."[13]

Aristotle believed that a natural scientist must understand this necessity "if he has to go beyond the inadequate explanation of those earlier philosophers who attempted to generate the configurations of things in the universe out of the assumption of some underlying material principle, such as water, fire, or earth, and of such moving principles, such as heat and cold or love and strife."[14] Similarly, as Crane says "if we are to know what the parts, and their characteristics, of a house or a poem of necessity are, and how they must be arranged, our starting-point cannot be the materials of bricks or language we are using, it can only be the conception of the house to be erected or the poem to be composed as a completed whole of a certain kind...."[15] So far the 'Chicago Critics' conception of the form or the final cause is the 'first principle' whereas for the New Critics it was the material cause or the language.

Therefore, the Chicago Critics like Aristotle consider the 'material cause' or language of a literary work to be just one of several factors in the creation of a literary work. Therefore, linguistic analysis plays a relatively a minor role in the theory and practice of the Chicago Critics. If poetic theory is a form of causal explanation, then any good poetic theory must take into account more than one cause. If only one cause is given an exaggerated importance, then the literary critics will unfortunately repeat the error which Greek physicists like Thales committed who attempted to "account for the phenomenal universe in terms merely of its material cause, the principle of water."[16] Thus what Aristotle did in the field of philosophy, the Chicago Critics attempted in literary criticism. It may also be said that it is the remedial character of Aristotle's principles which attracted the Chicago Critics, who were in quest of such principles and method that could remedy the defects of New Criticism which has terms for dealing with only one or a few of the many causes of poems, for example, only the psychology of the poet, or the poetic subject-matter or language. The primary concern of the Chicago Critics was to check the tendency of the contemporary criticism which they characterized as 'critical monism.' I have also already discussed that they were in search of a purely humanistic method. Therefore, it was difficult for them to approve of the monistic reduction of the critical principles, which appeared to them a type of scientific reductionism: "the spirit that denies the essence of the humanities by seeking always to direct our attention away from the multiplicity, to some lower or lowest common denominator...."[17] Again, the concept of 'immediate shaping cause' or the 'actual final cause' is nothing but a refined version of Aristotle's concept of 'final cause.' Aristotelian final cause includes function or the effect (*dynamis*).

The Chicagoan concept of 'form' is very near to Aristotle's conception of 'form,' in which all the three causes combine into one. In Aristotle's opinion, 'the final cause' is the 'form.' It is a sort of intuitive glimpse of the artistic form, which generates the artistic process that culminates in the production of an artistic or literary work. Explaining his conception of literary or artistic form, Crane observes:

> By form I mean simply the overall principle, whatever it may be, that makes of the materials of a work a single definite thing. It is the aspect of literary works which comes into view when we ask ourselves not simply what the meanings and the dictional devices and local effects are appropriately in the work (if they do indeed belong) and how, and how well, they function artistically with respect to one another and the whole— the meaning of 'why?' here being relative to the peculiar nature and the end of the individual nature and end of the individual work before us rather than the general intention or historical circumstances of the author.[18]

For Crane, "form," "over all form," "synthesizing principle" and "a shaping or directing cause" are all synonymous terms. All of them stand for an "intuitive glimpse of a possible subsuming form for the materials"[19] The 'form' of a literary work, says Crane, is a shaping cause in the sense that once it is grasped by a writer, it generates consequences and problems in the detailed working out of the subject of composition. It exerts a kind of impersonal and objective power over the organization of materials into an ordered whole. Crane says that the "artist's intuition of form capable of directing whatever he does with his materials in a particular work—is an essential cause of poetic structure, the most decisive, of all the causes of structure in poetry because it controls in an immediate way the act of construction itself."[20] And, of all the critical methods available to the Chicago Critics, both ancient and modern, Aristotle's method appeared to be most useful for the study of the constructional aspect of a literary work. Crane writes: "It is the merit of Aristotle...that he grasped the distinctive nature of poetic works as *synola*, or concrete artistic wholes, and made available, though only in outline sketch, hypotheses and analytical devices for defining literally and inductively, and with a maximum degree of differentiation, the multiple causes operative in the construction of poetic wholes of various kinds and the criteria of excellence appropriate to each."[21]

Crane was drawn to Aristotle because the latter supplied the principles and methods of inquiry, which he sought to explain the 'immediate shaping cause' of the literary works. Crane openly admits in the preface to LCSP that he is primarily interested in "the immediate causes, in the literal sense of that word, which have made the things what they are and rendered them capable of affecting our minds as they do, and more especially those causes which involve the efforts of human beings, whether politicians, scientists, philosophers, or artist, to solve successfully the particular problems inherent in their situations and tasks."[22] In this way we find that there are solid reasons behind the temperamental affinity between Aristotle and the Chicago Critics.

ARISTOTLE'S METHOD

Aristotle's method is *a posteriori* and inductive. It is *a posteriori* because Aristotle argues back from a given poem to its fourfold causes: final, formal, efficient and material. It is inductive because critical judgments on a literary work, are passed only after analyzing the principles of construction of a particular literary work. The method puts emphasis on the investigation of particular literary works before making generalizations about them. "In logic the word induction is customarily used to refer to an argument in which the premises do not entail the conclusion but rather (or are presented as being) evidence or grounds for the truth of the conclusion."[23] Therefore inductive method involves reasoning from particular facts or individual cases to a general conclusion. It throws light on the 'poetic reasoning,' and is based on the following assumptions:

> All art is concerned with coming into being, *i.e.*, with contriving and considering how something may come into being which is capable of either being or not being, and whose origin is in the maker and not in the thing made; for art is concerned neither with things that are, or come into being, by necessity, nor with things that do so, in accordance with nature (since these have their origin in themselves).[24]

Aristotle's method is precisely the method of a 'productive science' which studies only the "rational element in art"[25] or the 'poetic reasoning' through "hypothetical regressive reasoning." The poetic reasoning begins "from the character of the end to be achieved to the necessary or desirable means— that is reflected in this process when it terminates in an artistically successful product."[26] According to Olson, it proceeds "from the distinctive whole which is the product of the art to determine what parts must be assembled if such a whole, beautiful of its kind, is to result."[27] It is hypothetical because it is based on the hypotheses that "if such and such a work which is a whole, is to be produced, then such and such parts must be assembled in such and such a way; and if the work is to have excellence as a whole, then the parts must be of such and such a kind and quality."[28] He further adds that "The reasoning is regressive because it works backward from the whole, which is to exist, to the parts which must have existence previous to the whole."[29] Thus we find that Aristotle's method is based upon 'hypothetical regressive reasoning.'

The 'matter of fact method' discussed by Crane as a possible alternative to the 'other scientific method,' in his essay "The Multiplicity of Critical Languages" is nothing but Crane's version of Aristotle's method. Describing the salient features of the method, Crane says:

> Its starting-point is always some literary form or actuality that has been and hence can be achieved by art...and its procedure consists in reasoning back from this to the necessary and sufficient conditions of its existence or of its existence in the best possible state. The distinctions it looks for and employs are distinctions of "nature" rather than of "reason" in as much as their relevance is determined not by the exigencies of the critic's hypothesis but some kind of inductive consideration of the particular phenomena he is studying: for example, of the various kinds of wholes that poets may construct (as in Aristotle's differentiations of tragedy, comedy, and epic), or of the different elements necessary to the production of an effect or of a work of a certain kind (as in...Aristotle's discrimination of plot, character, thought, diction, melody, and spectacle as the constitutive parts of tragedies).... And it is characteristic of the method that it prefers multiple and overlapping classifications of literary things.... .[30]

Thus, it is clear that the Chicago method was largely influenced by Aristotle's. "A well-made poem or literary work," says Crane, "can be understood by depending upon inquiries of an *a posteriori* type which move inductively (in Aristotle's sense of induction) from the particulars to the universals they embody and form or forms thus defined, by hypothetical necessity to the essential conditions of their realization in poetic matter."[31]

WHOLE-ANALYSIS

"Whole-analysis" which is discussed in the *Poetics* examines the specific constitution and 'power' or a literary work or a "concrete whole." It is applied to the critical analysis of mimetic works only. The analytic devices, which he gives, determine the number, character, and ordering of the functional parts of various species of poetic wholes and defines "the often quite different conditions of success or failure implied by the nature of each."[32] Steps in such a type of analysis will be as follows: firstly, to determine "what the specific constitution and power of the whole the writer has achieved or aimed at really is"[33]; secondly, to determine how far that 'whole' tallies and differs from similar wholes and in what respects; thirdly, to determine as "to what extent, and with what degree of artistic compulsion, any of the particular things the writer has done at the various levels of his writing, down to the details of his imagery and language, can be seen to follow from the special requirements or opportunities that are bound to differ more or less sharply according as the whole being constructed as a mimetic rather than didactic form, a dramatic form intended for the stage rather than one meant primarily for recitation, a tragic platform of the order of Macbeth rather than of Othello, or of The Duchess of Malfi rather than of King Lear, and so on."[34]

In this kind of analysis, the critic tries to relate his conclusions and statements about parts to his statements about the "poetic" wholes. Thus, as Crane explains, "an adequate study of the plot-form of *The Duchess of Malfi* would necessarily involve a detailed consideration of Webster's use of language in that play, and a study of the language in (say) the scene of the Duchess's death would necessitate asking to what extent the choice and collocation of words, the invention of imagery and metaphor, etc., were dictated among other things, by Webster's sense of the particular mean between horrified indignation and pity which his plot-form required him to maintain in this part of his drama."[35] A literary work is a synthesis of parts: objects, means, manner and effect (*dynamis*). According to Crane it is a whole "that produces its effect not instantaneously but gradually in order of time; and its parts are consequently of two sorts: sequential parts, from beginning through middle to end, and functional parts that depend on the specific nature of the elements combined in the synthesis and on the mode of their combination."[36] Therefore, in the analysis of an imitative poem, Aristotle, first of all, grasps the poetic form which permits him to infer what its peculiar necessities and possibilities are; but, it cannot be grasped unless the critic takes into account the form and matter together.

Object, means and manner are the three necessary conditions of the existence of a literary work or a "concrete whole." These are the three bases of differentiations—the three material determinants of poetic structure. The object may be an argument, or an action or a state of character or feeling. The means or the mode used may be prose or meter of some kind. The manner of representation may be narrative or dramatic. Each of these determinants may vary in its specific character independently. It is due to this fact that mimetic works differ from one another, mainly in three different ways: "either in that they imitate in different media or matters or in that they imitate different objects or forms or in that they imitate differently and not in the same manner."[37]

The parts are independent variables. Therefore, according to Aristotle, says Crane "the same type of poetic medium may be used to imitate different kinds of objects (as when a combination of rhythm," melody and verse is employed in both tragedy and comedy), that the same object may be brought before us in different manners (as when the action of serious epic or part thereof is dramatized in a tragedy), and the same manner is consistent with widely differing poetic means (as when a prose-drama is rewritten in verse)."[38] As all the component parts vary independently, they must be analyzed with respect to the possibilities of independent variation. In the *Poetics* 1-3, Aristotle dwells upon the possibilities of using means: medium of rhythm, discourse and harmony both separately and in combination and, if in combination, simultaneously or in succession. He also discusses here the possibilities of using the objects of imitation, for example, the possibilities imitating the action of men better than we are or worse than we are or like ourselves. He also discusses the possibilities of independent variation of the manner of poetic imitation into the possibilities of representing the object dramatically throughout or narratively throughout or by some mixture of these two techniques.[39] Thus, the method "of multiple differentiation and systematic resolution of maximal composites into their least parts"[40] operates in whole-analysis. First, a 'whole' is differentiated into object, means and manner and, then each is further differentiated. One part is determined by another until the principal part is discovered which determines all. In this way the relative importance of the parts is established. The 'plot,' according to Aristotle, is the principal part of a 'whole.' If no 'plot' (in the Aristotelian sense) is found out then something analogous to 'plot' is found out by the Chicago Critics, as in the case of lyrics.

Aristotle says that the characteristics of a whole largely depends on the characteristics of its 'plot.' So, first of all, the principal part or the plot is identified and then the order of importance of the remaining parts is examined. The 'plot' is treated as a whole within a whole. This whole, which is actually the principal part of an artistic whole, is itself a whole composed of parts, having beginning, middle and end. Therefore, they are also determined and the character of their conjunction—necessity and probability—is shown. Every whole, in order to be a beautiful whole, is a whole of certain magnitude. The magnitude of the whole, according to Olson "lies in a mean between excess of the part and excess of the whole, the former producing such vast extension that the whole cannot be comprehended, the latter such minuteness that the parts cannot be apprehended."[41]

After determining the wholeness, completeness, and unity, the principal part is divided into its species. Aristotle says that plot can be divided into simple and complex. A complex plot, according to him, "consists of differentiable parts (*peripety* and discovery) according to the efficient cause of the change of fortunes with which tragedy is conceived."[42]

The 'plot' or the principal part is only materially a whole; and formally, it has a definite emotional effect—the "working or power," which is the form of the whole. Therefore, as Olson says, "the poetics of any species must be addressed to the differentiation of its principal parts, since it is this that primarily determines the emotional effect."[43]

Finally, we may conclude with Olson's remarks:

> The whole-analysis, thus, not merely indicates the possibilities of poetic construction but discriminates among them as better or worse, to exhibit the construction of a synthesis beautiful as a whole, composed of parts of the maximum beauty consistent with that whole, and productive of its proper emotional effects to a maximum degree.[44]

The influence of the Aristotelian whole-analysis can be easily traced in the theory and practice of the Chicago Critics. Let us first examine Olson's view which finally developed into the poetics of lyric. He writes:

> The method—one of multiple differentiation and systematic resolution of maximal composites into their least parts—may obviously be extended to poetic species which have emerged since Aristotle. Aristotle distinguishes broadly and between extremes; later theorists in his method must follow the basic lines and go farther. For example, his poetics, as we have it, deals only with such poetry as has plot, *i.e.*, such as imitates a system of actions. These are maximal forms; there are, that is, no "larger" poetic forms or any which have more parts than these; smaller forms, such as the species of lyric, can be treated by carrying such systems back to their elements.[45]

Olson further refines the basic 'concept of action' "far beyond the relatively primitive state in which Aristotle left it."[46] He writes: Four kinds of action or behaviour can thus be distinguished, without regard to seriousness or comicality,

(i) a single character acting in a single closed situation. By "closed situation" I mean here one in which the character's activity, however it may have been initiated or however it may be terminated, is uncomplicated by any other agency. Most of what we call lyric poetry belongs here: any poem in which the character commits some verbal act (threatening, persuading, beseeching) upon someone existing only as the object of his action (Marvell's "To His Coy Mistress"), or deliberates or muses (Keats's "Ode to Nightingale"), or is moved by passion (Lander's "Mother, I cannot Mind My Wheel").

(ii) Two or more characters in a single closed situation. "Closed situation" here means "uncomplicated by any other agency than the characters originally present and remaining so throughout." This parallel is the notion of "scene" in French classical drama; here belong all the real colloquies of persons acting upon and reacting to one another (*e.g.*, Browning's "The Bishop Orders His Tomb"), although not the metaphorical colloquies, such as dialogues between Body and Soul, etc.

(iii) A collection of such "scenes" as I have just mentioned about some central incident, to constitute an "episode" (Arnold's "Sohrab and Rustum").

(iv) A system of such episodes constituting the grand plot of tragedy, comedy, and epic which is treated by Aristotle.[47]

Olson's observation suggests a useful line of differentiation of the object of imitation, needed in whole-analysis of lyrics. He firmly believes that similar analysis of means and manner, already discussed in detail, "would extend Aristotle's system to include all poetic forms."[48] The Chicago Critics are of the view that Aristotle had developed not only a permanently true but indefinitely operable method which could be applied to newly developed forms of mimetic art which have emerged after Aristotle. They strongly felt the need of pushing the Aristotelian type of whole-analysis far beyond the point where Aristotle left it. They always felt that poetics is a progressive science "always lagging somewhat behind poets, but never, if it is to keep alive, remaining indifferent to what new poets are trying to do."[49] Crane says that "*Poetics* is a statement, or at least an outline sketch of a science, and as such it deals with principles and causes rather than with conventions or poetic Traditions with the artistic necessities and possibilities of particular forms rather than with accepted rules and models... ."[50] In short, they never treated poetics to be "something fixed,"[51] as they always held that critical knowledge, like all knowledge must be constantly extended; but no one is very likely to extend it who is not fully aware of what has already been accomplished or of what consequences follow from such accomplishments. This is the reason that they never blindly followed Aristotle, as some scholars think.

III

The Chicago Critics, despite their loud protests, continue to be considered as "Neo-Aristotelians" by a large number of critics, in and outside America. Crane says: "It is not a question of regarding the *Poetics*, in Mr. Blackmur's phrase, as a 'sacred book' and certainly not of looking upon ourselves, in any exclusive sense, as forming an 'Aristotelian' or 'Neo-Aristotelian' school. It would be a desirable thing, indeed, if we could do away with 'schools' in criticism as they have been done away with in most of the disciplines in which learning as distinguished from doctrine has been advanced."[52] Here an attempt will be made to examine the claim of the Chicago Critics in the light of what they say and do in criticism.

The Chicago Critics have borrowed Aristotle's basic concepts and mode of reasoning, without distorting them in numerous ways as the Renaissance and the 17th century French Aristotelians did or without completely confining themselves to Aristotle's logic, arguments and deductions, operative in this *Poetics*. Richard Mckeon remarks that "The long history of the influence of Aristotle has rarely produced an 'Aristotelian' dedicated to his diversity of method... ."[53] Since the Chicago Critics have reconstructed their own Aristotle, they are not to be taken as modem versions of the Renaissance and neoclassical Aristotelians.[54] Crane says that in the hands of these Aristotelians, "the method of 'Aristotelian' *poetics* has ceased to be that of an inductive science based upon hypothetical necessity and has become what for Aristotle would be a kind of dialectic—a discourse about poetry in general and its various species the 'first principle' of which are sought, not where Aristotle sought his, in the being of the things included in his sciences by virtue of his hypotheses, but rather in the generally accepted opinions of men of taste and learning and concerning what the pleasure and instruction of poetry ought to be."[55] Bernard Weinberg points out below four main defects of the Aristotelians:

> First, they came to the text of Aristotle with habits of textual interpretation, habits of fragmentation and methodological anarchy which made it impossible for them to understand this closely constructed and tightly argued. Second, they read the *Poetics* in the light of a rhetorical tradition which reduced all aspects of literary documents to considerations stemming from the audience. Third, they could not dissociate from their thinking about poetic matters

> the numerous details of Horace's *Ars Poetica*, which they had long known, and they insisted on reading Aristotle as if he were a kind of Ur-Horace. And finally they tried to "modernize" Aristotle, to adapt him to their own times and their own peoples in a manner scarcely authorized by the Aristotelian text.[56]

He called them pseudo-Aristotelians. Then, the question arises who are the true Aristotelians? If a group of critics engaged in reconstruction, refinement and extension of the 'first principles' of Aristotle in its original form refuse to be called "Neo-Aristotelians," then I do not know who else deserve this label. The prefix 'neo' means new, recent, latest, in a new, different or modified way. All these epithets cover the efforts of the Chicago Critics who were deeply interested in the revival of the general method of Aristotle. Even Crane admits that "if they are to be called 'Neo-Aristotelians,'" it should be in the same limited sense in which it is accurate to call these biologists "Neo-Mendelians."[57]

The name "Neo-Aristotelian" was first given to them, says Crane, by one of their friends, Kenneth Burke, in one of his earliest discussions of the Chicago critics. At that time, Burke was quite aware of their active study of the *Poetics* and other treatises of Aristotle.

If "Neo-Aristotelianism" is taken to be blind commitment to the critical theory of the Poetics, then the Chicago Critics are not "Neo-Aristotelians." But, if their active interest in certain basic principles and regressive hypothetical reasoning for grasping the 'immediate shaping cause' of a literary work, are taken into account, naturally one feels inclined to call them "Neo-Aristotelians." But the difficulty arises when the Chicago Critics prefer describing themselves as critical pluralists rather than as Neo-Aristotelians. The gap between what they say and do is certainly paradoxical and invites criticism from disinterested critics. Wayne C. Booth, who took serious exception to Ransom's remark that the Chicago Critics are pure Aristotelians, defends them on the basis of what they say. Booth argues that had Ransom cared to consider Crane's following pronouncement, he would not have remarked like that. Crane says:

> No one, it is true who uses the method for any length of time can help becoming aware of its limitations and hence of the need of supplementing it with other critical devices more sensitive to the various aspects of poetry which its characteristic selection of terms leaves out.[58]

It is true that Crane is fully aware of the limitations of Aristotle's method, yet, in practical criticism, he has not been able to supplement this method with any other method, as he repeatedly suggested in his writings. Ironically enough, even at the end of a brilliant whole-analysis of *Tom Jones*, we find him rarely saying: "We have obviously to go beyond formal criticism if we would assess Feilding's originality as a writer of 'comic romance' or account for that peculiarly eighteenth-century flavour in *Tom Jones* which causes us to reflect that, unique and unrepresentative as Fielding's novel is when considered as a whole, it could yet have been written at no other time." He has not been able to show as to how criticism of form could be supplemented with criticism of qualities, and also by historical enquiries of various sorts.[59] Thus, from the point of view of performance, they are "Neo-Aristotelian" critics.

Crane argues that Aristotle's method, like any other critical method, is limited in several ways, but, as compared to other methods, it is far more comprehensive. The comprehensiveness of the method, as he tells, rests on the following grounds:

> It is comprehensive...because it embraces all the elements necessary, in some particular determination and ordering, to the existence of a poem of any kind as a mind, and because it considers these (as in *Poetics* 1-3 as independent variables in a fashion quite different from the reductive, and frequently monistic, treatment of poetic elements to be found in much criticism of the present time.... The method is comprehensive...by virtue of the devices it affords for discriminating *a posteriori* an indefinite number of different poetic forms or principles of construction, and for dealing differentially with the common elements these involve, in terms not merely of their material content or technical configuration but of the functions they can be made to serve, directly or indirectly, in the constitution of different kind of poetic wholes; with the result that, when the method is properly used, it permits a far wider range of relevant differentiations in the discussions not only of poems but of poetic devices and materials than any method in which such a functional treatment of elements has no place.[60]

Thus it is the comprehensiveness of the method that draw them closer to Aristotle and not its perfection. Crane rightly comments that "the Chicago Critics have viewed their 'Aristotelianism' as a strictly pragmatic and non-exclusive commitment...to hypotheses about poetry and poetics that seem to them capable of being developed into a comprehensive critical method."[61] The method works well so long as a critic wants to understand and appreciate how well the "writers have accomplished the particular sorts of poetic tasks which the natures of the wholes they have attempted to construct imposed on them... ."[62]

After examining the claims and counter-claims of the Chicago Critics and their detractors, I feel that the Chicago Critics could be better called 'quasi-Aristotelians' instead of 'Neo-Aristotelians.' For all practical purposes they appear to be "Neo-Aristotelians." I do not know what different label can describe their deep-rooted faith in the concept of "concrete whole," *dynamis*, four causes, and "hypothetical regressive reasoning," which have been directly derived from Aristotle. I fully endorse Ransom's view that "in theory they are 'pluralists,' but 'pragmatically' they are occupied with 'Aristotelianism.'"[63] What I feel is that Crane's protest is based more on logic than on reality. They contend that they are more un-Aristotelians than Aristotelians. I think this paradox stems from their basic attitude to criticism, which was "progressive-conservative." They are, certainly, not going to apply it to the study of pre-constructional and post-constructional aspects of literary works for which better methods are available. Crane says that:

> the concept of imitation in its most general meaning, is more than an empirically verifiable hypothesis for distinguishing objects of art from natural things; or, taking the term in the more restricted sense in which it denotes one possible final cause in poetry, that all poems are imitations, though unquestionably many of them are...that the critic must define the end of poetry or art as pleasure simply or consider its function...to be only that of 'ornamenting pleasurably, in a moment's leisure, the life of its beholder...that the critic must think of distinctions among poetic species either as labels for conventionally determined classes of poems or as concepts signifying ideal values in the light of which individual productions may be compared and judged by considering the degree of their approximations to a precisely determined norms...that poetic kinds can even be completely enumerated or always differentiated accurately for one another...finally, there is nothing in the method that implies the impossibility, once the critic has grasped the principles of construction peculiar to different poems, of discussing their common elements and devices and arriving thus at comparative judgments or historical generalizations.[64]

Had Eliseo Vivas cared to go through this passage carefully, he would not have remarked that "the term imitation is a very poor term to achieve that end; that pleasure can neither define the end of poetry nor serve as a sign of poetic kinds."[65] What the Chicago Critics say regarding the concept of imitation[66] that they borrowed from Aristotle, does not invite the type of comments which Vivas makes in his review of *Critics and*

Criticism which was first published in the *Sewanee Review* in January, 1953. In the same year Crane's LCSP was also brought out from Toronto. I think either Vivas did not get the opportunity of going through the detailed discussion of Aristotle's theory and method by Crane in LCSP or he deliberately distorted Crane's interpretation. Crane was fully conscious of the powers and limitations of Aristotle's method. He never thought that the term 'imitation' was an ideal one; but, certainly, he considered it to be most comprehensive.

After examining the relationship of Aristotle and the Chicago Critics, we may conclude that their temperamental affinity has roots in their common interest in the structure of poetry. Aristotle's method, as they felt, had great remedial value for them. As literary critics, they had two main concerns: first, to check the use of *a priori* approach; and, second, to put a curb on the tendency of the contemporary critics towards monistic reduction of critical theories. Aristotle's *a posteriori* approach was the best alternative available to the Chicago Critics who considered the *a priori* approach of the contemporary critics inappropriate for understanding and appreciating literary works. Most of the contemporary critics were preoccupied with a single aspect of poetry, its 'material cause' only. But, Aristotle discovered multiplicity of structure in poetry not capable of reduction to a single cause, as wrongly emphasized by the New Critics tried to find out 'common structure' "which organizes works as dissimilar in other respects as the *Odyssey* and *The Waste Land*, "Tears, Idle Tears" and *The Rape of the Lock*."[67] But, Aristotle's differential analysis did not blur the distinctive character of the different literary works. Therefore, the Chicago Critics, for whom the end of a humanistic study in literature was to exhibit works as distinct human achievements, were naturally drawn to Aristotle for some basic assumptions and mode of reasoning. Thus, we find that the Chicago Critics found some vital elements in Aristotle which contemporary criticism lacked in. By and large, it is the remedial value of Aristotle's solution to certain basic literary problems that exercised a magnetic pull over the Chicago Critics. Being "progressive-conservative" reformers of literary studies they were in favour of using the 'usable past.' Crane says that "But our loyalty at any rate should be to problems rather than to ancient masters; and if it happens that we have problems for which Aristotle can give us the means, or some of the means, of solution, we should be prepared to benefit from his initiative in precisely the same way as many of our contemporaries have benefited from the more recent initiatives of Coleridge, Richards, Frazer, and Freud without necessarily becoming disciples of any of these men."[68]

The upshot of the discussion is that the Chicago Critics were greatly influenced by Aristotle, both in theory and practice. It is true that their commitment to Aristotle is purely pragmatic. They went to Aristotle in search of remedies that could remove the defects of the contemporary criticism, because they were basically reformers of literary studies. But, it would be a mistake to think that they found all the remedies that they sought in Aristotle only. Had it been the case, they would not have gone to Plato, Longinus, Dr. Johnson and others. Thus, despite their strong Aristotle's method they are basically critical pluralists in theory.

NOTES

1. LCSP, p. 154.
2. Physics, 194a 4-6.
3. *On the Parts of Animals*, Translated by W.D. Ross, 540^b 20-25.
4. LCSP, p. 150.
5. *Ibid.*, pp. 150-51.
6. *Ibid.*, pp. 151-53.
7. Crane, "The Critical Monism of Cleanth Brooks," *Critics and Criticism*, p. 93.
8. *Metaphysics*, VII, 7, 1033^1 15-20.
9. "An Outline of Poetic Theory," *Critics and Criticism*, n. 8, p. 21.
10. *On the Parts of Animals*, translated by William Ogle, p. i, l. 642.
11. *Ibid.*, see pp. 18-33.
12. LCSP, p. 184.
13. *Ibid.*, p. 45.
14. *Ibid.*, p. 45.
15. *Ibid.*, pp. 45-46.
16. *Ibid.*, p. 46.
17. *On the Parts of Animals*, 640^b 5-25.
18. *The Humanities*, I, xiv.
19. *The Humanities*, II, 184.
20. LCSP, p. 141.
21. *Ibid.*, p. 142.
22. *Critics and Criticism*, p. 17.
23. LCSP, p. xvi.
24. James D. Carney & Richard K. Scheer, *Fundamentals of Logic* (New York, The Macmillan Company, 1968), p. 351.
25. *Nicomachean Ethics*, translated by W.D. Ross, VI, 4,1140a 10-15.
26. LCSP, p. 46.

27. *Ibid.*, p. 46.
28. Aristotle's '*Poetics and English Literature*, p. 181.
29. *Ibid.*, p. 181.
30. *Ibid.*, p. 181.
31. LCSP, p. 23.
32. *Ibid.*, pp. 154-55.
33. Crane, *Critics and Criticism*, p. 13.
34. *Ibid.*, p. 13.
35. *Ibid.*, p. 16.
36. *Ibid.*, p. 16.
37. *The Humanities*, II, 56.
38. *Ibid.*, p. 48.
39. LCSP, p. 51.
40. *Ibid.*, p. 52.
41. "An Outline of Poetic Theory," *Critics and Criticism*, p. 560.
42. *Ibid.*, p. 559.
43. *Ibid.*, p. 559.
44. *Ibid.*, p. 559.
45. *Ibid.*, pp. 559-60.
46. *Ibid.*, p. 560.
47. Crane, *Ibid.*, p. 18.
48. *Ibid.*, p. 560.
49. *Ibid.*, p. 561.
50. LCSP, p. 65.
51. *Ibid.*, p. 65.
52. *Ibid.*, p. 65.
53. LCSP, p. 149.
54. "Rhetoric and Poetic in Aristotle," *Aristotle's 'Poetics' and English Literature*, p. 236.
55. Crane, *Critics and Criticism*, p. 17.
56. LCSP, p. 83.
57. "From Aristotle to Pseudo-Aristotle," *Aristotle's 'Poetics' and English Literature*, p. 199.
58. Crane, *Critics and Criticism* (abridged edition, 1957), p. iv.
59. *Critics and Criticism*, p. 19; cf. p. 645.
60. *Ibid.*, p. 645.
61. *Ibid.*, p. 646.
62. *Ibid.*, p. 20.

63. *Ibid.*, p. 13.

64. *Ibid.*

65. "Humanism at Chicago," *Kenyon Review*, Autumn, 1952, xiv, 302.

66. *Critics and Criticism*, p. 18.

67. "The Neo-Aristotelians of Chicago," *The Artistic Transaction* (Ohio, State University Press, 1963), p. 19.

68. *Critics and Criticism*, pp.160-68; Olson, *Ibid.*, pp. 553-54; Cf. Crane, LCSP, pp. 6, 18-19, 47-49, 81-82, 85-86, 150-60.

5

Critical Pluralism of the Chicago Critics

I

The object of this chapter is to be define the correct critical position of the Chicago Critics and to examine their powers and limitations. It will begin with a brief sketch of their pluralistic method, followed by a discussion of its application in practical criticism.

CRITICAL PLURALISM

The concept of critical pluralism was developed to end the chaos in criticism which was created by conflicting critical doctrines and judgments of the time. Expressing his concern in this regard, Olson observed:

> Criticism in our time is a sort of Tower of Babel. Moreover, it is not merely a linguistic but also a methodological Babel; yet, in the very pursuit of this analogy, it is well to remember that at Babel men did not begin to talk nonsense; they merely began to talk what seemed like nonsense to their fellows.[1]

> Olson's observation suggests that the crisis could be resolved by finding out "some critique which shall examine radically how such diversity arises... ."[2]

There are three principal ways, as Crane and Olson point out, in which the problem of extreme diversity in contemporary criticism have been tackled by the scholars.[3] The Chicago Critics analyze the solutions of their predecessors and contemporaries in the following way. Firstly, the skeptical writers hold "that no solution to the problem can be hoped for in as much as criticism, like philosophy, is only a matter of opinion."[4] Secondly, others think that what earlier critics have said about poetic structure are mere collection of errors or fragmentary truths founded on such assumptions that cannot be subjected to scientific enquiry.[5] Thirdly, some scholars might try to reconcile the partial critical insights, and try to integrate them into "a new and more comprehensive critical scheme."[6] In this way, we find that skepticism, dogmatism and syncretism are the three philosophic attitudes to solve the problem. But, Olson says: "Dogmatism holds the truth of a single position and the falsity, in some degree at least, of all others; syncretism the total falsity of all. All these take into their consideration doctrine alone; pluralism, taking both doctrine and method into account.... "[7] Therefore, 'pluralism,' as he suggests, is the fourth philosophic attitude which emerges out of a critique, which examines radically how such diversity arises. The three different ways of interpreting and dealing with oppositions in critical doctrines and judgments unfortunately rest upon a common assumption that there is "a single correct answer"[8] of the question regarding the structure of poetry. But, as Crane and Olson point out, it is erroneous to think so. Crane says that the meaning and character of a critical statement depends on "three independently variable factors."[9] Of these factors, says he, "one is the critic himself, as a man endowed with a certain set of interests, a certain intellectual capacity, a certain range of reading and information, a certain degree of taste and sensibility; and the second factor is the subject in which he is engaged, in the ordinary sense of the objectively existing text or body of texts to which he refers us when he speaks, for example, of *Macbeth* or Shakespeare or tragedy."[10] The third important factor that determines any critical writing, is the "internal necessities and possibilities of the discourse which he is constructing about"[11] the texts. "Any critical book or essay that makes coherent sense," says Crane, is "a body of propositions the meaning and validity of anyone of which cannot be properly judged until we have uncovered the precise question in the critic's mind to which the proposition is intended to be an answer."[12] Furthermore, he tells "that no question or problem ... has any absolute status or isolable meaning, but is always relative, as to both its content and the conditions of its answer, to the total context of the discourse in which it occurs... ."[13] Crane further adds that "the referent of any term is conditioned by the logical relation in which it stands to all other terms, or conceptual elements, employed in the discussion, and ultimately to the special set of assumptions concerning subject matter and method upon which the discourse rests."[14] Crane's semantic theory, by which he explains the critical controversies, is based on the above mentioned assumptions.

THE SEMANTIC THEORY OF CHICAGO CRITICS

Crane's theory, which accounts for the disagreements among critics, is called semantic theory because it involves an analysis of how critical statements mean. Crane says: "The view of critical question I want to suggest is based on the simple premise that no statement we make about literature in general or a given literary work can have any determinate meaning or relevance, or permit of any intelligent appraisal of its validity, so long as it is considered merely as an isolated statement."[15] Again, in his essay on Cleanth Brooks, he says that "all words as they present themselves to a writer, are ambiguous (there being many more things or ideas than verbal symbols for them) and therefore have to have their significances fixed by the particular contexts, of whatever sort, in which they are used."[16] Thus, Crane, at several places in his writings, holds that critical statements have determinative meaning within a context. According to him, a context consists of a subject matter and a procedure for deriving statements about that subject matter. What he precisely means by a subject matter can be best understood in his own words:

> There can be no intelligible discourse about literature or poetry...(or, for that matter, about any other subject) that does not rest upon...a conceptual scheme: and, once chosen...it delimits what the critic can say about any of the questions with which he may be concerned—and this for the simple reason that we can discuss only those aspects of existent objects which are represented or implied in the terms we select or have available for the discussion.... The subject matter of a given critical discussion is accordingly identical with its formulation in the necessarily finite system of general terms the critic uses in framing his problems and stating his conclusions: and it follows that before we can judge fairly of either the meaning or the validity of any critical statement, we must first reconstruct the underlying... conceptual scheme in which the statement appears—considering, for instance, whether it derives from principles that define and analyze poetry as a kind of knowledge or as a mode of speech...or as a variety or psychological, moral or political activity....[17]

Crane's explication of the nature of a subject matter is too brief to have a clear view of what he says. Therefore, it is necessary to supplement his brief explication with the work of his other Chicago colleagues. Elder Olson also says that the number of possible critical positions is relative to the number of philosophic positions; and, the latter are determined by two other main considerations; the number of aspects of a subject which can be brought into discussion, as constituting its subject matter and the kinds of basic dialectic which may be exerted upon the subject matter. He makes a distinction between the subject and the subject matter. I have already touched upon Olson's distinction of subject and subject matter in brief in Chapter 1 and have quoted passages from him which throw light upon it. According to Olson, "the subject is what is talked about; the subject matter is that subject in so far as it is represented or implied in the discussion. Philosophers do not discuss subjects themselves; they can discuss only so much as the term or materials of the discussion permit; and that is the subject matter."[18] Although Crane implies the distinction between the subject and the subject matter, in the passage quoted above, yet he fails to emphasize clearly the distinction between the two terms, as Olson does.

A subject, as Olson points out, is an area of intellectual activity or study such as poetry or economics, while a subject matter is the particular aspect of that subject area, such as poetry considered as a form of communication, that is actually under discussion in a critical essay. Like Crane, he too says that "any discussion of a 'subject' is relative to its formulation. But, further, any discursive reasoning must employ some method of reasoning, or inference; and, since there are various possible systems of inference, we may say that a given discussion is a function of its subject matter and of the dialectic, *i.e.*, system of inference, exerted upon that subject matter."[19]

According to Olson, conflict among critics arises when they fail to recognize the basic fact that when aspects or subject matters differ, they are bound to conclude differently. The conflicting views, according to him, are simply different and not inconsistent or 'contradictory,' as generally assumed by the critics. Only when critics refer to the same aspect or subject matter they contradict; and, never when their references are different.

Critics, as Olson indicates, explain a particular aspect of art with reference to certain causes and reasons. Such critics, for instance, who are concerned with the product of art try to explain "the nature of the product by reference to its matter or medium, to the subject represented or depicted, to the depictive method of the artist or some other productive cause, or to the end or effect of the product; and some have employed merely one of these causes or reasons, while others have used several or all."[19] Thus, when two critics refer to the same cause they may contradict each other; but, they certainly do not when they focus on two different causes. For example, Aristotle "employs differentiations of object, means, manner, and effect to define tragedy, whereas a critic like Richard Hurd finds the nature of poetry adequately defined by its subject matter."[20]

The mode of inference or dialectic also determines the nature of the context. This is a view that is more or less shared by all the Chicago Critics. Mckeon says that there are three main models of inferences or methods in use in the history of philosophy, that can be said to subsume all others: dialectical, logistics and problematic methods. Dialectical methods, according to him, "employ words in broad analogical meanings which permit the comparison of things different in kind and the reconciliation of opposites."[21] Logistic methods are employ "to construct systems of proof on the model of the mathematical deductions of geometry by giving simple terms literal and univocal definitions, by establishing simple relations among them, and by proceeding in long chains of deductive reasoning to the construction of more and more complex wholes."[22] Finally, as he says, problematic methods, "define terms relative to the problem under consideration and to the circumstances by which the problems are determined."[23]

Mckeon further explains that each of these methods employs principles that may be described as starting-points. He writes:

> The starting-point may be found in the beginning of a sequence, in the basic material underlying it, in the determination of the direction or order followed, or in the purpose to which the sequence is oriented. The method a philosopher uses determines his procedures, but his principles determine what he assumes as the beginning of philosophy, what he treats as its subject matter, what he constructs in ordering it, and what he seeks as its purpose. The principles of a philosophy, considered relatively to its method, are the assumptions with which the characteristic process of the method starts: the numerous forms of principles which have furnished the starting-places of dialectic, logistic, and inquiry may be classified under three heads as comprehensive, simple, and reflexive principles.[24]

Thus, we find that Mckeon states that the subject matter of a discussion should be identified by the basic principles of the discussion. If, for example, in a discussion of a literary work, say a novel, the principles are drawn from sociology, then the subject matter of discussion will be the sociological aspect of the novel. I have already quoted a passage[25] about Crane in which he implies a relation between a subject matter and principles, however, he does not state, as explicitly as Mckeon does, that in any argumentative discussions principles determine their overall procedure or method. For example, Mckeon clearly points out that any dialectical discussion "depends ultimately on comprehensive principles to reconcile or remove the basic oppositions which separate subject from object, thing from thing, and mind from mind...."[26] Thus, he suggests that a critic who examines the critical pronouncement of other critics must not overlook these controlling principles.

Mckeon's elucidation of the argumentative contexts helps us to understand that the determinate meaning of a critical statement, as Crane also suggests, is its meaning determined by normal grammatical and lexical analysis plus a description of its function with respect to the needs of the basic principles of its argumentative context.

What I feel here is that the Chicago colleagues influenced one another in formulating the concept of 'critical pluralism.' Exactly how much Crane was influenced by Mckeon is difficult to determine here, though some remarks by Olson suggest that the influence was considerable. He says: "It was Mckeon whose researches into critical and philosophic methodology both established the basis and determined the direction of critical pluralism."[27]

Thus it may be concluded that the semantic theory, which the Chicago Critics developed to account for the critical disagreements among critics, enjoins upon a critic's critic to place a critical statement in the larger context of its method, before he endorses or rejects it. Once the apparently contradictory critical statements are related to their original contexts, according to the Chicago Critics, they are usually found to be not contradictory, but simply statements about different subject matters. Thus we find, that the semantic theory of these critics as of great remedial value, as it clearly indicates that the mass of critical conflicts, recorded by literary historians, is largely an illusion. Crane observes:

> What I would propose...is that literary criticism is not, and never has been, a single discipline, to which successive writers have made partial and never wholly satisfactory contributions, but rather a collection of distinct and more or less incommensurable "frameworks" or "languages" within any one of which a question like that of poetic structure necessarily takes on a different meaning and receives a different kind of answer from the meaning it has and the kind of answer it is properly given in any of the rival critical languages in which it is discussed.[28]

The critique of disagreement among the critics, as Olson says, is of great remedial value indeed, as it is capable of ending a lot of confusion among critics.

The semantic theory of the Chicago critics is compatible with the current philosophic interest in language, as Crane quotes Edward Sapir's statement that linguistic "forms predetermine for us certain modes of observation and interpretation."[29] Drawing upon Sapir's view, he argues that the starting-point of any science or discipline is "a highly specialized linguistic construction—a coherent 'framework'...of selected terms and distinctions and of rules for operating with them into which we must translate all our observations of particular subjects if we are to succeed in making verifiable sense out of their characteristics and relations."[29] He also believes that there are various frameworks or systematic languages.

Critical pluralism of the Chicago Critics, in brief, is an attitude that welcomes the diversity of critical approaches and recognizes the powers and limitations of each, when properly handled, to say significant things about its subject.[30]

They have adopted an attitude to critical theories, which easily emancipates them from the stultifying notion "that there must be some 'proper' or 'right' approach to literature, poetry or Shakespeare... ."[31] This attitude towards critical methods is the outcome of their concept of critical pluralism, which permits the use of more than one method.

Mckeon says that a pluralistic critic "may successfully employ more than one of these modes of criticism and may even combine two or more of them, crudely or effectively, in a single theory or application of criticism."[32] Mckeon permits a pluralistic critic to combine more than two or more modes of criticism. But Crane disfavours any integration of critical modes. If by combining more than one method, Mckeon means use of more than one method, then his approach is not at variance with that of Crane; but, if he means integration of more than one critical mode, then he is certainly contradicting the general Chicago view regarding the matter. Mckeon's statement might be confused with the eclecticism of Hayman, Blackmur and Cargill.[33] Crane's view, which is by and large the Chicago view, is clearly incompatible with the view of "those who yearn for a more comprehensive 'synthesis' or 'integration' in criticism... and propose to achieve this by a more or less eclectic putting together of various distinct systems or approaches or at least of what appear to be their sounder parts."[34] He observes:

> I am quite unable to imagine what the "integrated" criticism proposed by Hayman would be like; but it is surely evident that the offspring of Mr. Blackmur's suggested alliance would have only the most remote resemblances to either of its parents: it might or might not have important virtues of its own as a newly invented language, but these would be no adequate substitute for the separate and distinctive virtues of either Coleridge or Aristotle, and we should

end, were his suggestion to lead to the rise of a new critical orthodoxy, in being worse off in analytical resources than we were before, just as criticism in the Neo-classical period was rather impoverished than enriched, on the whole, by the similar effort of the Renaissance to "marry" Aristotle with Horace.[35]

Thus, no two critical modes could be combined without doing harm to either of them. I think Mckeon's view should be interpreted in the first manner as I have suggested above. Mckeon insists on supplementing one critical mode with the other. Such an insistence rests on the basic assumption of the Chicago Critics that every critical mode has its own characteristic powers and limitations, owing to the fact that "any critical system must rest upon a finite number of terms and connections."[36] A pluralistic critic believes that "There are kinds of questions which Aristotle...can treat but Coleridge not, and other kinds of questions which Coleridge can deal with that find no place in Aristotle's poetic."[37]

Now, the question arises as to how a pluralistic critic will select his method or methods in literary criticism. Crane's answer to this fundamental question is based on a distinction that he borrowed from an essay by Rudolf Carnap, a logical positivist of the Vienna Circle, who tended to identify philosophy with analysis, especially the analysis of science. It appears that Carnap's writings exercised a great influence on the foundation of critical pluralism of the Chicago Critics. Crane derives certain consequences of major importance for the practice of criticism in general from Carnap's view about science and philosophy as a whole. "The essence of the view," says Crane, is "that the same critical 'sentence' about no matter what subject 'may by demonstrably true or demonstrably false, empirically confirmable or not, significant or nonsensical'...relevant or irrelevant of central or only marginal importance—'depending upon the framework to which we appeal.' "[38] Or, in other words, it may be said that there is "strict relativity, in criticism, of statements to questions and questions to 'frameworks' with respect to one another."[39] Crane drew this inference from Carnap's observation on the substance of any statement in science, about which two kinds of questions can be asked—'internal' and 'external.' The first kind of question, as he says, can be answered "within the conceptual and logical bounds of the framework."[40] And, the second kind of questions cannot be solved within the terms and rules of the 'framework.' The two kinds of questions are not theoretical but practical questions, for instance, "shall I use this or some other alternative framework."[41] Likewise, in considering the basis for choosing between a critical language that would relate poetry to other things (internal questions in Carnap's sense) or one that would examine poetry, (external questions), Crane says that:

> the issue, plainly, cannot be decided by a direct appeal to facts, for it is equally true that poetry is organically connected with everything else in life and that it is something with a distinctive reality of its own.... I can justify my choice only by arguing, and possibly persuading others to agree with me, that, by means of the particular framework I have selected, certain important questions about poetry...can be answered which I could not even raise, much less answer, intelligibly, in a framework of the other sort. There is thus a strict relativity, in criticism, not only of questions and statements to frameworks but of frameworks to ends, that is, to the different kinds of knowledge about poetry we may happen, at one time or another or for one or another reason, to want. And who is there with authority sufficient to entitle him to inform critics what these must be.[42]

The selection of aspect, which a critic does, depends on "a common sense apprehension...of the multiple likenesses and differences exhibited by literary works and of the variety of causes necessary to their production."[43] According to Crane, this selection of aspect is a pre-critical activity, which directly controls the choice of a critical mode. In the light of his pre-critical knowledge, a critic will discriminate between comprehensive and partial critical systems for the task in hand. Naturally, he would not go in for a critical mode which tends "to explain poetry in terms of only one or a small number of its causes, such as language, subject matter, or the psychology of the poet or his readers."[44] And he would not employ a critical mode which tends "to concentrate attention on the likenesses among poems to the neglect of all except their accidental differences or at least to have one preferred mode of analysis for all poems."[45] He would not use a critical mode which tends "to reduce all operative distinctions to one or two pair of contrary terms and to leave other terms...unanalyzed."[46] Finally, he would not prefer a critical mode which tends "to set up restrictive canons of poetic excellence and, in the name of these, to 'revaluate' negatively large parts of the established tradition."[47] The methodological limitations that Crane points out here can be found in abundance in contemporary criticism. Thus, a pluralistic critic would prefer, as far as possible, a critical mode which permits many-sided or comprehensive phenomena of a literary work. It must be reminded here that the Chicago Critics prefer the Aristotelian mode simply because it is more comprehensive than the other prevailing critical modes; and, not because they are blind Aristotelians. The pluralism of the Chicago Critics is not contradicted in anyway by their exclusive reliance on the Aristotelian mode, as they are fully aware of its limitations. The

Chicago Critics never assume Aristotle's *Poetics* as invulnerable. However, they contend that it can provide a number of remedies. Therefore, the concept of critical pluralism, which they have developed, was designed to supplement the deficiencies of the Aristotelian mode.

II

But there is a gap between the theory and practice of the Chicago Critics. In the previous Chapter, it has been discussed at length as to how the Chicago Critics, despite their claim to be pluralists, appear to be monists. John Crowe Ransom comments that "the Chicago Critics fail almost completely to use the plural method in their dealing with literary works. In theory they appear to pluralistic critics; but, pragmatically, they are occupied with their Aristotelianism." He further adds: "The Aristotelians in their book attack a number of contemporary critics, engrossed in their own specialties by accusing them of 'critical monism.' But towards the end of my writing, I felt I could proceed to categorize the Aristotelians themselves as 'monolithic.'"[48]

Crane's essay "The Concept of Plot and the Plot of *Tom Jones*" is considered to be one of the best practical criticisms. In this essay, he points out the limitations of the definitions of plot. Other critics have discussed plot as merely one topic among several others, and that too, in isolation from the remaining elements of thought, character, diction, style, narrative, techniques, ironical tone and the comic force of the novel. Crane comments: "All this points to a strictly limited definition of plot as something that can be abstracted, for critical purposes, from the moral qualities of the characters and the operations of their thought. This something is merely the material continuity of the story considered in relation to the general pleasure we take in any fiction when our curiosity about the impending events is aroused, sustained, and then satisfied to a degree or in a manner we could not anticipate."[49] As Crane points out, the contemporary fiction critics had found a plot good "in terms simply of the variety of incidents it contains, the amount of suspense and surprise it evokes, and the ingenuity with which all the happenings in the beginning and middle are made to contribute to the resolution at the end."[50] They have considered plot not as the end but as a means, as "mere mechanism." Crane comments: "When plot is conceived thus narrowly, in abstraction from the peculiar characters and mental processes of the agents, it must necessarily have, for the critic, only a relatively external relation to the other aspects of the work."[51] According to him, such narrow definitions of plot resulted from the "neo-classic degradation"[52] of the analytical scheme of Aristotle which "turned on the nature and functional interrelations of the four parts as elements in an artistic synthesis of a particular kind... ."[53] The disjunction of the four elements: "fable," "characters," "sentiments" and "language" produced a limited view of plot. Crane's restatement of Aristotle's view in the essay is significant from the point of view of its remedial value, because it provides him a vantage-point from which he launches his attack on the critics of *Tom Jones*. Crane's typical procedure consists of diagnosis of defects, followed by suggestion of remedies. He, first of all, examines, the critical estimates of the critics of *Tom Jones*—say of Arthur Murphy, Oliver Elton, Wilbur L. Cross, Aurelien Digeon, Elizabeth Jenkins and George Sherburn. The question which deeply concerns Crane "is not the justice of any of these estimates but rather the nature and critical adequacy of the conception of plot in general and of the plot of *Tom Jones* in particular that underlies most if not all of them."[53] Thus, the Aristotelian doctrine is conspicuously behind what Crane observes here.

Crane, in his formal analysis of the novel, discovers that the 'formal principle' of *Tom Jones* is peculiarly comic. He shows how the gradual attenuation of fear, pity and indignation produce cumulatively the comic effect. The sense of fear for Tom and Sophia, the two sympathetic characters as they move toward the successive climaxes of their troubles, is prevented from becoming the predominant emotion in the novel. A discerning reader can easily mark that Bilfil and Allworthy, whose actions threaten serious consequences for the hero and heroine are essentially laughable persons. Crane shows that Fielding handles the constituent parts of the novel "to sustain and maximize the special pleasure which is its form."[54] He says that "there are not many novels of comparable length in which the various parts are conceived and developed with a shrewder eye to what is required for a maximum realization of the form."[55] Crane's analysis of Fielding's artistic reasoning in the novel is based on "hypothetical regressive reasoning." His whole-part analysis is based on the assumption that a work of art is a dynamic whole which affects our emotions in a certain way through the functioning together of its elements in subordination to a determinate poetic form.[56] Crane has employed the Aristotelian method which has been discussed at length in Chapter 4. But, immediately at the end of the formal analysis of *Tom Jones* he points out the limitations of the method which can at best answer only one type of question. He writes that:

> the method is one which depends on the analytical isolation of works of art, as finished products, from the circumstances and

> processes of their origin. It is, therefore, better fitted to explain those effects in a work which would be specifically the same in any other work, of whatever date, that was constructed in accordance with the same combination of artistic principles, than those effects which must be attributed to the fact that the work was produced by a given artist, in a given period, at a given stage in the evolution of the species or tradition to which it belongs: we have obviously to go beyond formal criticism if we would assess Fielding's originality as a writer of "comic romance" or account for that peculiarly eighteenth-century flavor in *Tom Jones* which causes us to reflect that, unique and unrepresentative as Fielding's novel is when considered as a whole, it could yet have been written at no other time.[57]

After examining Crane's formal analysis of *Tom Jones* and his remarks therein, I feel that John Crowe Ransom did not care to take into consideration the concluding remarks of Crane, where he clearly points out the obvious limitations of Aristotle's method and the need to supplement it with other critical mode. Again, Ransom appears to have missed another important fact that, whenever, the Chicago Critics appear to have employed Aristotle's method in practical criticism, "they have employed Aristotle's general method not the doctrine of the *Poetics*,"[58] Wayne C. Booth says that the Chicago Critics "are careful to point out that the conclusions of the *Poetics* are for the most part, pertinent only to one small area of poetic drama; they are attempting only to adopt the method which underlay these conclusions, in order to produce criticism of other kinds of works which will have something of the same usefulness within its own limits which, according to (Ransom), the *Poetics* still has in dealing with Greek tragedy."[59] Thus, to Booth, it appears presumptuous on Ransom's part to take the Chicago Critics as the blind followers of Aristotle. What I feel is that if the Chicago Critics are to be labelled at all, they, instead of being called "Neo-Aristotelians," should be called "quasi-Aristotelians," which I think would be a better description of the activities they were engaged in.

They employed the Aristotelian mode of analysis to discover the immediate shaping cause of *Tom Jones*, without assuming that this would illuminate other aspects of the novel also. Crane is vulnerable to attack because he has not employed the other mode of analysis, as he has suggested, which could have supplemented the Aristotelian mode. Despite the gap which we notice in their theory and practice, we find them basically pluralists. Wayne C. Booth rightly observes "that Crane's critical pluralism is not the easy eclecticism that generally travels under the name. Until one has seem how a man is able, without inconsistency, to pursue a mode of thought rigorously and even passionately and at the same time to see that mode as only one of many valid modes, one cannot really catch what Crane is about."[60]

Again, in the analysis of Jane Austen's *Persuasion*, Crane employs Aristotle's general method and shows how he effectively moulded the "parts" of the novel to its comic form. A large number of incidental happenings and minor characters of the novel are geared to the "intended-overall effect" of the novel—to evoke a particular kind of happiness, which is only produced by a 'serious comedy.' According to Crane a "serious comedy is one, in which, what makes its events interesting and moving for us, is not so much its intrinsic painfulness and pleasurableness as the fact that they happen to persons for whom we have a special concern by reason of their merits as individuals."[61] After defining the form, Crane examines how this 'form' controls other expedients of the story. But this cannot be understood unless Jane Austen's primary task in writing this novel is fully grasped. By writing a 'serious comedy,' she wanted to evoke a particular kind of emotion in the readers—a feeling of happiness by sharing the lover's new-found happiness, which is actually not the love of lovers only but of all moral individuals. This sort of happiness cannot be attained by ordinary lovers but by "persons of superior minds and characters." Therefore, the kind of happiness that readers derive from *Persuasion* is "an effect compounded of sympathy and moral approbation."[62] As Crane says, it "is not simply that a marriage is to take place, but a good marriage, of the kind we would wish all persons we particularly value to have."[61] Crane concludes his analysis by saying: "But whatever the degree of her success, it is clear that she was aware of what had to be done, and knew, what kinds of devices of 'treatment' would best help her in the circumstances of the novel, to do it."[62]

In the analysis of Hemingway's story "The Killers," Crane infers that the "intended-overall effect" of the story is shock—the most probable 'form' of the story. Crane discovers this element of shock in different parts of the story. He writes:

> It is faintly shocking that the action in prospect from the beginning is a gangster murder. It is more shocking that this is to take place in a quiet small town far removed from the normal sphere of such killings. It is still more shocking that it is being carried out, in a completely passionless and impersonal spirit ("Just to oblige a friend, bright boy"), by creatures as obnoxiously inhuman as Al and Max. And it is greatly more shocking still that the intended victim

of this horrible "vaudeville team," whatever he may have done to get in wrong, is a big, friendly, and polite Swede, whom no one meet in Summit thinks other than pleasantly of ("An awfully nice man. He was in the ring you know").[63]

In the analysis of the last voyage of *Gulliver's Travels*, Crane's hypothesis regarding the 'form' of the fable is based on the evidence found in the next. According to him, Swift's main artistic problem was to employ such devices as would arouse extreme kind of abhorrence and disgust against the appearance, actions and habits of the Yahoos, as Gulliver felt. The story was to be imaginatively convincing as a vehicle for his satirical thesis. Crane contends that Swift conceived of the Fourth Voyage as an "anti-Porphyrian" satire in order to "vex" the "honest men."[64] Crane's interpretation of the 'Fourth Voyage' appears to be convincing as it is based on a confirmatory evidence that Swift was seized with the problem of anti-Porphyrian definition of man at the time of writing the satirical book. Crane's analysis of the 'Fourth Voyage' of *Gulliver's Travels* is based upon the theory of 'multiple working of hypotheses.' Here he accepts the most probable hypothesis which is supported by a textual evidence. He takes into account the 'overall intended effect'—which was to shock the honest men of his time, and examines its execution at different levels of the narrative. Crane exhaustively considers Swift's immediate artistic task, and points out the defects of Frye's analysis of the 'Fourth Voyage.'[65]

Crane says that "Many of Swift's recent critics have thought it necessary to find special reasons for both the character and the quantity of this imagery; and, almost without exception, they have assumed that the explanation must involve reasons not directly deducible from the 'Fourth Voyage' itself, when this is read simply as a literary composition."[66] Some critics find the clue to the highly repulsive kind of imagery in the personality-traits of Swift—"his obsession with cleanliness and the nastier bodily functions."[67]

Some relate it to "his secret theological intentions in the writing of the Fourth Voyage."[68] We are told by them that Swift "represented in the Yahoos...the condition into which man had been brought by original sin."[69]

Again, Crane's habit of finding fault with the practical criticism of the contemporary critics, can be illustrated by examining his analysis of Jane Austen's *Persuasion*. He tells us that what is wrong with Mudrick's analysis[70] is that, he too tries to allude certain episodes, as depicted in chapters 6 and 8 of *Persuasion*, to "Jane Austen's attitude toward certain kinds of people."[71] According to him, such critics would have produced better practical criticism of the novel, "if he had asked himself seriously beforehand just what was Jane Austen's problem as a novelist—her literary problem—at the point in *Persuasion* where this episode occurs?"[72]

In his practical criticism of Ernest Hemingway's story, "The Killers," Crane follows the same method. First of all, he analyses the defects of the analysis of the same story as done by Cleanth Brooks and Robert Penn Warren in *Understanding Fiction*. At the very outset of his functional analysis, Crane writes; "The question I want to raise is one that has been overlooked or evaded in most of the discussions of Hemingway's tale I have read or heard. It is the technical question of how the characters, actions, and speeches of the boys in the lunchroom are related to the situation involving the Killers and Ole Andreson."[73] Again, he takes the view that the characters of the story do what the 'form' of the story compels them to do—a fact, which the New Critics and overlooked in their analysis. About the functional role of the characters, he says that "They belong to the 'subject' of the story not directly but indirectly; they belong intimately to the 'treatment,' as devices of disclosure and commentary which enable Hemingway to bring his essential 'subject' before us with a maximum of concentration and dramatic liveliness and a minimum of ambiguity as to its desired emotional effect."[74]

Crane also realized that the contemporary dramatic criticism was defective in the sense that it hindered the realization of Arthur Mizener's aim; which was "to promote a union of the living stage and the stage as a formulated art."[75]

Here, Crane shows his concern for the second element of Mizener's combination—that is, "with the condition under which,...the reading and study of dramatic criticism may help to advance rather than hinder the realization of its double aim."[75] Surveying the critical theories from Thomas Rymer and Voltaire to William Archer and Wilson Knight, he observes:

> What is lacking in both of these of dramatic criticism is a critical view of criticism itself. It is the business of critics of the drama to make propositions about plays or about the art of which plays are products, and it is our business, as students of the drama, to utilize these propositions to the end of improving our capacity for contemplating and discussing the plays we read or see. But we cannot do this intelligently or fruitfully if we are content to concentrate merely upon what is explicitly said about this or that topic. For the propositions of critics, or at least of those most likely to repay our

> study, are never neither fully intelligible or completely verifiable in themselves as independent judgments or statements of doctrine. They are not propositions simply but reasoned propositions, and as reasoned propositions they derive their meaning and validity not only from their relations to the objective dramatic things they refer to, but, more immediately, from their place in a network of other propositions, not all of them expressed, which serve both to fix their terms and to provide a warrant for their assertion. If we are really to profit, therefore, from our study of critical writings about the drama, we must form the habit of reading them with a view not merely to what they say about a given subject but to why they say this, whatever it may be, rather than something else. We must consider, that is, not only the doctrines and judgments of critics but the basic reasons, or, as Dryden puts it in his essay on tragedy, the "grounds of criticism," upon which these rest.[76]

Thus, we find that, whether it is fiction criticism or drama criticism, the primary aim of R.S. Crane is remedial. In this connection, Keast's practical criticism of *King Lear* may be discussed here. As the title of his essay, "The New Criticism and King Lear," suggests Keast is mainly concerned here with the criticism of New Criticism. Keast critically examines the tradition of criticism that started with the analysis of the imagery of Shakespeare's plays by Caroline Spurgeon's, as early as 1935. In this essay, he analyzes Robert Bechtold Heilman's critical analysis of *King Lear*. Heilman, following Spurgeon's pattern, discovers the meaning of the play in the patterns of recurrent images. Crane categorically points out that there is nothing in the text of the play which warrants a symbolic interpretation of *King Lear*."[77] He writes: "Anyone who wishes to take this position is, of course, free to do so; but he must discharge the initial critical and logical responsibility of showing his assumption to be needful and relevant, by making it clear that an interpretation of the play as a literal action is inadequate to the author's intention as revealed in the details of the work."[78] It is unjustified act on critic's part to subject a literary work to symbolic interpretation which does not demand such treatment.

Elder Olson, in his essay "A Symbolic Reading of the Ancient Mariner" also raises his objection to the unwarranted symbolic interpretations of literary works. In this essay, he analyses the interpretation of Coleridge's poem by Warren,[79] that the poem "has a meaning—not a literal one, not an allegorical one, but a symbolic one."[80] He writes:

> The words have a meaning; they mean the poem, but why should the poem itself have any further meaning? And, if there is any point to this asking, shall we not have a further meaning still, and so on *ad infinitum*, so that interpretation becomes impossible, as being an infinite process? Moreover, these "meanings of poems" are at best something very trivial, prosaic and obvious: Oedipus means that man walks in darkness, Hamlet that man is utterly alone, the Ancient Mariner that life is one and that the imagination revenges itself, etc. Such interpretation springs from the use of a very arid grammatical apparatus and wholly blinks the question of how powerfully we are affected by the spectacle of human fortunes, as well as that of how the situation, character, passion, and thought of the poetic *personae affect their speech.*[81]

Thus, Keast and Olson try to interpret literary works in the light of their New Critics' "ruling hypothesis." Their critical approaches are based on *a priori* reasoning. Keast points out that:

> Heilman's error in interpretation are thus the inevitable consequences of his theory. He begins with a determinate structural scheme which, since the work must express meanings, must be embodied in the work if it is to have artistic value. He knows, in all important respects, what he is going to find out before he begins, and it is no wonder that, having begged all the important respects, what he is going to find out before he begins, and it is no wonder that, having begged all the important questions he should find it. His interpretation is, moreover, in the proper sense, materialistic: form and structure are for him derivative form, and therefore strictly dependent on, the matter which the work expresses; the form of the play, indeed, is its total meaning, and this obviously not be characters, or their actions, or their thoughts, or even the language in which their thoughts are cast, but what these all represent.... His theory, furthermore, is essentially a system of very simple dichotomies, which he attributes to the play itself. And "meanings" are elaborated from a private and non-artistic theory of morality and religion, and then the necessary symbolic counterparts for the term of the theory are "discovered" in the play.[82]

After examining the critical performance, of the Chicago Critics, we are easily led to believe that their primary aim in criticism was to get it *rid of* defects.

Although Chicago Critics have produced very little of practical criticism; yet, the little they have produced, is important from the point of view of its remedial character and not for its critical ingenuity. They have attempted the practical criticism of only such works as have been already explicated by the contemporary critics. They have found fault with their methods of criticism.

Murray Krieger calls a practising critic a player.[83] If practical criticism is to be regarded as a play, then, it appears, that the Chicago Critics like good coaches know how to train good players more than to play well. They are all the time preoccupied with what is foul-play and how to avoid that. And, it is commonly seen that a player, who is conscious of the rules and regulations of a play, cannot be a good player. The Chicago Critics, being academic critics, considered literary criticism as teaching item through which they could help their students in developing right kind of critical habits. Consequently, the basic character of their criticism became remedial.

Explaining the special characteristics of the Chicago Critics, Crane avers: "For we possess what these other methods have conspicuously lacked: a means of isolating and defining those principles of structure in individual poems which distinguish them from other poems or kinds of poems and determine thus in highly specific way what their distinctive elements are and the artistic reasons that justify the particular configurations we observe them to have."[84] As already discussed in detail, they have made, "the shaping principle of form and emotional 'power' without which no poem could come into existence as a beautiful and effective whole of a determinate kind,"[85] the starting-point of their practical criticism, which has been left out by modern critics like I.A. Richards, T.S. Eliot, F.R. Leavis, Cleanth Brooks, Robert Penn Warren, Allen Tate, John Crowe Ransom, Yvor Winters etc.

The advantages, which they have over the New Critics, can be best summed up in Crane's words:

> We can therefore talk with a fulness and precision of distinction impossible to them about the particular and widely variant relations which exist in different poems between their formal and their material natures. We are not limited to any one conception of poetic unity, or to any one set of concepts for defining structure. We are not forced to speak of the working together of the parts of a poem merely in terms of simple contrarieties of theme or tone or in a vocabulary of which the most exact words are expressions like "goes with," "associated with," or is "related to" or "carries out," "reflects," "repeats," "qualifies," "balances," "contrasts with," "contradicts" and so on. We are not compelled, in order to show our recognition

that the best poetry is not indifferent to thought or "meaning," to interpret all poetic masterpieces in which ideas are contained or evoked as if they were compositions of the same order as *The Divine Comedy*, or, at any rate, in some sense or in some degree metaphorical or symbolic expressions, or, at the very least, "studies" of something or other. We shall be aware that there are indeed many poetic works to which such descriptions can be applied, but we shall go on the assumption—which all experience and literary history surely warrants—that ideas can function in poems in radically different ways: sometimes as sources of inspiration, sometimes as formal and shaping ends, sometimes as means for constituting the characters, purposes, or states of mind of the *dramatis personae*, sometimes as choric devices for enhancing or universalizing the actions: and the distinctions of our theoretic analysis, and notably our distinction between imitative and non-imitative forms, will enable us to discriminate these various uses when we come upon them and to judge of the significance of the thought in-any poem or passage according as one or another of them is its primary cause. And finally, in dealing with the problems of imagery that have been so prominent during the past generation, especially in the criticism of Shakespeare, we are not restricted to either a merely material classification and psychological interpretation of images (as in Miss Spurgeon and her followers) or to a merely generalized and indefinite discussion of their functions in drama (as in some of the more recent Shakespeareans): with our basic distinction of object, manner, and means and our more specific devices and our more specific devices for relating the parts of individual works to their controlling forms, we should be able, at the very least, to introduce greater particularity and artistic intelligibility into the subject that are apparent in most of the current discussions.[86]

Thus, we find that the blue-print, which the Chicago Critics prepared for the criticism of poetic structure will be certainly free from the limitations of the contemporary criticism. Their motive is essentially remedial, therefore, "there must be many readers of such criticism who would be grateful for more precise indications than they usually get of what are the formal as well as the material and technical novelties to be found in the latest serious novels, plays and volumes of verse, and above all the kinds of 'peculiar pleasures' they are fitted to give us and why."[87]

The Chicago Critics have supplied us with a method which, on being skillfully handled, can improve the writing of literary history as well as practical criticism, by taking into consideration "the immediate artistic causes of literary productions along with the relatively more external and remote causes to which historians of literature have mainly confined themselves."[88] The principles of the Chicago Critics is capable of bringing about appreciable improvement in the field of literary education, as they have given a critical apparatus for reading and appreciation "which would be exempted, on the one hand, from more impressionism and the evocation of irresponsible opinion and, on the other hand, from the imposition on students of ready-made literary doctrines or canons of taste."[89] About this kind of improvement, of all the Chicago Critics, Crane had plenty of things to suggest. Crane's "Comprehensive scheme of questions to be asked about all the different kinds of literary works"[90] and his "criterion for discussing the appropriateness and adequacy of the answers in the light of the particular texts,"[91] will be discussed in the following chapter. But, it must be indicated here that Crane along with his colleagues always made efforts to improve the theory and practice of literary criticism. Thus, the chief contribution of the Chicago School of Criticism lies in their quest for an appropriate method in literary studies that would be free from the defects of the contemporary methods. The development of such a method, "centred, as it would be, in the statement and free comparison of hypotheses, would help to bring into literary studies something they have commonly lacked—a subject matter, namely, in the sense not merely of facts but of compendent general concepts for their interpretation; concepts, moreover, that can be translated into habits of observation and reflection such as will tend to make the student independent of his teacher; a potential scholar in criticism rather than a disciple or member of a school, and a scholar who would do credit to his training precisely in proportion as he was able to correct and develop further the things he had been taught."[92]

Thus the main motive behind their practical criticism is to improve the contemporary practical criticism, which was an ultra academic exercise in 'lemon-squeezing,' by focusing its attention on the 'writer's immediate literary task.' Crane's I views on the function of practical criticism is as follows:

> It would seem therefore that the first business of practical criticism, in dealing with a given work, must be to ask what were the literary problems the writer was faced with, why these were problems for him in relation to his overall literary work, we may come out with explanations or judgments either wholly or partly beside the point: Psychological, philosophical, or historical construction on the work

that will appear unnecessary or far-fetched when we descend to the simpler level of the writer's literary task.[93]

The Chicago Critics attempted only a criticism of practical criticism already done by their contemporaries, like T.S. Eliot, I.A. Richards, Cleanth Brooks, John Crowe Ransom and Allen Tate. Thus they themselves limited the scope of their practical criticism. They mostly indulged in criticism of practical criticism already brilliantly done by other critics.

If critical pluralism means simply the use of more than one critical method then the Chicago Critics seems to have failed; but, if it means framing more than one hypothesis then they have succeeded. Except in Crane's analysis of Gulliver's fourth voyage, we do not find any use of Dr. Johnson's "Circumstantial method." As I have already pointed out, the Chicago Critics invariably employed Aristotle's mode of analysis. But, what still makes them pluralists is their openness to other critical modes. They are anything but dogmatic and restrictive. Their "problematic functional analysis" is quite flexible. The habit of reading literary works in the light of their particular 'literary' ends, problems, and reasons, as they urge, will surely emancipate critics from falling a victim to critical monism—a kind of dogmatism—which shows that what is irreducibly manifold can be described through a single approach based upon a "ruling hypothesis." The Chicago Critics in their practical criticism have never viewed a literary work in the light of one favourite hypothesis. They frame their hypothesis tentatively. Their pluralism may be defined as a kind of anti-dogmatism.

NOTES

1. "An Outline of Poetry," *Critics and Criticism*, p. 546.
2. *Ibid.*, p. 546.
3. LCSP, pp. 8-9; also see Olson, *Critics and Criticism*, p. 547.
4. LCSP, p. 8.,
5. Cf. "But if vie now turn to consider what are the results yielded by the best minds pondering these questions in the light of the eminently accessible experiences provided by the Arts, we discover an almost empty garner. A few conjectures, a supply of admonitions, many acute isolated observations, some brilliant guesses, much oratory and applied poetry', inexhaustible confusion, a sufficiency of dogma, no small stock of prejudices, whimsies and crotchets, a profusion of mysticism, a little genuine speculation, sundry stray inspirations, pregnant hints and random apercus; of such as these, it may be said without exaggeration, is extant critical theory (I.A. Richards, *Principles of Literary Criticism*, London, Routledge & Kegan Paul Ltd.), p. 6.

6. LCSP, p. 9.
7. "An Outline of Poetic Theory," *Critics and Criticism*, p. 547.
8. LCSP, p. 9.
9. *Ibid.*, p. 10.
10. *Ibid.*, p. 10.
11. LCSP, p. 10.
12. *Ibid.*, pp. 10-11.
13. *Ibid.*, p. 11.
14. *Ibid.*, p. 11.
15. "Questions and Answers," *The Humanities*, II, 177.
16. "The Critical Monism of Cleanth Brooks," *Critics and Criticism*, p. 102.
17. *Critics and Criticism*, p. 7; see also LCSP, pp. 10-11; "Questions and Answers," *The Humanities*, II, p. 178.
18. "An Outline of Poetic Theory," *Critics and Criticism*, p. 547.
19. *Ibid.*, pp. 547-48.
20. *Ibid.*, p. 549.
21. *Ibid.*
22. Richard Mckeon, *Freedom and History* (New York, 1952), pp. 14-15.
23. *Ibid.*, pp. 14-15.
24. *Freedom and History* (New York, 1952), pp. 14-15.
25. "Philosophy and Method," *The Journal of Philosophy*, XLV1II (October, 1951), 665.
26. See p. 6 fn. 1.
27. "Philosophy and Method," *The Journal of Philosophy*, XLVIII (October, 1951), 665.
28. *Aristotle's Poetics and English Literature*, ed. Elder Olson (Chicago, 1965), p. xxviii.
29. LCSP, p. 13.
30. LCSP, p. 11. Also see *The Encyclopaedia of the Social Sciences*, IX (New York, 1933), p. 156.
31. LCSP, p. 12.
32. *Ibid.*, pp. 191-94.
33. *The Humanities*, II, 180.
34. "The Philosophic Bases of Art and Criticism," *Critics and Criticism*, p. 544.
35. See *The Armed Vision: A Study in the Methods of Modem Literary Criticism* (New York, 1948), pp. ix, 395-407.
36. LCSP, p. 28.
37. *Ibid.*, p. 29.
38. Crane, *Critics and Criticism*, pp. 9-10.

39. *Ibid.*, pp. 9-10.
40. LCSP, p. 26.
41. *Ibid.*, p. 26.
42. *Ibid.*, p. 26.
43. *Ibid.*, p. 26.
44. *Ibid.*, pp. 25-26.
45. Crane, *Critics and Criticism*, p. 10.
46. *Ibid.*, p. 10.
47. *Ibid.*, p. 10.
48. *Ibid.*, p. 10.
49. *Ibid.*, p. 10.
50. Wayne C. Booth, "Communications on the Aristotelian Front," *Kenyon Review*, Vol. XV, Spring, 1953, No. 2, p. 302.
51. *Ibid.*, p. 302.
52. Crane, "The Concept of Plot and the Plot of 'Tom Jones,'" *Critics and Criticism*, p. 618.
53. *Ibid.*, p. 618.
54. *Ibid.*, p. 619.
55. *Ibid.*, p. 618.
56. *Ibid.*, p. 617.
57. *Ibid.*, p. 638.
58. *Ibid.*, p. 639.
59. *Ibid.*, p. 645.
60. *Ibid.*, p. 646.
61. Wayne C. Booth, "Communications on the Aristotelian Front," *Kenyon Review*, Vol. XV, Spring 1953, No. 2, p. 300.
62. *Ibid.*, p. 300.
63. *The Humanities*, I, xxi.
64. *The Humanities*, II, 289.
65. *Ibid.*, p. 289.
66. *Ibid.*, p. 289.
67. *Ibid.*, p. 299.
68. *Ibid.*, quoted on p. 305.
69. "Houyhnhnms, Yahoos, and the History of Ideas," *Ibid.*, p. 263.
70. See Roland M. Frye, "Swift's Yahoos and the Christian Symbols for Sin," Journal of the *History of Ideas*, 15 (1954): 201-15.
71. "Every Man His Own Critic," *The Humanities*, II, 210.
72. *Ibid.*, p. 210.

73. *Ibid.*, p. 210.

74. *Ibid.*, p. 210.

75. See Karvin Mudrick, *Jane Austen: Irony as Defence and Discovery* (Princeton, 1952), pp. 211-13.

76. *The Humanities*, II, 212.

77. *Ibid.*, p. 212.

78. *Ibid.*, p. 303.

79. *Ibid.*, p. 304.

80. Cf. “It is our ambition,” Arthur Mizener says, “to pull together the drama as a thing alive on the stage and the drama as a thing read, contemplated, and discussed” (quoted on p. 215 of *The Humanities*, II).

81. *Ibid.*, p. 215.

82. *Ibid.*, p. 216.

83. *Ibid.*, p. 136.

84. *Ibid.*, p. 136.

85. See *Samuel Taylor Coleridge*, “The Rime of the Ancient Mariner” with an essay by Robert Penn Warren (New York: Reynal & Hitchock, 1946).

86. *Critics and Criticism*, p. 138.

87. *Ibid.*, p. 139.

88. *Ibid.*, p. 118.

89. *Play and Place of Criticism* (Baltimore, The John Hopkins Press, 167), p. viii.

90. LCSP, p. 184.

91. *Ibid.*, p. 185.

92. *Ibid.*, p. 186.

93. *Ibid.*, p. 187.

6

Every Man his Own Critic

I

Any assessment of the Chicago school of criticism will remain incomplete unless R.S. Crane's contribution to it is fully understood. Crane in his various capacities—as an editor, a bibliographer, an educator and a reviewer—helped the Chicago school of criticism to fulfil its aim, it is difficult to sum up his career as he has been simultaneously charged with being a renegade historian and an apostate critic.[1] He started his career as a specialist of the eighteenth century literature. In the eighteenth century, he found an ideal state of relationship among the humanist scholars—grammarians, historians, philosophers and critics. Harmony among the practitioners of various disciplines characterized the spirit of the age. Any kind of separation or antithesis was considered to be unhealthy for the humanities during that period. Efforts towards solutions, howsoever partial, of the oppositions between advocates of useful knowledge and humanists; between rhetoricians and philosophers; between partisans of the moderns and the admirers of the ancients, created a peaceful atmosphere. According to Crane, the eighteenth-century was a great humanistic age in which the purpose of literary studies was seldom seriously doubted even by the teachers of natural sciences. The central problems of the philosophers of this period were problems of powers and achievements of human beings. On the one hand, the grammarians, critics, and historians attempted to be philosophical, and on the other hand "...philosophers concerned themselves in a humanistic rather than merely scientific spirit with language, criticism and history...."[2] The breadth and harmony of interest which Crane noted in the eighteenth century formed the philosophic base of the Chicago School of Criticism which he founded later on. As I have already discussed, he disagreed with those critics of his time who set up a sharp antithesis between a scholar and a critic. He attempted to unite the function of a critic and a scholar. Therefore, he disapproved the methods of those critics who completely rejected the methods of the ancient critics. He tried to re-establish the eighteenth century ideals in contemporary criticism which was opposed to separation and controversy. The literary humanists of his time (critics) were engaged in open war with the scholars as they felt that whereas the historical scholars dealt only with the extrinsic factors of literature and concentrated on facts,—"often useless and insignificant facts, instead of values,"[3] they were concerned with the intrinsic factors of literary works. Crane always favoured a balanced approach, which he defined as a kind of "progressive-conservatism."

What appeared like a kind of betrayal to Crane's early collaborators, who had established criticism in the universities, was, in fact, the right kind of approach, which every sensible critic should possess. It was a strategic retreat—an act of the great virtues of Crane was that he was always ready to modify his earlier stand, whenever he felt convinced about its incorrectness. This shows his capacity for self-knowledge, understanding and adjustment. In his essay "Criticism as Inquiry," he modified his earlier stand which he had taken in "History *Versus* Criticism" (1957). He says that in 1935 he supported those men who "set criticism in sharp antithesis to the established mode of literary scholarship,"[4] because it "had some rhetorical or political justification two decades ago, but surely no other justification then or since."[5] After twenty-two years, he firmly holds that there "can be no adequate criticism that is not solidly based on the history of the art with which it is concerned."[6] Thus we find that Crane was completely free from dogmatism. Whenever he discussed the powers of a critical method, he simultaneously discussed its limitations also. In the essay, "The Teaching of Literary Texts," he clearly points out the strength and weakness of the five major critical methods. Here he tells us that no critical method should be completely relied upon by a critic, because, howsoever comprehensive it may be, it cannot answer all the questions which a literary work raises. He says: "I have presented these five kinds of criticism as so many distinct lines of inquiry into literary works, each with its characteristic questions, presuppositions, and data. . . ."[7] Whenever a critic selects a method, in his critical analysis, he must be aware of its powers and limitations so that he may not misuse it. Crane thought all critical methods to be valid but never thought that a particular method was the only proper method for answering all kinds of questions that relate to a particular literary work. The nature and number of critical methods to be employed in the critical analysis of a literary work will be decided according to the "concrete problems presented by the authors or texts."[8] In Crane's view different lines of critical inquiries have independent status. One line of critical inquiry answers only one kind of critical question; and, when two lines of inquiry are employed simultaneously in the critical analysis a particular literary work they complement each other because they are half-truths. The systematic espousal of one, as Crane says, will necessarily entail leaving out, "at least, temporary an essential aspect of literary reality."[9] In this way, Crane suggests that various approaches to a literary work is possible. For example, *Oedipus Rex*, can be considered both as a tragic plot-form and a form resembling that of a primitive religious ritual. The two kinds of solutions which we find with regard to the structure of the play are answers to two different types of questions; and therefore, they do not contradict each other. The multiple truth regarding a literary work can be answered by framing multiple hypotheses. Such an approach will minimize the possibility of disagreements among critics. The habit of constructing alternative hypotheses about the structure of a literary work would end dogmatism which takes the form of "'ruling' hypotheses."[10] Crane's faith in the use of more than one hypothesis and method, reflects the concept of critical pluralism which he largely shared with his Chicago colleagues. Crane's pluralistic approach was an antidote to the critical monism of the New Critics. His essay "The Critical Monism of Cleanth Brooks" points out not only the narrowness of Brooks's critical approach but also the critical monism of all the New Critics. Allen Tate's doctrine of "tension," John Crowe Ransom's principle of "texture," Robert Penn Warren's obsession with "symbols" and I.A. Richards's concern with the "behaviour" of words are all different brands of monism. They do not convey the whole truth but the partial truths about poetic structure. Crane's description of the "monism" of the New Critics reminds me of a poem, by John Godfrey Saxbe, entitled "The Blind Men and the Elephant." Like the imaginary elephant a poetic structure is a "concrete whole"— a totality, which cannot be perceived by considering the part for the whole. As an elephant is not like a wall, or a rope, so poetic structure is not merely "paradox" or "ambiguity." I think by putting the phrase New Criticism in place of Hindustan in Saxbe's poem, we can draw the moral of Crane's essay. Saxbe wrote:

> And so these men of Hindustan
> Disputed loud and long

Each in his own opinion
Exceeding stiff and strong
For each was partly in the right
And all were in the wrong!

Crane did great service to criticism by exposing the monism of the New Critics. We know that monism begets dogmatism: and dogmatism begets hostility, rivalry or belligerence. Therefore Crane's concept of critical pluralism must have put the timely curb on the monistic tendencies of these partial critics.

Crane's main contribution lies in the field of the theory of criticism. He tells us that so long the cult of "concrete" prevailed, the so-called emperics dominated the science of medicine and very little progress was made. After the end of their reign, considerable progress was made in the field of medical sciences. In other disciplines too, he argues that notable advances were made only after theoretic revivals. On the strength of this kind of observation, he maintained that, advances in contemporary literary criticism could also be made if proper attention was paid to theory. The "cult of concrete"[11] in the contemporary criticism,—critic's excessive concern for dealing with particular facts—had largely impaired critic's capacity for theorizing; therefore, Crane attempted to revive critics' interest in theory. According to him three variable factors are essential for good practical criticism: (i) particular knowledge, (ii) conceptual definition and analysis, and (iii) sensitive response.[12] The second factor is the peculiar object of theory. It is the most important factor in literary criticism, as everything depends on the basic assumptions of the critic regarding the nature of a literary work. According to Crane criticism is "a reasoned discourse and not merely an irresponsible recording of impressions."[13] Therefore, in order to a reasoned discourse, it must depend on some kind of literary theory.

For the analysis of imagery in a poem, a critic, as Crane says, must possess the knowledge of general theory about metaphors. Again, for the analysis of a particular tragedy, he should know about the general nature of tragedy. The theory of art was completely neglected by Crane's contemporaries. He argues that even the impressionistic critics employ theories of some kind or other; and we can discover them, on a close examinations. Crane's colleague, W.R. Keast, pointed how "the circumstantial method" innocently operates behind Samuel Johnson's criticism.[14] The method takes into account the external or accidental factors—the circumstances of the work, which condition its construction or the shaping principles. Dr. Johnson, as he quotes, in the *Miscellaneous Observations on the Tragedy of Macbeth* had observed that "in order to make a true estimate of the abilities and merit of a writer, it is always necessary to examine the genius of his age, and the opinions of his contemporaries."[15] Therefore, history and biography are the necessary tools of Dr. Johnson's method. On analyzing the formal principle of Johnson's greatest critical work *Lives of the Poets*, Keast finds that a systematic critical theory is lurking behind it, which rests on the analysis of three factors: (i) the external circumstances, (ii) the intellectual character of the writer, and (iii) the qualities of his works.[16] Keast's examination of the theoretical foundation of Johnson's criticism explains how a great critic like Dr. Johnson, who possessed great critical sensibility, also could not avoid or escape theory.

Under the influence of the prevalent "anti-intellectualism,"[17] in the '30s and '40s, the critics of the day, had completely subordinated the importance of critical theory to mere exercise of sensibility. Lionel Trilling, says Keast, praised F.R. Leavis as a critic, because the latter did not work by elaborated critical theory and "required no formulated first principles for his judgment but only the sensibility that is the whole response of his whole being."[17] Keast's essay served two purposes, firstly, it corrected the opinion of contemporary critics that Dr. Johnson's criticism had no theoretical foundation and, secondly, it re-kindled critics' faith in theory.

Crane also suggests that Dr. Johnson's mode, which he calls "criticism of circumstances,"[18] can complement the other three critical modes: (i) the "criticism of elements," (ii) "the criticism of form," and (iii) "the criticism of qualities."[19] The practitioner of this critical mode will understand why works like *Lycidas, An Elegy Written in a Country Churchyard, In Memoriam, The Waste Land*, based on almost similar themes, are so different in character and treatment. The differences of these works, says Crane, may be due to differences in the genius and "vision" of their authors, which were shaped differently by different circumstances of their creation. The first poem was published in 1638; the second, in 1751; the third, in 1850; and, the fourth, in 1922. And a student of literary history knows that in four different periods of history, four different types of conventions of subject matter, language, and technique existed.

Therefore, for the proper handling of the "circumstantial method," a good grounding in literary history is needed, which will require a knowledge not only of periods, movements, and literary schools in the conventional sense, but also a grasp of the essential chronology, based on the discussion of individual authors and their particular texts; a sense of period styles—the ability of drawing inferences from the internal characteristics of texts; and, finally, "a habit of asking questions about works that will yield such information concerning their occasions, their sources or models, the philosophic and the traditions they carry on...."[20] Crane indirectly suggests here that, a critic who intends to investigate the circumstances of literary creation, cannot do without explicit or implicit theoretical principles. He writes that no one can think or speak or write literary works "except through the medium of some set of general concepts...which constitute for him his literary theory, whether he is consciously aware of its influence on him or not."[21] Critical theories, says he, may function in criticism in two principal ways. When it functions positively, it acts as "stimulus to observations and judgments"; and when it functions negatively, in the form of "doctrinal adhesions," as I.A. Richards described them, they colour our value-judgment.[22] It is a fact that a critic cannot avoid commitment to some basic principles of literature in literary reading and appreciation. But he should not possess them as "unexamined dogmas," and feel unnecessarily compelled to apply them to whatever they critically examine, rather he should form the habit of treating them as "limited hypotheses that may or may not be relevant to a particular case."[23] Crane's stress on the basic principles of literature aimed at counter-balancing the stress on "practical criticism" by his contemporary critics. In their practical criticism, the New Critics mainly focused on the meanings, structures, and values of particular literary works in the light of predetermined conceptual frameworks. In 1956, he recalled how the vogue of practical criticism, which was originally started to counteract historicism and impressionism gradually acquired too dominating a position over the last twenty or thirty years in literary criticism. It found such a great prominence in literary studies that, by criticism, students of literature meant merely practical criticism; and, the success and failure of a critic was judged by his practical performance or the close-textual "readings" of literary texts only. Here focus on the structure of a literary work may be a necessary condition of literary criticism but it cannot be a sufficient condition. Unless the practical criticism is well grounded in literary theory, it will not produce good criticism. Therefore, no permanent strategy can be drawn by critics. It is always determined by the demands of the time. Therefore, Crane attempted to achieve a kind of balance between literary theory and close textual analysis.

Now the problem was how to acquire this fundamental theory of literature and from where. The theories, which the New Critics derived through dialectical reasoning, as I have pointed out in Chapter two, were fallacious in different ways. Every critical doctrine, says Crane, depends on two things: firstly, the underlying principles and, secondly, the method of theoretical discourse by which the doctrine, and the "critical common sense" or the general knowledge, which is acquired through direct practical knowledge of literary principles operating in literary works. Thus, the "common sense literary knowledge,"[24] consists of the practical understanding of the literary works which is handed down, independently of doctrine, from one age to another and the ability of the common readers or theatre goers to react to what they read or see. So literary theory should be acquired by a critic in both the ways. He should consult literary theorists and constantly experience literary works of different ages and different kinds also. Crane, strikes a note of balance by emphasizing the importance of literary theories as handed down by critical theoreticians and educators, and the practical insights of common sense. Such a balanced view was taken by Crane to counteract the growing restrictive tendencies in literary theory among his contemporary critics. It also explains why the Chicago critics were drawn towards Dr. Johnson, the great exemplar of the fusion of principles and common sense in criticism.[25] A kind of "common sense practical intelligibility"[26] the ability to translate the abstract statements of the critics into concrete operations with words, thoughts, and incidents, as Dr. Johnson did, can be an ideal solution. Dr. Johnson's theorizing, as Crane tells us, "was founded on premises of a kind that allowed him to appeal constantly to what every man is aware of in literary matters against the dogmas of the theorists who had based themselves...on 'narrower principles.'"[27] The interest taken in Dr. Johnson, by Crane and Keast, is more than a merely antiquarian interest. They found in him a method, as explained above, which could be still useful in modern contexts. They were interested not in Dr. Johnson's critical judgment but in his methodology. Keast states that "It is very difficult to learn or improve the art of criticism by a study of the particular judgments of past critics on authors and works. In the service of developing the art of criticism, the chief significance of such particular judgments will be in helping us ascertain the principles of more general import which underlie them and which may be instructive or useful in other contexts."[28]

Crane was always pre-occupied with the problems of literary theory and methodology, as he always attempted to bring about improvements in these fields. His deep concern for the proper training of students in critical methodology can be noted in the following statement. He said: "It is well to bear in mind from the onset that the proper end of training in and [of the arts of English study] is not knowledge of principles divorced from the concrete subject matter of particular literary works or linguistic documents but rather a set of trained habits of reflection and inquiry which can be formed only by the constant application to a great variety of special problems of whatever principles of analysis the student may have learned."[29]

As I have already pointed out in Chapter Two, the Chicago School of criticism was greatly influenced by the revaluation of educational methods that took place in the University of Chicago in the thirties. We find that Crane and his colleagues were mainly concerned with the reform of contemporary critical methods, Their remedial aim was directly shaped by the educationists like Richard Mckeon, Robert Hutchins, and Mortimer Adler, the chief architects of the educational reform at the University of Chicago, during that period.

Their central concept of general education laid emphasis on the study of "first principles." Hutchins said: The fundamental problems of metaphysics, the social sciences, and natural sciences, are then, the proper subject matter of higher learning.... I have used the word metaphysics to include not only the study of the "first principles" of change in the physical world, which is the philosophy of nature, and about the analysis of man and his productions in the fine arts including literature."[30] Crane also put stress on the study of "first principles." As explained earlier, he believed that the humanities (here literary criticism) are best defined in terms of certain arts or methods.

What a critic does largely depends upon are his taste, temperament and training. As Crane joined the English Department of the University of Chicago in 1924, he must have been exposed to the deliberations of the Chicago humanists who had launched a new kind of general education. Just after his appointment as the President of the University of Chicago, De Witt Burton initiated a faculty study on reorganizing the university's departmental structure and curriculum. Under President Max Mason's tenure this work continued and was finally completed in Hutchins's time, who joined the University in 1929. In course of a personal talk[31] with Mrs. R.S. Crane (Julia Crane), Mr. Bruce Bashford came to know that, until late thirties, several educationists and scholars at Chicago met at Crane's place to discuss the policy regarding the changes in the methodology of teaching literature. All the Chicago humanists emphasized the importance of teaching "first principles." By metaphysics, Mckeon means "the study of methodological starting-points, not the establishment of statements about the nature of the world which is true in some absolute sense."[32]

Adler also underlies the importance of teaching "first principles." From *Dialectics* (1927) to *The Conditions of Philosophy* (1965), he continuously upheld a system that will allow a fruitful ordering of methods and knowledge.[33]

Besides the influence of his colleagues at Chicago, Crane's mind was also shaped by one Professor B, who had deepened his faith in the study of first principles, in his undergraduate days. Professor B, as Crane says always held that "all teaching of literature...ought to occupy itself much less than...with superstructures and much more with foundations."[34] Remembering the qualities of Professor B, he adds that "he was quite consciously concerned with implanting in us, through his analytical mode of lecturing and above all through the independent studies he engages us in, something over and above his immediate subject matter that might possibly remain with us for the rest of our lives... ."[35] Professor B, says he "taught us as a guide rather than a master" and lectured "in a problematic rather than a didactic spirit...taking us inside the processes of reasoning he brought to bear on his problems."[36] When he became himself a professor of literature, he always remembered Professor B as a model. He largely shared Mr. Hutchins belief that "It is principles, and everlastingly principles, not data, not facts, not helpful hints, but principles which the rising generation requires if it is to find its way through the mazes of tomorrow."[37] He wanted to free his students from the shackles of critical dogmas or common places which they absorb during their student days. He did not offer any new critical method. He felt that a student's mind should not be stuffed with readymade phrases like "dissociation of sensibility," "objective correlative," and "poetry is an extinction of personality," etc....but be equipped with analytical tools or methods so that they may handle them independently when they are out of the portals of the University. Thus he always took an 'instrumentalist view' of criticism. This attitude explains his constant pre-occupation with the "problem of method."[38] We know that any discussion of method involves a discussion of theory. Because, according to Crane, a method (in a broadened sense of the term) consists of two things: "a particularly formulated subject matter and a particularly determined mode of reasoning about it... ."[39]

II
CRANE'S METHOD

One of the important tasks that Crane set before himself was to find out a method to analyze and appreciate the "humanistic properties," that is, the "uniqueness" of a particular work of art. A particular work of art is unique because its principle of construction cannot be duplicated even in a similar work of art. The uniqueness of a work of art can only be understood by analyzing its "immediate shaping cause."[40] A critical, method, says Crane, which studies the uniqueness of a literary work. Their methods worked well when common principles of construction were to be discovered in literary works of different times and kinds. The methods, says Crane, were scientific or pseudo-scientific or "unhumanistic" because they only looked for what is reducible to a common denominator.[41] Therefore, Crane observed that "a method committed to proper differentiation [was] needed...to avoid reductions to a common ground."[42] A passion for marking out the distinctive feature of a particular work led Crane "quite naturally to an effort to understand the principles of construction that differ from genre to genre and finally from work to work."[43]

Crane adapted Aristotle's method—the hypothetical regressive reasoning—to grasp the artistic rationale of construction. His basic assumption was that, in making an individual work of a certain kind, a writer faces a number of aesthetic problems, which are more or less peculiar to that work and which allow him certain range of choices. If they are to be appropriately solved. Therefore, the first business of a critic, says he, "must be to ask what were the literary problems the writer was faced with, why these were problems for him in relation to his overall literary task, and what literary reasons or justifications may be found for what he actually did in solving them."[44]

The critical procedure which tries to analyze and understand "the writer's immediate literary task"[45] may be described as "problematic and functional analysis."[46] An attempt will be made here to explain the advantages and disadvantages of this method, when employed in the practical criticism of particular works; and its comparative merit over the method of New Critics will be ascertained. Let us discuss the practical criticism of *Macbeth* as done by the critics of the two schools.

AN ANALYSIS OF THE PROBLEMATIC ANALYSIS OF *MACBETH*

Crane observed that a play is "a work for whose peculiar principles of structure there are nowhere any usable parallels either in literary theory or in our experience of other works."[47] His observation is based on the assumption that a work of art is "a particular that cannot be known through the universal."[48] Crane employs the procedure of framing "multiple working hypothesis" to grasp the "plot-form" of the play. Before we proceed further, we must understand his concept of plot. According to him, a plot-form is the distinctive "working power" (*dynamis*) of a particular literary work which affects "our opinions and emotions in a certain way."[49] It is a complex of principles that synthesizes various parts into an artistic whole and produces the intended effect upon the reader. The process of grasping a plot-form is a kind of inferential activity;[50] naturally, in the critical analysis of every new work, it has to be done afresh, and cannot be taken for granted before the analysis of a particular work starts.

Explaining the nature of reader's reaction, he says: "...we are bound, as we read or listen, to form expectations about what is coming and to feel more or less determinate desires relatively to our expectations."[51]

Thus, a reader while reacting to "what happens" in a work, infers the power (*dynamis*) of the peculiar synthesis of character, thought and action from the consequences of words to move his feelings powerfully and pleasurably in a certain definite way."[52] Therefore in determining the plot-form of *Macbeth*, Crane imagines the natural response of a common reader. A common reader, says Crane, will react to situation in a drama as a normal human being reacts to natural situations in his real life. Therefore, Crane, first of all, focuses upon the human appeal which a mimetic work, being an imitation of a human action of feeling or thought, possesses for readers.

In the practical analysis of *Macbeth*, Crane takes into account various possibilities of its plot-form. Beginning with a broader form, he goes on narrowing its range. First of all, he starts with the general hypothesis that *Macbeth* is "an imitative tragic drama based on historical materials."[53] On further investigation he discovers that the plot-form of the play is a combination of the plot-forms of *Othello* and *Richard III*. Explaining the special plot-form of *Macbeth*, he observes that the form of the play is really the interaction of the two opinions and emotions.... "It is a form that turns upon the difference between what seemingly advantageous crime appears to be in advance to a basically good but incontinent man and what its moral consequences for such a man inevitably are; and the catharsis is effected not merely by the man's deserved overthrow but by his own inner suffering and by his discovery, before it is too late, of what he had not known before he began to act."[54]

After determining the plot-form of the play, he proceeds to find out how the structural parts of the play conform to it. He discovers the duality of the plot-form on different levels especially in Act V.[55]

The process of reasoning back from the known character of the plot-form to the necessary character and relation of its parts is a way of discovering the choices that a writer, at different stages of his creativity, has to make. When writer's "first principle" becomes the critic's "first principle," then the right kind of practical criticism emerges. And this can be achieved through reconstructing the problems of construction that the writer might have faced in constructing a literary work. In this way, the critic might know whether a writer has been able to fulfil the requirements of the plot-form which he tried to impose upon his material consciously or unconsciously.

The writer will be deemed to have erred, if he either does too little or too much of what is expected of him. Borrowing the idea of the aesthetic mean, that is, choosing between 'too much' and 'too little,' from Aristotle, Crane says that "the mean in art, as in morals is a relative mean which has to be determined in adjustment to the particular necessities and probabilities of the form the artist is trying to achieve."[56] In addition to examining the requirements or necessities of a plot-form, a critic will have to examine its various possibilities. An ordinary artist does all that the distinctive plot-form of a particular literary work demands. But a good artist always does a little more than what is expected of him. Therefore, besides examining the necessities of the plot-form, the critic should examine its possibilities or "probabilities," in order to assess the power of human inventiveness, as great literary geniuses often exceed the normal power of human inventiveness. For assessing the probabilities, the critic will have to put himself in the writer's position and try to imagine whether he could conceive of a more satisfactory solution than the one found by the writer. For examining the necessities and probabilities, the critic will compare the efforts of the writer he examines with those of other writers, confronting similar problems in their works. Thus we find that Crane like Eliot emphasizes the importance of analysis and comparison in literary criticism.

As Crane suggests, the "problematic and functional analysis" will help us in forming value-judgments. He says that "...if the writer has done, somehow, all the essential things he would need to do on the assumption that he is actually writing the kind of work we have defined, then to that extent the work is good, or at least not bad... ."[57] Explaining the excellence of the scenes of Act V, he says that "The artistic triumph of the scene lies in the completeness with which both problems are solved: the first in the words of and actions of Macduff, the speeches about young Siward, and Malcolm's closing address; the second by a variety of devices, both of invention and of representation, the appropriateness of which to the needed effect can be seen if we ask what we would not want Macbeth to do at this moment."[58] For the New Critics the play is good because it is rich in symbolical suggestions.

In an essay, while decrying the tendency of modern critics to interpret older literature symbolically, he says: "We have no business to conclude that (a poem is symbolic) unless we are forced so to conclude by the poem itself when we look at it, independent of theory, as the work of a given poet a given time, and examine it with the other possibility (the non-symbolic) actively in mind."[59] Crane points out that the text of *Macbeth* hardly demands a symbolic interpretation. The New Critics, says Crane, "have inferred the central form of the play chiefly from the thought and imagery that serve to emphasize the unnatural character of the hero's crimes and the inevitability of a just retribution, without attempting to correlate with this the many signs, both in the construction of the plot and in its extraordinarily artful representations of the distinctive moral quality of Macbeth's actions when they are seen from the inside."[60] The New Critics concentrate on the attributes of language whereas Crane concentrates on the humanness of Macbeth's speech and action. According to him the hypotheses of the symbolic interpreters of the play are incomplete because they do not take into account "the peculiar sequence of emotions we feel when we read the work unbiased by critical doctrine."[61] None can deny the soundness of Crane's logic that proves the incompleteness of the hypotheses of the New Critics, regarding the structure of the play. Yet we cannot ignore the magic of their incomplete hypotheses which have given us brilliant symbolic interpretations of *Macbeth*.

According to Crane, "the principle of construction is the concrete human action which it (Macbeth) represents—an action to which we are intended to respond emotionally, as we would respond to a similar situation in life by virtue of the illusion the drama creates that the hero and most of the other *dramatis personae* are in all essential respects men and women like ourselves."[62] For the New Critics, says he, the controlling structure of *Macbeth* "must be one not of literal actions... but of meanings."[63] Their hypotheses neither imply nor are implied by the particulars of the text. So they are simply postulates. He says: "It is an error...that does little credit either to Shakespeare's genius as to our understanding of his age or of poetry to think of *Macbeth*...as primarily a drama at all, at least, in the sense ordinarily given to the 'word' from Aristotle to Bradley and William Archer."[64]

In my opinion, Crane deserves credit for drawing the attention of contemporary critics to certain human qualities of human products; but, it is difficult to agree with him when he says that "it is an error" on the part of the New Critics to interpret *Macbeth* symbolically and show its special pattern of meanings. Crane refers to four instances of such erroneous interpretations of the play by Roy Walker, Harold Goddard, L.C. Knights and G. Wilson Knight.[65] To consider the structure of the play as a political allegory, or a manifestation of two universal myths, or a 'poem' in the dramatic form like *The Waste Land*, or metaphysical vision of death and life forces, all appear to Crane as exercise in futility. I feel that he has taken a rather unsympathetic view of these brilliant critics of our time. It is difficult for a student of literature to understand, in what way these interpretations of *Macbeth* do great disservice to Shakespeare. The variety of interpretations, though not literal as Crane points out, add new dimensions to the meaning of the play. It is said that every new age reads its own meaning in the great works of art. Then what is wrong with the New Critics, if they discover symbolical meanings of the play. How cap these critics completely free themselves from the influence of the contemporary philosophers like Ernest Cassirer, Susanne Langer, A.N. Whitehead etc. who have concerned themselves more with the "character, organization, and uses of symbols."[66] So the New Critics considered "the structure of particular poetic in the terms...of poetic form as 'meaning' and of literature as 'ultimately metaphorical or symbolic.' "[67]

Crane, in order to draw the attention of contemporary critics to the humanistic and the constructive aspects of literary works, completely ignored their other aspects, especially the symbolic aspects. Crane did not interpret the works of modem American writers. Had he done so, we could have compared his practical criticism with that of Charles Feidelson's in *Symbolism and American Literature*. Feidelson says: "In the central works of Hawthorne, Whitman, Melville, and Poe symbolism is at once technique and theme. It is governing principle: not a stylistic device, but a point of view; not a casual subject, but a pervasive presence in the intellectual landscape."[68] I doubt whether Crane's "problematic analysis" is comprehensive enough to come to grips with the symbolic aspect of modern literature. Thus, we find that Crane has himself limited the scope of his critical method by putting greater emphasis on the humanistic point of view, which he found absent from contemporary criticism.

One more example of his practical criticism will throw clear light on the merits and demerits of his method. In the analysis of Gray's Elegy, Cleanth Brooks, the representative of the New Critics, shows how the poem reflects the ironical contrast of the "two possibilities of burial and his (Speaker of *Elegy*) unmotivated choice between them."[69] Crane argues that if Brooks's account of the poem is to be believed, it seems to be an expression of "a piece of moderately subtle dialectic"[70] rather than an expression of a human experience. The typical procedure of discovering ironic contrast in *Elegy* by Brooks is summed up by Crane as follows:

> The essay considers successively, first the effect of the many "echoes" of Milton and others in making the *Elegy* in ironical rather than a "simple" poem; then the ironic contrast implied in the opening description of the churchyard; then the ironic function of the personifications, together with their "supporting ironical devices" in phrases like "homely joys," "the short and simple annals of the poor," "animated bust," the stanza beginning "Full many a gem," and the lines on Hampden, Milton, and Cromwell; then the passage on the tombstones in the churchyard, which, according to Brooks, brings together opposites so far held apart; and, finally, the poet's lines about himself and his imagined epitaph, which are said to centre in the speaker's "choice" between the two alternatives of burial contrasted earlier in the poem.[71]

In Crane's view *Elegy* portrays:

> a situation in which a virtuous, sensitive, and ambitious youngman of humble birth confronts the prospect of his death while still to "Fortune and to Fame Unknown," and eventually, after much disturbance of mind...reconciles himself to his probable "fate" by reflecting that none of the rewards of successful ambition can "soothe the dull cold ear of Death," which comes as inevitably to the great as to the obscure; that a life passed "from the madding crowd's ignoble strife," though circumscribing the exercise of virtue and may yet be means of preserving innocence; and that he can at any rate look forward to—what all men desire as a minimum—living on in the memory of at least one friend, while his merits and frailties alike repose "in trembling hope" on the bosom of his Father and his God. What is embodied in the words of the poem is the final stage or this "action"—the resolution of the speaker's internal conflict (hinted at 11 101-08); with respect to this, his evening meditation in the churchyard on the "unhonour'd Dead" serves the double function of dramatizing and externalizing device and, more importantly, of an analogy in his reconciling argument. He stands apart from both the great of the world and the humble rustics whose tombs are before him; but he resembles more closely, in his fortune, the latter than

> the former. Hence it is natural for him to infer that the advantages and consolations he finds in their lot can likewise be advantages and consolations for himself.[72]

Thus we find that Brooks and Crane focus on two different aspects; and, therefore they do not contradict each other. The two methods light up two different elements of the poem. A pluralistic critic like Crane should not have reacted so violently against Brooks's "reading." The way Brooks argues his thesis of ironical contrast in the *Elegy* is quite interesting; and, to a great extent, he succeeds in discovering the common structural properties, which he finds in other poems, as discussed in *The Well Wrought Urn*. But Crane's analysis of the poem does not appear like proving a thesis, rather it is an open inquiry about the structure of the poem. If Brooks's analysis is taken out of *The Well Wrought Urn* and is given to a reader who is not aware of the defined objective and deliberate plan of the book, which was to examine a few poems in terms of a common approach, I think he would not be as shocked as Crane was when he came across it. What shocked Crane most was not the analysis of the poem, but Brooks's method which he employed in the analysis of other poems of that book. Crane's objection is that Brooks found only one structure in *Elegy* and focused on only one aspect of the poem. Brooks's analysis of the poem runs into eighteen pages. Had he discussed its other aspects also, then he would have taken more space and would have taxed the patience of his readers. No critic, however brilliant, can cover all the aspects of a poem in its practical criticism. Crane himself could not do so in the practical criticism of the poem, which concerns itself chiefly with its human aspect. At best a critic can tackle only or two aspects at a time. The analysis of the *Elegy* by both the critics can be equally charged with being narrow. Further, it is difficult to determine whether Crane's analysis has greater appeal than that of Brooks. As a practical critic Brooks impresses us more than Crane, who was primarily a critic's critic. Brooks handles his so-called bad critical method well, whereas Crane fails to achieve the desired result by the use of his so-called better critical method. Brooks's method, as Crane says, is bad because it is extremely monistic in character. For a man of letters, it hardly matters whether a critic employs only one or more than one critical mode, because he does not read a critic for finding fault with his critical procedure. Criticizing a critic is an academic exercise and it might interest a philosophic critic, who is mainly pre-occupied with the theoretical problems of criticism. Criticism of criticism is a specialist's job and can be done by only those who possess a high degree of intellectual sophistication. Crane was a first-rate humanist scholar, philosopher and a critic all rolled into one. He makes a very heavy demand on his readers. It is difficult to understand him without possessing a fair amount of scholarly equipment. He is a difficult critic and has a limited appeal to only serious students of literature. He was an educator first then a critic, for whom writing good practical criticism was only subordinate to imparting the right kind of training in critical methods. Most of his critical writings were addressed to advanced students and serious teachers of literature, because he always approached the problems of criticism from an academician's point of view. His motive was predominantly pedagogical,— "to advance the enlightenment to put down error and wrong."[73] The critic in him was always dominated by the pedagogue. A professor is "a man devoted to diluting and retailing the ideas of his superiors."[74] As a professor, Crane was more interested in the problems of literary theory and methodology than in the practical criticism of individual literary works. The little practical criticism he did by way of demonstrating the efficacy of the method, which he declared better than that of the New Critics. They are just samples of good criticism according to him.

Criticism of criticism is a valuable philosophical activity, especially from the point of view of its remedial potentiality. It not only throws light on the nature of criticism "but also help us read individual works with greater understanding and appreciation, the active appreciation of literature is not always dependent on such theorizing."[75] As in interpreter of critical theories. Crane has carved his niche in the history of literature. The critique of criticism, which he produced along with his Chicago colleagues, will help students of literature to clarify, focus, and increase, literary appreciation. Crane's appearance on the American critical scene may be likened to the coming of a Hindu *avatara*. His main purpose was to correct the errors of contemporary criticism. Crane was a critic's critic, hence he cannot be easily compared with the professional critics of our time. He did not directly aim at expanding our awareness of literary values in literary works but he worked for sharpening our critical tools, that might help us, in the long run, in developing an increased awareness of literary values. Literary critics like Crane must appear on the critical scene from to time to put the house of criticism in order and save it from becoming the "tower of Babel."

III

Crane cannot be easily compared with the professional critics of our time due to two reasons: Firstly, because his method is diametrically opposed to that of I.A. Richards, Empson, Cleanth Brooks and their followers; and, secondly, because he was not a professional critic in the strict sense. Actually, he was a scholar critic more like David Daiches than the New Critics, Leavis and their admirers. If we read the professional critics of our time, we find that they are mostly partial critics and have added merely "specialized critical vocabulary and professional tricks" to literary criticism instead of supplying a "total vision,"[76] Crane has admirably worked in this direction, at least, in theory be tried "to blend the insights yielded by many critical approaches."[77] By blending, I do not mean integration or alliance, but a dynamic co-operation among critical methods to grasp the whole truth of the literary works. When a critic combines more than one method without a sense of dogmatism, he reaches near the pluralistic ideal of Crane.

Both Crane and David Daiches took a critical view of criticism. Both of them were concerned with the problems of critical methods. David Daiches says in the preface to *Critical Approaches to Literature* that "I am concerned with methodology, with the varying ways in which the art of literature and work of literature can be profitably discussed… ."[78] Crane took a similar stand throughout his critical career. Once he observed: "The important practical problem for us…is the problem of method…in the intellectual sense of the kinds of questions about literary works we ask students and train them to ask themselves, and of the techniques we cultivate in them for getting and justifying answers."[79]

It is a truism to say that early Eliot and Richards had been the most pervasive literary and critical forces in the first quarter of this century. F.O. Mathiessen says that these two critics instigated a kind of revolution in the field of literature.[80] If they brought about a revolution, then Crane and his colleagues launched a counter-revolution, in the form of the Chicago school of criticism. The counter-revolution was motivated by a belief that "what the world turns to, when it has cured of an error, is usually simply another error, and may be one worse that the first one."[81] But in literary revolutions, what is "overthrown remains undestroyed and capable of being rediscovered at the next turn of the wheel of taste."[82] The Chicago school of criticism, under the leadership of Crane, made an effort to re-establish the claims of certain useful things which were completely neglected or rejected by the New Critics. The courage which Crane showed in challenging the authority of I.A. Richards and Cleanth Brooks, the reigning gods of contemporary criticism, is of great historic importance, as it jolted them out of their complacency and made them aware of their defects.

Eliot, Richards, Leavis and the New Critics concerned themselves with the revaluation of individual authors and their texts, but Crane and his Chicago colleagues mainly concerned themselves with the revaluation of critical tools. They overhauled the old critical tools and made them capable of their modern use. We know that no surgical operation can be properly done if the instruments are not appropriate to the task in hand. Therefore, we may say that those who manufacture surgical appliances also perform an important duty. But we also know from our experience that sometimes good instruments are also mishandled. Naturally, the success and failure of a surgeon is finally decided by the way he handles the tools. So, for a patient who is going to be operated upon, the skill of a surgeon matters more than the skill of technician who fashions new surgical instruments. This analogy might clearly explain. Why common readers prefer New Critics to Chicago Critics.

Despite his limitations, as a practical critic, Crane will be always remembered for his great contributions to critical theory. He has received some attention from American and British critics in recent years. David H. Richter applied his pluralistic approach, as a solution, to the conflicts arising out of various theories of genre. He says: "It is the ideal of pluralism as preached (whether or not practised) by R.S. Crane: the notion that it has been designed to answer a particular kind of question about literary texts. The questions critics ask and the explanations they seek are determined by their various purposes, and these purposes often are mutually exclusive, though equally valid in themselves." Gradually, Crane's concept of critical pluralism is gaining grounds among British critics also. Malcolm Bradbury, a renowned British critic says that "the ideal state of affairs in criticism is a kind of pluralistic one... ."[83] In a way, Roger Fowler, also upholds Crane's view when he argues that "the range of literature—is enormous, as is the range of readers, motives for reading, performances, audiences, markets of publications, teachers and studying communities. In these circumstances diversity of method and interpretation is inevitable and if the alternative is repressive and authoritarian bigotry, desirable."[84] Crane's influence on Roger Fowler is so deep that the title of his essay "Structure of Criticism and Languages of Poetry," immediately reminds Vs of Crane's *The Languages of Criticism and Structure of Poetry*. Like Crane Fowler says that "...one of the benefits of a true pluralism, one would think, would be healthy and productive interchange of views, informed agreement to differ, and certitude on what it is one is differing about."[85] Strong echoes of Crane's views can be noted in the following extract from Malcolm Bradbury where he urges that we now need a poetics derived in the first instance from literature itself, rather than from linguistic or cultural theory...a poetics that is empirical, in the sense that is responsive in a *post facto* way, to the character of any given work to which critical attention is taken. It (is) criticism without predetermined set of hypotheses; yet the means of making hypotheses in sympathetic relation to the work that it is reading. For it is precisely with the conscious, created, pervasive elements of literary texts, those features of making and shaping that give it its essential independence, that the test of an adequate literary criticism lies.[86]

Wilbur S. Scott also shares Crane's pluralistic approach when he says that "...since critics tend to emphasize a particular approach, there is always the danger of their excluding valuable points of view which lie outside the particular creed."[87] "Blackmur," as he points out, also "argues against excessive faith in a single approach, against what has been called 'critical monism,' and on behalf of the provisional entertainment of any point of view that may send a reader to a work of literature with illumination."[88] Crane's first revolutionary essay "History *Versus* Criticism in the Study of Literature" was published in the *English Journal* as early as 1935. The role that this document played in resolving the opposition between history and criticism had a greater relevance for literary critics in the 30's. In 1967, on being reprinted in *The Idea of the Humanities*, it partly lost its original appeal, as no sharp antithesis existed then between historical scholarship and criticism. His second important essay, "Criticism as Inquiry," or "The Perils of the 'High Priori Road,'" still has some appeal to students of literature. Even though published in book form after a gap of seventeen years, the essay had not lost its original appeal in late 60's. Even today we cannot reject Crane's main contention that literary criticism should always remain a form of open inquiry, and a critic should possess a scholar's habitual distrust of the *a priori*: "...all ways of arriving at particular conclusions, which assume the relevance and authority, prior to the concrete evidence, the theoretical doctrines or general propositions concerning the subject matters in question."[89] Crane's considered view was that a critic should possess all the qualifications of a good scholar and he urged that literary studies be redirected towards the text without overlooking the marginal utility of the historical method. It may be mentioned here that Eliot, in his celebrated essay, "The Frontier of Criticism" said that "we must not identify biography with criticism: biography is ordinarily useful in providing explanation which may open the way to further understanding: but it may also, in directing our attention on the poet, lead us away from poetry."[90] The main argument of this essay is that factual knowledge, acquired through historical scholarship, can only be used with care, as it may serve as a "necessary preparation for understanding the poetry...but for the appreciation of the poetry, it can only lead us to the door we must find our way in."[91] He argues that "If in literary criticism, we place all the emphasis upon understanding, we are in danger of slipping from understanding to mere explanation."[92] Eliot's essay "The Frontier of Criticism" was first published by the University of Minnesota in 1956, and the points which it raised had already been thoroughly discussed by Crane in his revolutionary essay "History *Versus* Criticism" in 1935. His another significant essay "Principles of Literary History and Criticism" which examines the relationship of history and criticism, was first produced as an unpublished monograph in 1950. Thus what Crane thought in the United States of America earlier, Eliot seems to have touched upon much later in England. But, it is surprising that when two critics hold almost similar views, one is over discussed and the other almost wholly ignored.

Like Eliot Crane was also dissatisfied with the reviewers of the Sunday supplements of the journals and magazines. Expressing his concern, Eliot once observed: "We should all try to be critics, and not leave criticism to the fellows, who write reviews in the papers."[93] But Crane's concern seems to be deeper than that of Eliot when he extends Eliot's last phrase to include "the fellows like (himself) who teach literature in universities and colleges or write essays on literary subjects for the learned or the critical journals."[94] Crane's attitude towards literary criticism was very serious, as he treated it as a distinct discipline—"a form of inquiry to be cultivated in the same questioning spirit, for the sake of a disinterested understanding and appreciation of its objects in their own nature's, as is proper to the study of history, language, and ideas, and with an approach to the same rigour of analysis and statement."[95] Crane rightly distinguishes himself from Hazlitt, Sainte-Beuve, Matthew Arnold and their descendants in whose hands literary criticism had taken the form of "cultivated causerie;"[96] and, again from those who applied the general systems of religion, philosophy and political thought "after the manner of later Eliot, the Marxists, Liberals, Humanists, Kirkegaardians, and Existentialists."[97] Crane appears to be a type by himself. Being a pluralistic critic, he, at least, theoretically, welcomes the methods of all the major critics, but especially clings to Aristotle. He does not integrate various methods, as Stanley Edgar Hayman does.[98] He also disapproves of R.P. Blackmur's way of "alliance" or "marriage" between Aristotle and Coleridge.[99]

The early Eliot, who conditioned the mind of the New Critics to a great extent, had contended that "to make value judgments was 'no part of the critic's serious business' and, in fact, categorically prescribed that in matters of great importance the critic...must not make judgments of worse or better... ."[100] Therefore, Crane's emphasis on making value-judgment should be appreciated in' the context of the needs of his time. I think he was perfectly justified in shifting the emphasis from mere explication to evaluation. In fact, no good critic can avoid for long value-judgments of one kind or the other. Crane rightly holds that a critic's main function is to judge. The term *Kritikos*, meaning "a judge of literature," occurs as early as the end of the fourth century B.C.[101] Crane revived the importance of judgment in criticism. He firmly held that "criticism...is simply the disciplined consideration, at once analytical and evaluative of literary works as works of art."[102] Crane analyzes and evaluates a particular literary work in the light of general principles of aesthetics. He focuses on the internal causes of a literary work for judging its artistic merit.

It may be mentioned here that the early Eliot and Richards, the precursors of the New Critics, maintained that the main job of a critic is "never to judge a poem (never, that is, to use either valuative or hortatory terms), but only to place the poem in its historical context and to elucidate, to compare, and to analyze."[103] This is a rather extreme view. Richards had to modify his earlier stand in course of time. He wrote: "There is, it is true, a valuation side to criticism when we have solved completely, the communication problem, when we have got, perfectly, the experience, the mental condition relevant to the poem, we have still to judge it, still to decide upon its worth. But the later question nearly always settles itself: or rather, our own in most nature and the nature of the world in which we live decide it for us."[104] Although the early Eliot spoke against the act of value-judgment, but he himself could not help it. He said:

> The critic must not coerce, and he must not make judgments of worse or better. He must simply elucidate: the reader will form the correct judgment for himself.[105]
>
> If the critic has performed his laboratory work well, his understanding will be evidence of appreciation; but his work is by the intelligence, not the emotions...where he judges or appreciates he simply...is missing out a link in the exposition.[106]
>
> In the dogmatic or lazy mind comparison is supplied by judgment, analysis replaced by appreciation. Judgment and appreciation are merely tolerable avocations, no part of the critic's serious business.[107]

Eliot's emphasis was on "comparison and analysis,"[108] in which literary criticism of the late 20's—dominated by historical scholarship—sadly lacked in. But, a remedy when abused, requires another remedy. Eliot's emphasis on "impersonality" and his distrust of emotions were necessary antidotes to impressionism of the 20's; but, when it became a critical creed with his followers, it required another antidote. This is the reason that Crane revived the question of artist's intention in a very careful manner lest he should be charged with "intentionalist fallacy." Crane, apprehending the charge of "intentionalist fallacy" against himself, said that the intentions which he took into account "would be those, except accidentally, which the writer had explicitly before or after writing or those which can be defined for the writer by saying that he must have intended to write the work because this is what he has written."[109] It must be made clear here that by intentions he never meant conscious intentions. Attempting a defence against the charges he said that "they do not hold...when we identify intention with the hypothesized form of a poetic work and then consider how fully what we know of necessities and possibilities of this form are achieved in the work, on the assumption that, if the work shows any serious concern with art at all, the writer must have wished or been willing to be judged in this way."[110] The New Critics had completely rejected the theory of genres. Crane did not want that modern criticism should be completely deprived of the benefit of the theory of genres, so he revived it in a modified way. Crane's conception of genre should not be confused with the traditional concepts of *genres*. A critic, using his method, says Crane can "properly continue to talk...of literary form, meaning by the term not traditional *genres* like 'epistle,' 'ode,' or 'ballad opera,' or constructed subject matter classes like 'revenge tragedy,' 'graveyard poetry,' or any of the many dialectically derived literary types such as 'the poetry of synthesis' but species of works, inductively known, and differentiated, more or less sharply, in terms of their peculiar artistic elements and principles of construction."[111] Crane concentrates on the plot-form. Therefore, works based on similar plot-forms can be classed together as a species or works or genre. Such a conception of *genre* is different from the traditional concept. Crane calls *Persuasion* a "serious comedy."

It is a comedy because its plot moves from unhappiness to happiness. But it is a "serious comedy" because "what makes its events interesting and moving for us is not so much their intrinsic painfulness and pleasurableness as the fact that they happen to persons whom we have a special concern by reason of their merits as individuals."[112] The category like "serious comedy" is an improvement upon the traditional concept of *genre*, which was neglected by his contemporary critics. Thus we find that Crane was always pre-occupied with the search for suitable remedies to remove the defects of contemporary criticism. Therefore, he described, compared, analyzed, interpreted, explained different critical systems. His excursions into poetic theory, and disputes with the fellow critics aimed at a reconstruction of contemporary criticism on sounder foundations.

It is a pity that a critic like Crane, who was so much interested in all-round development of criticism, should continue to be an obscure figure in contemporary criticism. The reasons behind his obscurity are many.

The first reason, as I have already indicated, is the very late publication of his critical writings in book-form. Due to the late publication of his books, his reputation as a critic, mostly remained confined to a limited academic circle. His first book, *The Languages of Criticism and Structure of Poetry*, was published when he was sixty-one-year old. His second and the last book *The Idea of the Humanities* (2 Vols.) was brought out when he was eighty-one-year old. Such is not the case of other major critics of past and present who occupy important places in the history of literature.

It is of interest to note here that when *Defence of Poesie* was published, Sidney was forty-one; when *Essay of Dramatic Poesy* was published Dryden was forty-seven; when *The Essay on Criticism* was published Pope was thirty-one; when *Tatler* was published Addison was thirty-six; when *Rambler* was published Johnson was forty-one; when *Lyrical Ballads* was published Wordsworth was twenty-one; when *Biographia Literaria* was published Coleridge was forty-five; when *A Defence of Poetry* was published Shelley was twenty-nine; when *Specimens of English Dramatic Poets* was published Lamb was thirty-three; when *Lectures on the English Poets* was published Hazlitt was forty; when *Essays on Criticism* was published Arnold was forty-three; when "Tradition and the Individual Talent" was published Eliot was twenty-nine; when *The Principles of Literary Criticism* was published when I.A. Richards was in his early thirties; and so on. But when Crane's first important book was published he was already sixty-year old.

The second reason of Crane's obscurity may be very small number of his critical works. Only two prefaces to the two different editions (1952, 1957) of *Critics and Criticism, The Languages of Criticism and Structure of Poetry* (1953), part III of *The Idea of the Humanities* (II), some critical essays in the *Modern Philology* and reviews in the *Philological Quarterly* constitute his critical corpus.

The third reason of Crane's obscurity is his very scanty practical criticism. Crane mostly analyzed eighteenth-century works of English writers: Jane Austen, Jonathan Swift, Henry Fielding. Among modern writers, he only dealt with Hemingway. He completely neglected the contemporary literature of the United States of America. Besides this he focused his attention only on well-constructed works. Contemporary American fiction which is heading towards formlessness cannot be adequately dealt with Crane's critical method.

The fourth reason of his obscurity may be his long quarrel with contemporary scholars of the universities who constituted the establishment. He earned their wrath by pointing out their shortcomings. Consequently, his method could not be popular with students who came into contact with such teachers who were antagonized by him. Crane was a rebel critic of his time.

The fifth reason of his obscurity may be assigned to his awkward prose-style. Each paragraph of his essays is generally full of dependent clauses, synthetic parallels, anaphoric monotony, which make his prose murky and turgid. Such laborious prose-style has a very limited appeal to average students of literature. Lawrence Lipking rightly observed that "...it is a prose we read doggedly and do not always pick up again."[113] Criticism of criticism is specialist's job and can be done by only those who possess a high degree of intellectual sophistication. Crane was a first-rate humanist scholar, philosopher who made a very heavy demand upon his readers. It is difficult to understand him without a fair degree of intellectual equipment. We know that a style is shaped by writer's specific purpose, environment and personality. His prose-style was too ponderous and pedantic. Crane, is a first-rate scholar who wrote only for serious students and scholars.

Crane's criticism is a sort of classroom criticism. So its character is basically different from "workshop criticism" of Eliot and other poet-critics like Sidney, Ben Jonson, Johnson, Arnold, Coleridge, Wordsworth, Shelley etc. because Crane was not a creative writer. He never wrote criticism in defence of his own writings. His aim was not to create a new kind of literary taste but to create a new kind of critical habit among students. His aim was to make "every man his own critic" and not to increase the number of doctrinaire or rubber-stamp critics, and establish gurudom in literary criticism.

Crane belongs to a mixed tradition: the Euro-American tradition of literary criticism. He has affinity with the early Eliot and Richards in their fight against impressionism and subjectivism; but his main critical ideas were essentially those of Aristotle. Crane's approach was highly pragmatic. He was an instrumentalist. He was an innovator as well as a conservative. He reconciled the claims of yesterday and tomorrow for a brighter future of criticism. Unlike the New Critics he did not consider the basic assumptions and general method of Aristotle as oddly anachronistic. On the contrary, he permitted its limited use for a limited purpose.

The critical pluralism, which Crane advocates, is the typical American accent in modern American criticism. Americans, as we know, constantly harp on pluralism, as a powerful remedy against all sorts of social, political, cultural and ethnic conflicts. Therefore, Crane's belief that friction among critics could be minimized through pluralism, both in theory and practice, as it is fully in tune with the general American way of thinking.

NOTES

1. Lawrence Lipking, "R.S. Crane and the Idea of the Humanities," *Philological Quarterly* (Nov. 1968), 457.
2. Crane, "Shifting Definitions and Evaluations," *The Humanities*, I, 122.
3. *Ibid.*, p. 165.
4. "Criticism as Inquiry," *The Humanities*, II, 26.
5. *Ibid.*, 27.
6. *Ibid.*, 17.
7. "The Teaching of Literary Texts," *Ibid.*, p. 188.
8. *Ibid.*, p. 188.
9. *Ibid.*, p. 189.
10. *Ibid.*, p. 191.
11. LCSP, p. xiv.
12. *Ibid.*, p. xii.
13. "History Versus Criticism," *The Humanities*, II, 12.
14. W.R. Keast, "The Theoretical Foundations of Johnson's Criticism," *Critics and Criticism*, p. 406.
15. Quoted in *Ibid.*, p. 406.
16. *Ibid.*, p. 407.
17. Crane, "History Versus Criticism," *The Humanities*, II, 13; Cf. *The Humanities*, II, 204.
18. "The Moral Tradition," *New Yorker*, September 24, 1949, p. 89.
19. "The Teaching of Literary Texts," *The Humanities*, II, 186.
20. *Ibid.*, pp. 182-85.

21. *Ibid.*, p. 187.
22. "Every Man His Own Critic," *Ibid.*, p. 201.
23. *Ibid.*, p. 202.
24. *Ibid.*, p. 202.
25. "Every Man His Own Critic," *Ibid.*, p. 204.
26. *Ibid*,, pp. 204-05.
27. *Ibid.*, p. 205.
28. *Ibid.*, p. 204.
29. "The Theoretical Foundations of Johnson's Criticism," *Critics and Criticism*, p. 392.
30. See Bruce Bashford's unpublished dissertation, p. 23, where it is given that this extract forms the part of a pamphlet, whose authorship is assigned to Crane by Gwin Kolb, who was the Chairman of the English Department of the University of Chicago in mid 70s.
31. *The Higher Learning in America* (New Haven, Connecticut, 1962), p. 107. The book was copyrighted in 1938.
32. Bruce Bashford, "*The Humanistic Criticism of R.S. Crane*," 71-1790, University Microfilms, A Xerox Company, Ann Arbor, Michigan.
33. "The Battle of Books," *The Knowledge Most Worth Hairing*. Ed. Wayne C. Booth (Chicago, 1967), p. 194.
34. Henry Johnstone, Jr., *Philosophy and Argument* (University Park, Pennsylvania, 1959), p. 132.
35. "Every Matt His Own Critic," *The Humanities*, II, 139.
36. *Ibid.*, p. 196.
37. *Ibid.*, p. 199.
38. *The Education We Need* (Chicago, 1947), p. 10.
39. "The Teaching of Literary Text," p. 177.
40. Crane, "Introduction," *Critics and Criticism*, p. 8.
41. LCSP, p. 140.
42. Wayne C. Booth, "Introduction," *The Humanities*, I, XV.
43. *Ibid.*, p. xvi.
44. *Ibid.*, p. xvi.
45. "Every Man His Own Critic," p. 209.
46. *Ibid.*, p. 209.
47. *Ibid.*, p. 209, footnote no. 5.
48. LCSP, p. 167.
49. "On Value Judgment in the Arts," *Criticism as Inquiry*, Vol. I (September, 1971), 75.
50. "The Concept of Plot and Plot of Tom Jones," *Critics and Criticism*, p. 261.

51. *Ibid.*, p. 621.
52. "The Concept of Plot...," p. 621.
53. *Ibid.*, p.622
54. LCSP, p. 170.
55. *Ibid.*, p. 172.
56. *Ibid.*, p. 172.
57. *Ibid.*, p. 156.
58. *Ibid.*, p. 181.
59. *Ibid.*, p. 173.
60. *Ibid.*, pp. 178-79.
61. *Ibid.*, pp. 178-79.
62. *Ibid.*, p. 179.
63. *Ibid.*, p. 76.
64. *Ibid.*, p. 7.
65. *Ibid.*, p. 7.
66. *Ibid.*, pp. 7-8.
67. LCSP, p. 11.
68. *Ibid.*, p. 116.
69. *Symbolism and American Literature* (Chicago: The University of Chicago Press, 1953), p. 43.
70. "The Critical Monism of Cleanth Brooks," *Critics and Criticism*, p. 99.
71. *Ibid.*, p. 99.
72. *Ibid.*, p. 98.
73. "The Critical Monism of Cleanth Brooks," *Critics and Criticism*, p. 99, footnote no. 35; Cf. LCSP, pp. 176-77.
74. H.L. Mencken, "The Critical Process," *Literary Criticism in America*, edited by Nostrand (New York: The Liberal Arts Press, 1957), p. 240.
75. *Ibid.*, pp. 242-43.
76. David Daiches, "Epilogue," *Critical Approaches to Literature* (London, Longmans, 1957), p. 391.
77. *Ibid.*, p. 392.
78. *Ibid.*, p. 393.
79. *Ibid.*, p. 393.
80. *Ibid.*, p. viii.
81. "The Teaching of Literary Texts," *The Humanities*, II, 177.
82. "The Responsibility of the Critic," *The Writer and His Craft*, edited by Roy W. Cowden (The University of Michigan Press, 1957), p. 244.
83. *Ibid.*, p. 244.
84. *Ibid.*, p. 244.

85. 'Pandora's Box Revisited': A Review Article," *Critical Enquiry*, Vol. 1 No. 2 (December, 1974), p. 427.
86. "Structure of Criticism and Languages of Poetry," *Contemporary Criticism (*London: Edwin A. Arnold), p. 36.
87. *Ibid.*, p. 174.
88. *Ibid.*, p. 37.
89. "Synthesis," *Five Approaches of Literary Criticism* (New York: Collier—Macmillan Ltd., 1968), p. 313.
90. *Ibid.*, p. 313.
91. "Criticism as Inquiry," *The Humanities*, II, 29.
92. *On Poetry and Poets* (London: Faber & Faber, 1957), p. 117.
93. *Ibid.*, p. 117.
94. *Ibid.*, p. 117.
95. Quoted on p. 194 of *The Humanities*, I. 2. *Ibid.*, p. 194.
96. *Ibid.*, p. 194.
97. LCSP, p. x.
98. *Ibid.*, p. x.
99. *Ibid.*, p. x.
100. LCSP, p. 28.
101. *Ibid.*, p. 28.
102. Ingo Seidler, "The Iconolatric Fallacy: On the Limitations of the Internal Method of Criticism," *Journal of Aesthetics and Art Criticism*, XXVI (Fall, 1967), 13.
103. Rene Wellek, "The Term and Concept of Literary Criticism," *Concept of Criticism* (Yale University Press), p. 21.
104. "History *Versus* Criticism," *The Humanities*, II, 12.
105. Explication as Criticism (New York, Columbia University Press, 1965), p. 17.
106. *Practical Criticism* (New York, 1935), p. 11.
107. *The Sacred Wood* (New York, 1930), p. 11.
108. "Studies in Contemporary Criticism," *The Egoist*, V (October, 1918), p. 113.
109. *Ibid.*, p. 113.
110. *Selected Essays* (New York, 1932), p. 32.
111. LCSP, p. 182.
112. *Ibid.*, p. 182.
113. "Principles of Literary History," *The Humanities*, II, 59.

7

Conclusion

The Chicago school of criticism is one of the major movements in modern American criticism after the Kenyon school of Criticism or New Criticism. The disagreement between the two schools of criticism is not just a "family quarrel,"[1] but a much deeper affair. Despite their common ancestry, they differ in fundamentals, for example the New Critics preach and practise an *a priori*, deductive and monistic approach, whereas the Chicago Critics favour *a posteriori*, inductive and pluralistic approach.

Generally, "schools" set up polarities and foster some sort of dogmatism which finally lead to confusion, tension and dissension. But, ironically enough, the Chicago school of criticism was founded to end all kinds of dogmatism in criticism and to achieve a kind of harmony, balance and a peaceful co-existence among critics. The internecine wars among critics which had enlivened the critical scene of the 30's and 40's greatly disturbed the Chicago Critics. Reporting on the war-like atmosphere among literary critics of the period, Allen Tate observed: "As for literary criticism, we here encounter a stench and murk not unlike that of a battlefield three days after the fighting is over and the armies have departed."[2] Norman Forester, in his introduction to *American Critical Essays* (1930), divided the critical battles in America into four dialectical positions: modernist sceptists *versus* expressionists; moralists *versus* realists; humanists *versus* naturalists; and scholars versus critics. A similar attempt to categorize the critical controversies in fourfold pattern of contraries: nationalism *versus* internationalism, formalists *versus* expressionists; moralists *versus* Menckenites; and aesthetes *versus* 'message-hunters' was already made by Jane C. Bowmon in his *Contemporary American Criticism* (1926). In his essay, "Shifting definitions and evaluations," Crane also mentions how the period preceding the eighteenth century, "set humanists, as advocates of useful knowledge against dialecticians; natural scientists, as advocates of useful knowledge, against humanists; partisans of the moderns against admirers of the ancients; and rhetoricians and scholars against philosophers."[3] Again, between 1920 and 1930, a war was waged between the self-styled radicals and the neo-humanists. In the 50's, fighting was still going on between relativists and positivists, formalists and historicists, monists and syncretists, and the like. The most recent war between the monists and the Chicago pluralists was to end all such wars.

As long as dogmatism persists, critical front cannot be quiet completely. The Chicago critics realized that doctrinal conflicts among critics merely spell doom for criticism. Through their semantic theories, Mckeon, Crane and Olson, tried to immunize their contemporary critics against futile polemics which merely wasted their critical energy. They clearly pointed out that when critics differ they often do not know what they precisely differ about. Their apparent contradictions, as they point out, are due to their lack of understanding of the aspects they deal with. They feel that a critic should clearly know the powers and limitations of his own method as well as those of others. They openly acknowledged the contributions of the New Critics in making teachers and students more capable of close textual analysis and lively appreciation than their predecessors, who were under the strong influence of the old guards of philology and literary history. They disagree with the New Critics most agreeably. Those who have not made in-depth comparative study of the two groups of critics, mistakenly jump to the conclusion that the Chicago Critics completely rejected the New Critics. The truth is somewhat different. On the contrary, the Chicago Critics, have consolidated the gains made by the New Critics over the historical scholars, and tried to improve upon them by supplementing their deficiencies. Like the New Critics they also focus on the text; but they do not focus their attention on semantic aspect.

The panacea which the Chicago Critics discovered for the doctrinal conflicts and methodological confusion in criticism was 'critical pluralism.' Pluralism is an anti-dote to arrogance which is born out of dogmatism of this or that type. I think that a pluralistic approach, if fully accepted, can be a great leap into the realm of tolerance among critics as it will always guard them against superiority complex, smugness, indifference, coldness and rivalry. In critical pluralism, the Chicago Critics found a way out to liberate their contemporary critics from critical neurosis. They tried to make critics free, flexible and open minded. Thus, we find that they sincerely worked for changing discord into harmony. The Chicago school for criticism, therefore, may be called a Criticism of Concord.

Richard Mckeon believed that the arts of the humanities must be brought to bear on the conflicts of our time. In his autobiographical sketch, he observed: "I backed into philosophy as a means of securing insights into the conflicts of theory and practice, values and actions, which became increasingly prominent at the time of the First World War."[4] Pluralism is the insight which he discovered, after making a comparative study of various philosophic systems. It is a permanent remedy against dogmatism, either in philosophy or in criticism. Its relevance, not only for the critical monists of the middle 30's but also for all critics of all times, can hardly be questioned.

It is often mistakenly held that the bias of the Chicago Critics for the Aristotelian method contradicts their pluralistic position. Neither Crane nor his Chicago colleagues were blind followers of Aristotle. They "viewed their 'Aristotelianism' as a strictly pragmatic and non-exclusive commitment."[5] They never considered Aristotle's method as a rival of any other method, but always as a supplement to the method commonly employed by T.S. Eliot, F.R. Leavis, Allen Tate, R.P. Blackmur and Kenneth Burke.

The Chicago Critics were "progressive-conservative" reformers of literary studies. They welcomed whatever useful they found in the long tradition of Euro-American criticism and tried to conserve them; but, simultaneously, they discarded whatever unnecessary, irrelevant and harmful they found in it for the growth of criticism. In their view an active co-operation among men of different disciplines, namely, criticism, philology, bibliography, history and analysis of ideas can help eradicate "guild prejudices"[6] of the specialists of the respective disciplines. Such as inter-disciplinary interaction will end "the perennial jealousies of rhetoricians and philosophers, grammarians and rhetoricians, historians and critics... ."[7]

The revivals, extensions and re-opening of some of the major issues, already initiated by the Chicago Critics in the 30's, in recent years indicate that the Chicagoan seeds have started sprouting forth like belated crops. The New Critics, as I have already stated, had completely rejected the genre theory and "cast it off the throne it occupied during the Neo-classical period, indeed, since the Middle Ages, and put it into the dog-house."[8] Unlike them, the Chicago Critics tried to modify it according to modern needs. "The first important reaction in favour of generic criticism," says David H. Richter,

> was that of the Chicago neo-Aristotelians, whose feisty polemics against the 'New' critics must have seemed in the 1940s and 1950s like voices crying in the wilderness.... And today, if the books covering my desk are anything to go by, genre criticism has emerged in force. The flood has brought forth historical studies of Renaissance analyses of traditional genres like the picaresque or of new one's like 'the fantastic,' efforts to systematize the genres of narrative fiction, and even an attempt, through the philosophic analysis of dozen genres systems, to go 'beyond genre.' Indeed, the late sixties spawned a journal entitled *Genre* entirely devoted to theoretical and practical criticism employing the concept.[9]

The rise of New Historicism in the recent times also shows how Crane's early campaign for maintaining a useful link with historical scholarship was a significant step in the direction of restoring health to contemporary criticism.[10]

The Chicago school of criticism, as some of the critics have gloomily observed,[11] is not going to wither away, or to die a natural death. The element of timelessness which characterizes its crusade against reductionism and dogmatism, will give permanence to it.

The Chicago Critics have produced a very strong impact on Wayne C. Booth, Robert Marsh, Sheldon Sacks, M.H. Abrams, Northrop Frye and many others. Wayne C. Booth's *The Rhetoric of Fiction* is the most important work in which the critical concepts of the Chicago school of criticism have been applied to the analysis of novels. In this book Booth studies the effect of novels on readers not by speculation about the function of the creative imagination or by analysis of reader's psychology but by focus upon the writer's technique, voice and narrative strategy. He focuses upon the how of art, the "technique as rhetoric."[12] In his recent publication *Rhetoric of Irony*, he "cuts through the various meanings we have come to give to 'irony' and analyze the problems of sharing specific ironies. After an extended discussion of how we can know 'when to stop' in pursuing 'the heady delights of ironic communion,' the author turns to ironies that resist interpretation."[13] Again, in his latest book, *Modern Dogma and The Rhetoric of Assent* he has developed the typical Chicagoan stance, which may be described as anti-dogmatism. In this book, he "exposes five dogmas of modernism that have too often inhibited efforts to answer these questions, and he traces their consequences through a wide range of inquiry and action: in politics, art, music, literature, in personal 4efforts to find 'identity' or a 'self,' "[14] Sheldon Sacks's *Fiction and the Shape of Belief* and Paul Goodman's *The Structure of Literature* have also been greatly influenced by the assumptions and method of the Chicago Critics.

No doubt, since Crane's death, 'the influence of the Chicago group has been waning'[15] but its impact on some individual critics can be easily traced. John Paul Pritchard rightly observed that "what the future course of these critics will produce, it is impossible to say; but they are undoubtedly one of the most interesting groups at present occupying the attention of the literary men."[16]

The weakest point of the Chicago School of criticism is its low output in the field of practical criticism; but I do not think that this drawback forfeits its claim to be recognized as a major school of criticism of our time. Whatever little applied criticism it has produced is rich in its depth and quality. They are to be treated as worked out examples.' The motive behind their practical criticism was to demonstrate how to improve the critical analysis of *Persuasion, "Killers," Tom Jones* and *Gulliver's Travels*, already done by the New Critics.

Having examined their meager critical performance, one feels tempted to compare them with those teachers of a medical college who know a lot about human anatomy, physiology and medicines but have treated very few patients. I think if a patient is freely allowed to express his preference, he would go in for a practising physician rather than a learned medical college teacher. Similarly, a student of literature or a common reader would prefer a New Critic to a Chicago Critic, even knowing fully well that the latter's criticism is far more comprehensive than that of the former. David Daiches admires the Chicago Critics for their brilliance and thoroughness, but does not discuss them at all in *The Critical Approaches to Literature* because their practical Criticism did not impress him.[17]

As I have already pointed out, the Chicago school of criticism will be chiefly remembered for its therapeutic effects; I must add now that the remedies which they suggested have also produced some adverse side-effects like the toxic action of high antibiotics. By examining the logical base: the postulates, definitions, hypotheses, and dialectics—of other New Critics, the Chicago Critics turned critical activity into a kind of logical activity. At times, what they talk about seems to be more a type of dialecticism than literary criticism. In addition to this, they heavily rely on Aristotle's general method in their practical criticism, which is ideally suited only for the analysis of well-structured works of literature. Their bias for Aristotle's method may give rise to a new kind of monism, which takes into account only the "immediate shaping cause" of literary works and nothing else.

The Chicago school of criticism, in a bid to reconstruct contemporary criticism, shifted the emphasis from 'monism' to' 'pluralism'; from *a priori* deductive approach, to *a posteriori* inductive approach; from "abstract method" to "matter-of-fact" method; from the Aristotelian "material cause" (language) to the "final cause" (*dynamis*); from the "part" to the "concrete whole" (*Synola*); from the antithetical relationship between history and criticism to a fruitful interaction of the two; from the ruling hypothesis to "multiple working hypotheses" etc. The remedies, which the Chicago Critics offered went a long way in achieving a kind of balance, because they put proper emphasis on aspects hitherto neglected by modern critics of America.

Crane, in his scheme of five sets of critical questions,[18] left out those aspects of literary works which have bearing on ancient myths and rituals. He did not even suggest the marginal utility of the psychological, mythological and archetypal approaches. A pluralistic critic like him should not have missed the "mythopoeic perspective" of literary works. How can we deny the usefulness of these two popular methods? I do not think that a literary critic will do any violence to literary criticism if he studies literary works in these perspectives also.

Crane's opposition to such critics is based on the fact that they subordinate "intrinsic factors" of literary creation to "extrinsic" factors, which have roots in cultural anthropology, psychology, religion, ritual, history, philosophy and fine arts and not in literature itself. I think this is carrying one's bias too far. The literary spectrum comprises history, myth, biography, psychology, sociology, religion and music.[19] Therefore, a pluralistic critic should not be unnecessarily prejudiced to mythical interpretations. Myth critics have applied a variety of techniques to the study of literary works with great profit. To deny the fruits of their insights, as Crane did, is to miss the advantages of an interdisciplinary approach. Who can deny the positive contributions to modern criticism of such works as: R.Y. Hathorn's *Tragedy, Myth, and Mystery*, I.G. MacCaffrey's *The Visionary Company*, Philip Wheelwright's *The Burning Fountain and Myth and Metaphor*. No discerning critic can afford to deny that some of the myth critics have produced excellent interpretations of The Greek classics in terms of mythic and ritualistic origins.[20] Under the direct influence of Sir James G. Frazer's *The Golden Bough*, brilliant studies of the works of such modern writers, as James Joyce, Thomas Mann, T.S. Eliot, Yeats and Conrad have been made. R.W.B. Lewis's *The American Adam* deserves special mention here.

It is difficult to agree with Crane's logic that myth critics have committed a deadly sin by deriving their "first principles" or insights from non-literary sources. Just because some myth critics sometimes lose sight of the aesthetic values of literary works, out of their sheer passion for mythical interpretation, we cannot deprive ourselves of the benefit of their approach. Similarly, Crane's repudiation of the psychological critics, in very strong terms, is also misleading. He says that the Freudian critics, despite Freud's warnings, have subsumed literary works under their dream theory and have developed ready-made systems of symbolic interpretations in terms of latent and manifest contents. The Jungian critics, too, hold that the structure and the emotional appeal of literary works are functions primarily of the psychological and ritualistic archetypes, despite Jung's warning that "that which constitutes the essential nature of art must always lie outside the province of analytical psychology."[21] It is true that a critic's obsession with sex-symbols, "collective unconscious," "racial memory," "Oedipus complex," "Electra complex" will do more harm than good to literary criticism. But this does not mean that the psychological critics are of no use to us.

The success and failure of a movement in literary criticism can be best understood in thę context of its age. The Chicago school of criticism was mainly started to supplement New Criticism, which was good but not good enough according to the Chicago Critics. It is a revised and enlarged edition of the Kenyon school of criticism. It has certainly improved upon the earlier school, at least, in theory. Now, we do not find some of the perversities in American criticism which confronted the Chicago Critics in the middle thirties. The strictures passed by them upon the New Critic must have worked as deterrents. The Chicago Critics concerned themselves more with the revaluation of methods than the revaluations of literary works and individual authors. They neglected contemporary creative writers in favour of contemporary critics, because they were primarily critics of "critics and criticism," as the title of their first critical symposium suggests.

The Cambridge school of criticism, as F.R. Leavis says, produced brilliant "revaluations," which finally brought about decisive change in "the conception of Jane Austen's art and achievement."[22] It also restored George Eliot to her position among the great novelists and "established Conrad in his now recognized place among the great, and *Nostromo* as his greatest novel."[23] The Chicago school of criticism cannot claim such spectacular achievements in respect of the revaluation of literary works. Nevertheless, its achievement in the sphere of the revaluation of critical methods is of very great significance. But to criticize the critics is not considered as a primary duty of a literary critic, though it is one of his jobs. A critic's job is to help us perceive the nature and worth of a literary work."[24] Helen Gardener also holds that "the primary critical act is judgment, the decision that a certain piece of writing has significance and value."[25] The MLA Committee on Research Activities, in 1952, also declared that "the essential nature of literary criticism turns on value judgments. The chief end of literary criticism is evaluation or value-judgment. It is this characteristic which distinguishes criticism from other forms of literary scholarship.[26] But the Chicago Critics, instead of judging sufficient number of literary works, have paid greater attention to the mechanics of value-judgment. Consequently, they appear more like critical theoreticians than literary critics.

It is difficult to determine the full impact of the remedial treatment of contemporary literary criticism by the Chicago Critics so early, as it is not yet harvest-time. Most of them, though quite old now, are still writing. History of literature shows that some movements gain late recognition. The Chicago school of criticism, being a constructive criticism of contemporary literary criticism, is bound to be recognized as an important movement of modern American criticism, because, it did the much needed servicing of the critical tools, which were in constant use since Aristotle. The critique of criticism,—a comparative examination of critical concepts and methods—which they attempted, yielded an objective criteria for interpreting the diversities and oppositions among critics and for judging the comparative merits of rival critical schools. They rightly questioned certain abuses of criticism by the New Critics; and, I think that their objections and suggestions for improvements benefited literary criticism in a number of ways. Crane, says Booth, rightly held that "stagnation comes when assumptions remain uncriticized, when hypotheses are taken self-proving, when methods are practised as routine, and when conclusions are debated as fragments torn from the context."[27] The Chicago school of criticism has, at least, ensured modern literary criticism against stagnation, by subjecting it to serious scrutiny.

NOTES

1. Wilbur Scott, "The Formalistic Approach," *Five Approaches of Literary Criticism* (New York: The Macmillan Company, 1968), p. 18.
2. Quoted from Allen Tate's The Forlorn Demon in Sujit Mukherjee's essay, "The Business of Criticism of America," in *The Indian Journal of English Studies*, Orient Longmans IX (1968).
3. *The Humanities*, I, 122.
4. *Moments of Personal Discovery*, ed. R.M. Maclver (New York, 1952), p. iii.
5. Crane, *Critics and Criticism*, p. 13.

6. *Ibid.*, p. 23.
7. *Ibid.*, p. 3.
8. David H. Richter, "Pandora's Box Revisited: A Review Article," *Critical Inquiry*, Vol. 1, No. 2 (December, 1974), 453.
9. *Ibid.*, pp. 453-54.
10. See Wesley Morris, *Toward a New Historicism* (New Jersey, Princeton University Press, 1972).
11. Rene Wellek, *Concept of Criticism* (New Haven: Yale University Press, 1963), p. 360.
12. Sheldon Norman and S.N. Grebstein, "The Formalistic Critic," *Perspectives in Contemporary Criticism*, 1968, p. 81.
13. Quoted in the *Critical Inquiry*, XVIII (1974), 292.
14. *Ibid.*, p. 292.
15. See Warren G. French's letter in the appendix.
16. *Criticism in America* (Oklahoma, University of Oklahoma Press, 1956), p. 282.
17. *The Critical Approaches to Literature* (New York: Longmans, 1957), p. viii.
18. "The Teaching of Literary Texts," *The Humanities*, II, 181.
19. James Thorpe, "Introduction," Relations of Literary Study edited by James Thorpe (New York: *Modern Language Association of America*, 1967), p. xi.
20. See Anthropology and the Classics (Oxford, 1968), an edited symposium by R.R. Marett; Jane Harrison's *Themis* (Cambridge, 1912); Gilbert Murry's *Euripides and His Age* (Holt, 1913); F.M. Cornford's Origin of Attic Comedy (Arnold, 1914).
21. Crane, "Criticism as Inquiry," *The Humanities*, II, 32-33.
22. "A Retrospect, Scrutiny," XX (Cambridge, The Syndics of the Cambridge University Press, 1963), p. 13.
23. *Ibid.*, p. 14.
24. Henry Seidel Canby, "An Age of Criticism," *Definitions* (New York: Harcourt Brace & Co.), p. 174.
25. "The Sceptre and Torch," *The Business of Criticism* (Oxford: The Clarendon Press, 1959), p. 4.
26. "The Aims, Methods and Materials of Research in the *Modern Languages and Literature*," PMLA, LXVII (1952), 29.
27. "Introduction," *The Humanities*, I, xxii.

APPENDICES

Appendix A

Biographical sketches of the Chicago Critics are given below.[1]

CRANE, PROF. R(ONALD) S(ALMON), b. Tecumseh, Mich, Jan. 5, 86; m. 17; C.2. English Literature, A.B., Univ. Mich, 08. L.H.D., 41; Ph.D., Univ., Pa, 11; D. Litt, Northwest Univ., 63, Instr. ENG, Northwest. Univ. 11-15, asst, prof., 15-20, assoc, prof., 20-24; Univ. Chicago, 24-25, prof., 25-50, distinguished serv. prof., 50-51, Emer Distinguished Serv. Prof. 51, Chmn. dept, 35-47, Ed, *Mod. Philol*, 30-52; Alexander lectr. & vis. prof., Univ. Toronto, 52; vis. prof. Cornell Univ., 52-53, 57; Carleton Coll, 53; Univ. Ore, 54; Stanford Univ., 54-55; Ind. Univ., 55-56; Univ. Fla, 58; Northwest Univ., 50; N.Y. Univ. 60-61; Univ. Rochester, 62; Univ. Iowa, 63. MLAA (v. press, 31); Am. Acad. Arts & Sci. History of literature and ideas in England in the 17th and 18th centuries; history of criticism "Languages of Criticism and the structure of poetry," U. of Toronto; "New essays of Oliver Goldsmith" & Co-auth., "*Critics and Criticism*: Ancient and Modern" U. of Chicago.

Add: Dept, of English, University of Chicago, Chicago 37, 111.

KEAST, William Rea, Univ. Pres.; b. Malta, III, Nov. 1, 1914; S. Perce Marwood and Helen Gertrude (Dusher) K.; A.B., U. Chgo., 1936, Ph.D. (Rockefeller Postwar fellow in humanities 1946-47), 1947; Doctor of Laws (hon.), University Michigan, 1967; m. Mary Alice Hart, Aug. 21, 1938; Children—Sara Hart, Stephen Calhoon, Emily Wrightsman. Instr. English, U. Chgo., 1938-47; asstt. prof., 1947-51; asso. prof. English, Cornell U., 1951-57. prof. English chmn. department, 1957-62, dean of Coll. Arts and Sciences, 1962-63, v.p. acad. affairs, 1963-65; pres. Wayne State University, 1965- , Mem. Pres. Adv. Council Developing Instns. Bd. dirs. Detriot Round Table, Detroit Symphony Orch.; trustee Cranbrook Sch. Served from pvt. to maj., Army Ground Forces, AUS, 1941-46. Recipient Univ. Fellowship U. Chgo, 1936-38; faculty fellow Fund for Advancement

Edn., 1955-56; Guggenheim fellow, 1958-59. Mem. Modern Lang. Assn. Am., American Civil Liberties Union (Detroit exec, bd.), Phi Beta Kappa, Phi Kappa Phi Clubs: Detroit, University Detroit Athletic (Detroit); Grolier, Authors: (with R.R. Palmer B.I. Wiley) Procurement and Training of Ground Combat Troops, 1948; (with others) *Critics and Criticism*, 1952; (with R.E. Strecter). The Province of Prose, 1956, 2nd edit, 1959; Seventeenth-century English Poetry, 1962; also articles prod, jours., revs. Home: 441 W. Fenny Av., Detroit 48202.

A select bibliography of Keast is given below as supplied by him on my personal request.

"Imagery and Meaning in the Interpretation of King Lear," *Modern Philology*, XLVII (1949), 45-64. Reprinted as "The 'New Criticism' and King Lear" in *Critics and Criticism*, ed. R.S. Crane (Chicago, 1952), pp. 108-37.

"Johnson's Criticism of the Metaphysical Poets," ELH, *A Journal of English Literary History*, XVII (1950), 59-70.

"Killigrew's Use of Donne in The Parson's Wedding," *Modern Language Review*, XLV (1950), 512-15.

"Dryden Studies, 1895-1948," *Modern Philology*, XLVIII (1951), 205-10.

"The Theoretical Foundations of Johnson's Criticism," In *Critics and Criticism, Ancient and Modern*, ed. R.S. Crane (Chicago: University of Chicago Press, 1952), pp. 389-407.

"The Preface to A Dictionary of the English Language: Johnson's Revisions and the Establishment of the Text, "Studies in Bibliography," V (1952-53), 129-46.

"Some Emendations in Johnson's Preface to the Dictionary," *Review of English Studies*, N.S. IV (1953), 52-57.

"Wallace Stevens's 'Thirteen Ways of Looking at a Blackbird,'" *Chicago Review*, Winter-Spring 1954, pp. 48-63.

The Shakespeare Folios in the Cornell University Library, Ithaca, N.Y., 1954.

"Johnson's Plan of a Dictionary: A Textual Crux," *Philological Quarterly*, XXXIII (1954), 341-47.

(With L.F. Powell, J.H. Sledd, & J.R. Sutherland) "The Language We Speak," *University of Chicago Round Table*, May 1, 1955.

(With R.S. Streeter) *The Province of Prose*. New York: Harper & Brothers, 1956.

"The Element of Art in Gibbon's History," ELH, *A Journal of English Literary History*, XXIII (1956), 153-62.

"The Two Clarissas in Johnson's Dictionary," *Studies in Philology*, LIV (1957), 429-39.

(ed.) *Seventeenth Century English Poetry. New York:* Oxford University Press, 1962. (This list omits small notes, reviews, and a volume of military history.)

"Dryden and Flecknow: A Conjecture," *Philological Quarterly*, XXXIII (1954), 338-52.

W.K. Wimsatt, Jr., *The Verbal Icon: Studies in the Meaning of Poetry* (Lexington: University of Kentucky Press, 1954. xviii, 229 pp). Review: *Modern Language Notes*, LXXI (1956), 591-97.

"The Theoretical Foundations of Johnson's Criticism." In *Critics and Criticism* (abridged ed.), ed. R.S. Crane (Chicago: University of Chicago Press, 1957), 169-87.

"Johnson and Intellectual History," In *New Light on Dr. Johnson*, ed. Frederick W. Hilles (New Haven, Connecticut: Yale University Press, 1959), 247-56.

"Johnson and 'Cibber's' Lives of the Poets, 1753," In *Restoration and Eighteenth-Century Literature*, ed. Carroll Camden (Houston, Texas: Rice University-Semicentennial Publications, 1962, 63), 89-101.

"Samuel Johnson and Thomas Maurice," In a volume of *eighteenth-century studies in memory of Donald F. Hyde.* To be published.

Bibliography to 1957.

McKEON, RICHARD PETER, educator; b. Union Hill, N.J., Apr. 26, 1900; S. Peter Thomas and Mathilda (Hrischfeld) Mck.; A.B., Columbia, Feb. 1920, A.M., Oct. 1920; grad, work, U. of Paris and Ecole des Hautes Etudes, 1922-25; Ph.D., Columbia, 1928; Litt. D., Jowish Theol. Sem. of America, 1942; Doctor honoris causa, Univ. of Aix Marseilles, 1951; m. Clarice Mauriel Thirer, July 10, 1930; Children—Peter, Nora, Michael, Inst, philosophy, Columbia, 1925-20, asst, prof., 1929-35, also instr. in Greek and Latin, Summer 1926; Visiting prof, history, U. of Chicago, 1937-47; dean of Div. of Humanities, 1935-47; distinguished service prof. Greek and philosophy since 1947, William H. Colvin research prof. Greek and philosophy since 1947, William H. Colvin research prof., 1965-66. Mem. U.S. del. Gen. Conf. Unesco, Paris, 1946, Mexico City, 1947, Beirut, 1948; U.S. counselor UNESCO Affairs, am. embassy, Paris,

France, 1947. Apprentice Seaman, USN, 1918, Pres. Internat. Inst. Philosophy, 1953-57; v.p. Internat. Fedn. Philos. Societies 1953. Fellow Mediaeval Acad. Am., Philos. Assn. (pres. 1952), Afn. Philo. Assn., History Sci. Scc., Institut Internat. de Philosophic Politique, Am. Council Learned Socs. (v. chmn. 1939), Phi Beta Kappa, Kappa Alpha Club: Quadrangle. Author: *The Philosophy of Spinoza*, 1928; *Freedom and History*, 1952; *Thought, Action and Passion*, 1954; (with R.K. Morton and W. Gellhorn). *The Freedom to Read*, 1957; co-author of several books; also editor and Translator of books; contbr. to sci pu; Home: 5632 Blackstone Av., Chgo. 37.

MACLEAN, NORMAN F(itzroy), educator; b. Clarina. Ia., Dec. 23, 1902: S. John Norman and Clara (Davidson) M.; A.B. Dartmouth, 1924; Ph.D. U. Chgo., 1940; M. Jessie Burns, September 24, 1931; children—Jean Burns, John Norman. Intr. English Dartmouth, 1924-26; with U. Chgo., 1931, successively inter., asst, prof., prof. English 1954, William Rainey Harper Prof, of English, 1963, dean of studies in coll., 1942-45, acting dir. Inst. Mil. Studies, 1943-45, chmn. com. on gen. studies in the humanities, 1952-66. Awarded prize for Excellence in Undergrad, teaching U. Chgo., 1932, 40 Mem. Modern Lang Assn., Beta Theta Pi Club: Quadrangle. Author: Manual of Instruction in Military Maps and Aerial Photographs (with Everett C. Olson), 1943; Critics and Criticism: Ancient and Modern (with others) 1952. Home: 1216 E. Madison Park Chgo. 60615.

OLSON, Elder James, educator, poet; b. Chgo., Mar. 9, 1909; S. Elder James and Hilda (schroeder) O.; B.A., U. of Chgo., 1934, M.A., 1935, Ph.D., 1938; M. Ann E. Jones, Feb. 13, 1937 (div. 1948); children—Ann (Mrs. David Burr), Elder; m. 2d, Geraldine Hays, Sept. 17, 1948; children—Ines Olivia, Shelley. Inter., Armour Inst. Tech. Chgo., 1935-38, mem. Faculty U. Chgo., 1936—prof. English, 1954; Rockefeller prof. U. Frankfurt (Germany), 1948, U. Philippines, 1966-67; vis. prof. U. P.R., 1952-53; Mahlon Powell prof, philosophy Ind. U., 1955, vis. prof. lit. criticism, 1958-59, fellow Seh. Letters, 1961, Patten lectr., 1964. Recipient Witter Bynner award, 1927; Guarantor's award Poetry mag., 1931, Tietjens award, 1953; Emily Clark Balch award, Va. Quar. Rev., 1965; Quantrell award U. Chgo., 1966; grantee Longview Found. 1958; award Poetry Soc. Am., 1955, Acad. Am. Poets, 1956. Mem. Modern Lang Assn., P.E.N. Internat. Soc. europeene de culture, Phi Beta Kappa. Author: Thing of Sorrow, 1934; The Cock of Heaven, 1940; (with others) *Critics and Criticism*, 1952; *The Poetry of Dylan Thomas*, 1954; *The Scarecrow Christ*, 1954; *Plays and Poems*,

1958; *Tragedy and the Theory of Drama*, 1961; *American Lyric Poems*, 1963; *Collected Poems*, 1963; *Aristotle's Poetics and English Literature*, 1965. Home: 5540 Kimbark Av. Chgo, 60637.

WEINBERG, BERNARD; Professor of Romance Language. Born in Chicago, III, 1909. Ph.B., Ph.D., Univ. of Chicago, Guggenheim Fellow, 1947-48, 1956-57; Fulbright Fellow, Italy, 1951-52, France, 1962-63. Taught at Washington Univ. and Northwestern Univ. since 1955, at the Univ. of Chicago;

department chairman, 1958-67. First Vice President, MLA 1963. Publications: French Realism: The Critical Reaction, 1830—1870 (1937); ed. *Critical Prefaces of the French Renaissance* (1950); *A History of Literary Criticism in the Italian Renaissance*, 2 vols. (1961); *The Art of Jean Racine* (1963); *The limits of Symbolism: Studies of Five Modern French Poets* (1966); *Trattati di Poetica e Retorica del Cinquecento*, 3 Vols. (forthcoming 1970-71); numerous articles on French and Italian literature.

NOTE

1. Biographical sketches of Crane, Keast, Mckeon Maclean and Olson are taken from *Who's Who* and *The Dictionary of American Scholars*. Only Bernard Weinberg's sketch is taken from PMLA, Sept. 1970, Vol. 85, no. 4, p. 844.

READING LIST

A reading list of the students of the three courses of the humanities is given below. It has been prepared on the basis of an account presented by Russell Thomas in his book *The Idea and Practice of General Education* (pp. 49-120) published by the University of Chicago Press (1950). As the books were taught by the Chicago Critics; naturally, they must have provided the theoretical base of the Chicago school of criticism.

Humanities 2

Philosophy: Dewey, John, *Essays in Experimental Logic* (Chicago: University of Chicago Press, 1916), pp. 75-102, 220-29, 230-49.

Plato, Phaedo and Protagoras, trans. B. Jowett, in the works of Plato, ed. Irwin Edman ("Modern Library" [New York: Random House, n.d.]).

Aristotle Metaphysics, trans: W.D. Ross, in Introduction to Aristotle, ed. Richard Mckeon ("Modern Library") (New York: Random House, 1947), i. 1-7.

— *Posterior Analytics*, trans. G.R.G. Mure, *Ibid*., i. 1-3.

— *On the Soul*, trans. J.A. Smith, *Ibid.*, 11; ii 1 and 2.

— *Nicomachean Ethics*, trans. W.D. Ross, *Ibid.*, i. 13; ii (entire).

Humanities 3

Criticism

Aristotle Physics, trans. R.P. Hardie and R.K. Gaya, in the *Basic Works of Aristotle*, ed. Richard Mckeon (New York: Random House, 1941), ii 1.

— *Metaphysics*, trans. W.D. Ross, *Ibid.*, vii 7-9.

— *Poetics*, trans. I. Bywater, in Introduction to Aristotle, ed. Richard Mckeon ("Modern Library" [New York: Random House, 1947]).

Plato Phaedrus, trans: B. Jowett, in the Works of Plato, ed. Irwin Edman ("Modern Library" [New York: Random House, n.d.]).

Hume David, "Of the Standard of Taste," in *Essays and Treatises on Several Subjects* (London, 1760), I 363-95.

Croce, Benedetto, *Aesthetics and Science of Expression and General Linguistics*, trans: Douglas Ainslie (2nd ed.; London: Macmillan & Co. Ltd., 1922), pp. 1-38, 67-73, 78-81, 0 87-103, III-39.

Arnold, Matthew, "The Study of Poetry," in *Representative Essays of Matthew Arnold*, ed. E.K. Brown (New York: Macmillan Co., 1936), pp. 156-68.

Jaine Hippolyte, Introduction, in *History of English Literature*, trans: H. Van Laun (Edinburgh: Edmonston & Douglas, 1871), pp. 1-21.

Pater Walter, "The School of Georgione," in *the Renaissance: Studies in Art and Poetry* (London: Macmillan & Co. Ltd., 1910), pp. 130-54.

Browen, Elizabeth, "Notes on Writing a Novel," *Orion*, II (1945), 18-29.

Humanities 3: Selected Readings (4th ed., Chicago, University of Chicago Press, 1948).

Appendix B

THE LETTERS

In course of my research work, I corresponded with a number eminent scholars. Some of the important letters are given below as they throw light on different aspects of the "Chicago School of criticism." The letters are arranged chronologically in their original form. The correspondence was done in late 60's and mid 70's.

THE UNIVERSITY OF CHICAGO CHICAGO. ILLINOIS 60637 DEPARTMENT OF ENGLISH 1050 EAST 59TH STREET

February 17, 1968

Dear Mr. Shrivastava,

I have just received your letter of February 6, and I will turn it over to Dr. Alexander Cappon, editor of the University Review to see if he can locate the three articles about which you request information. He may need some further data about the time of their publication. If we can locate them, we will see if arrangements can be made to provide you with copies. They may also at some time have been reprinted; perhaps Dr. Cappon will have this information available.

As for the men that you ask about, several of them are still teaching actively at the University of Chicago—Professors Norman MacLean and Elder Olson. Professor Crane died recently, I believe, but W.R. Keast has been Vice-President of Cornell University, Ithaca, New York, and I believe that he is still there. Professors McKeon and Weinberg, I am unable to locate. (Just located some further information—Professor Weinberg is retired from the University of Chicago, but still can be reached there; Professor Keast is now President of Wayne State University, Detroit, Michigan.) I can locate nothing about Professor McKeon, who is probably retired or possibly deceased. I am sure, however, that Professor Elder Olson can help you locate any of them and can assist you with any problems about the "Chicago Critics." The group has not been flourishing since Professor Crane's retirement, but there have been several collections made of their work.

I hope that this will provide you with the information that you need to proceed. You will hear subsequently about the articles.

Sincerely yours,
Sd/- Warren G. French
Chairman
English Department
University of Missouri
Kansas City

Dept, of Romance Languages and Literatures
The University of Chicago
1050 East 59th Street
Chicago, Illinois 60637

October 24, 1968

Prof. R.N. Shrivastava
Kala Bhawan, Shrinandan Road
P.O. Chapra (Bihar), India

Dear Professor Shrivastava,

The only response I can make to your good letter of October 7 is to say that I'm sending you, under separate cover, a copy of the abridged version of *Critics and Criticism*, which contains, on pp. 275-76, a partial bibliography of the so-called "Chicago Critics."

Good luck to you in your work on the group's critical theories and practices.

Yours sincerely,
Sd/- Gwin J. Kolb, Chairman
March 28, 1969

Professor Ravindra Nath Shrivastava
Kala Bhawan
Shrinandan Road
Chapra, Bihar
India

Dear Professor Shrivastava,

Contrary to your information, I am still very busily teaching and working at Chicago.

Most of my writings on criticism (The History of Literary Criticism in the Italian Renaissance, *The Art of Jean Racine*, and The Limits of Symbolism) have been published by the University of Chicago Press. Ronald Crane's *The Idea of the Humanities* was also published by the University of Chicago Press and his *The Language of Criticism and the Structure of Poetry* by the University of Toronto Press. *The Dictionary of World Literature* was published by the Philosophical Library in New York. Elder Olson's *Tragedy and the Theory of Drama* was published by the Wayne University Press and his *Theory of Comedy* by the Indian University Press.

I know of no manifesto of the school, but I think that Crane's two prefaces to the two edition of *Critics and Criticism* would be your best source.

Sincerely yours,
Sd/-Bernard Weinberg

UNIVERSITY OF MISSOURI-KANSAS CITY
COLLEGE OF ARTS & SCIENCES
DEPARTMENT OF ENGLISH

5315 Holmes Kansas City, Missouri 64110	College of Arts and Science Department of English	Telephone 816 276-1305

June 2, 1969

Prof. R.N. Shrivastava
Kala Bhawan
Shrinandan Road
P.O. Chapra, Bihar, India

Dear Professor Shrivastava,

I am sorry indeed that Professor Alexander Cappon did not have a chance to reply to your letter of February 17, 1969, and to send you the material that you requested from the University of Kansas City Review, Spring, 1942; but he is now quite an elderly man, and he has been extremely busy this year. He does not have an adequate office staff, either, so that it is difficult for him to comply with requests for assistance.

I have managed, however, to locate an unbound copy of the issue containing the articles that you wish in our departmental files, and I have had the two articles and the prefatory note Xeroxed for you. I enclose these copies with this letter. I hope that they will prove useful to you. The whole group of writings together does explain unusually well the practices of the Chicago Critics.

I'm afraid that I can't help you with the addresses of some of the magazines that you ask about. I have lists of only those devoted to articles about literature in English;

> ELH, Department of English, Johns Hopkins University, Baltimore, Maryland Modern Language Quarterly, 109 Parrington Hall, University of Washington, Seattle, Washington.
>
> ROMANIC REVIEW (I can find no such magazine as ROMANTIC REVIEW listed. The Romanic is devoted to
>
> Romance Languages and Literature.) 518 Philosophy Hall, Columbia University, New York, New York.
>
> COMPARATIVE LITERATURE, University of Oregon, Eugene, Oregon COLLEGE ENGLISH, C/o Richard Ohmann, Editor, Wesleyan University, Middletown, Connecticut, 06457.

I have to information about CLASSICAL PHILOLOGY, nor have I ever head of the *Carleton Drama Review, The Carleton Drama Bulletin* or *the Carleton College Bulletin*. All three may have been published at some time by Carleton College, Northfield, Minnesota, which now publishes the *Carleton Review*. I would suggest that you write the English Department there. The JOURNAL OF EDUCATION must be a professional education school magazine, and the JOURNAL OF PHILOSOPHY must also be a professional journal. You should be able to get information about them from any USIA library. The ENGLISH INSTITUTE ESSAYS are not a journal; they are a series of hardbound books. A selection of the essays read at each year's Institute is published by the Columbia University Press. There must be a set of these essays somewhere in India, as they are distributed throughout the world. It would be easier to locate them locally than to have copies made here. One would also have to know the particular year desired.

I hope that this information will be of some help to you I wish that we could offer more assistance, but we have no assistants to help us with requests and our library is preparing to move.

We were quite delighted, by the way, to have R.K. Narayan, the distinguished Indian Novelist here for a month. He is a most delightful visitor, and we hope that he can return. I hope also that your project will go well.

Sincerely yours,
Sd/- Warren G. French
Chairman

WAYNE STATE UNIVERSITY
Detroit, Michigan 48202

Office of the Director June 19, 1969

Professor R.N. Shrivastava
Kala Bhavan
Shrinandan Road
P.O. Chapra, Bihar
India

Dear Professor Shrivastava,

I am very pleased to know that you are writing on the Chicago Critics, and I am delighted to try to provide some materials that may be useful to you in your studies. I am most apologetic for this delay in answering your kind request. Your first letter was forwarded to me from Cornell University and I took it home with me intending to locate the documents and answer it. In the press of business I then misplaced your letter. If I have caused you undue inconvenience or delay I am very sorry.

Professor Richard P. McKeon is Distinguished Service Professor of Greek and philosophy at the University of Chicago, Chicago, Illinois 60637. The 1968 manuscript included is to be published by the Grolier Club in a volume of eighteenth-century studies in memory of Donald F. Hyde. You may want to write to the editor, Mr. W.H. Bond, The Houghton Library, Harvard University, Cambridge, Massachusetts 01238, for its date of publication. The bibliography enclosed is (except for the addition of the 1962 book) current only as of 1957. I hope to find time to bring it up-to-date soon. One item to which you refer, "Critical Essays, prefaces, and Notes" was not published; the bulk of the manuscript was destroyed in a fire in 1963 and I have not been able to find time to do the work over again.

I send best wishes for your success in your studies. I hope you will send me a copy when it is completed.

Sincerely yours,
Sd/- William R. Keast
President

30 June 1969
Northfield, Minn.
U.S.A.

Dear Professor Shrivastava,

The Chairman of our department of English at Carleton has asked me to answer your inquiry to him, and I am pleased to oblige since I was once a student of Professor Crane. He was a splendid teacher and a fine man and I only wish he were still alive to answer your requests, as I am sure he would have done with unfailing courtesy. Professor Crane died in 1967 and his career and criticism were summarized in the July, 1968, issue of *Philological Quarterly*, a journal I am sure would be available in India since it contains the bibliography of the studies in English literature from 1660-1800 published in 1967.

Ronald Salmon Crane was born in Tecumseh, Michigan, on January 5th, 1886, and took his A.B. degree from the University of Michigan in 1908 and his Ph.D. from the University of Pennsylvania in 1911. There I think he studied under Felix Scheling, the great Elizabethan scholar. His teaching career was centred at two universities: North-western from 1911 until 1924; the University of Chicago from 1924 through 1951 when he retired. He continued to teach at Chicago and elsewhere after his retirement and indeed his most distinguished critical works were published while he was in his late '60s and '70s. He continued teaching seminars at Chicago until shortly before his death.

The works published by Carleton which you ask for have all been reprinted in a book that has apparently not yet reached India. Since you would need to read the entire work for your study, I shall take the liberty of not sending you reprints of his Carleton essays but rather recommending to you his final work, *The Idea of the Humanities*, 2 volumes (Chicago: University of Chicago Press, 1967). Wayne Booth has contributed a fine introductory essay to that volume, and if you need further information you can write him in care of the Department of English at the University of Chicago.

In *The Idea of the Humanities* you will not only find the answers you inquired after but also the answer to many of the queries you submitted. Mr. Crane's concept of the humanities is discussed by Booth in his introduction and the title essay of the collection. Mr. Crane's position as a neo-Aristotelian and a critical pluralist is best seen in the introduction to *Critics and Criticism* (Chicago: University of Chicago Press, 1952).

For discussions of Mr. Crane's criticism see the following works which I hope are accessible to you: (1) Lawrence Lipking, "R.S. Crane and

The Idea of the Humanities," a review article in *Philological Quarterly, XLVII* (July, 1968), 455-71 (already cited above). (2) John Holloway, "The New and the Newer Critics," in *The Chartered Mirror* (New York, 1962), pp. 187-203. I do not know the English publisher. (3) William K. Wimsatt, Jr., "The Chicago Critics," in *The Verbal Icon* (Lexington, Kentucky: University of Kentucky Press, 1954), pp. 41-65. (4) Eliseo Vivas, "The Neo-Aristotelians of Chicago" in *The Artistic Transaction* (Columbus, Ohio: Ohio State University Press), pp. 243-59.

I hope I have been of help in your research project. I wish you the best of luck in your research project.

Sincerely
Sd/- Owen Jenkin

Florence, Italy
August 27, 1969

Dear Professor Shrivastava,

Once again, your letter was long in reaching me, since I am spending the summer in the Italy. I am happy to give you what little help I can.

For all the critics you mention, there are two public sources of biographical information: *Who's Who in America*, in any recent edition, and the *Dictionary of American Scholars*—in the latest edition, the separate volume devoted to the Humanities. Both these will give the essential data. McKeon, Olson, MacLean, are still at the University of Chicago and may be reached there; W.R. Keast is President of the Wayne State University, Detroit, Michigan.

Among the younger critics I might mention Wayne Booth and Robert Marsh, both now at the University of Chicago. As for critical reception. I know only of the negative attacks of such writers as Rene Wellek in *Concepts of Criticism*. John Crowe Ransom and Kenneth Burke have written and spoken favorably of the school, but at this distance I cannot give you any bibliographical details.

Let me wish you well in the successful pursuit of your project.

Sincerely,
Sd/- Bernard Weinberg

The University of Chicago
Chicago Illinois 60637
Department of English
1050 East 59th Street

December 15, 1969

R.N. Shrivastava
Kala Bhawan
Shrinandan Road
P.O. Chapra (Bihar)
India

My dear Sir,

Please accept my apology for not responding to your letter sooner. Life in an American university is at best a demanding one, and time is the one precious thing (in spite of what some people say about the American preoccupation with money).

You have asked for a number of difficult things. But, first of all, you should know that Mr. Crane died shortly after the publication of *The Idea of the Humanities*, and therefore there is no work, published or unpublished, by him written after that. You will find, however, a rather large number of reviews (some short, some long) which he did over the years for *Philological Quarterly*, beginning in the 1930's. No one has troubled to make of this a comprehensive list, but I assure you that he took those reviews quite seriously.

As for my own work, I have never gone to the trouble to construct a list, but the following are representatives:

1. Four Dialectical Theories of Poetry: *An Aspect of English Neoclassical Criticism* (University of Chicago Press, 1965).
2. "Historical Interpretation and the History of Criticism," in *Literary Criticism and Historical Understanding*, ed. P. Damon (Columbia University Press, 1967), pp. 1-24.
3. "Observations on the Criticism of Yvor Winters," *Spectrum* (Summer, 1960), pp. 146-62 [University of California at Santa Barbara publication].
4. "The Seasons of Discrimination," *Modern Philology*, LXIV (No. 3), February 1967, pp. 238-52.
5. "The 'Fallacy' of Universal Intention," *Modern Philology*, LV (No. 4), May 1958, pp. 263-75.

Biographical details: look at *Directory of American Scholars* and *Who's Who* in America.

I suggest that you write for further information to the following people:

Professor Walter Davis,
Department of English,
The University of California at Santa Barbara
Goleta, California, U.S.A.

Professor M.H. Abrams,
Department of English,
Cornell University,
Ithaca, New York, U.S.A.

If I can be of further assistance to you please do not hesitate to write again.

Yours truly and sincerely,
Sd/- Robert Marsh

26 February, 1970

Professor R.N. Shrivastava
Kala Bhawan
Shrinandan Road
P.O. Chapra (Bihar)

Dear Professor Shrivastava,

I am sorry, but I cannot give you much help in your research on the Chicago Critics. I know of no obvious influence on creative writers though possibly one could find an effect on the novels of Saul Bellow, who is a Chicago graduate, and now a part-time member, I believe, of the Chicago faculty.

As for reviews: an example of the kind of attack on these critics is William K. Wimsatt, "The Chicago Critics," in his *The Verbal Icon: Studies in the Meaning of Poetry*. A good man to write to for further information is Professor Wayne Booth, Department of English, the University of Chicago. Booth's very influential book, *The Rhetoric of Fiction*, is itself a fine example of a special application of the Chicago approach to aspects of the novel.

Yours sincerely,
Sd/- M.H. Abrams

Dear Prof. Shrivastava,

Please forgive me for my long delay in answering your letter of last fall; a death in my immediate family was partly responsible.

I really don't have a lot to say to you about the so-called Chicago school of literary critics, beyond what you can obtain from reading their works. I assume that you have seen Mr. Crane's final (posthumous) volume, *The Idea of the Humanities*, with my introduction, and my *The Rhetoric of Fiction*, which reflects their ideas in many many points. I do not have a bibliography here in London, but you seem to have all of the school. I'm sure you know that no "school" of independent minds are in agreement on all points.

One person whose name you do not mention and who may be able to help you is Prof. Sheldon Sacks, author of the fine book, FICTION AND THE SHAPE OF BELIEF. Perhaps you could write him at the Dept, of English, the Unive. of Chicago.

May your work go well.

Very sincerely,
Sd/- Wayne Booth

Walter Davis
Dept, of English
University of California, Santa Barbara
Goleta, California, U.S.A.

Dear Prof. Shrivastava,

I doubt if I can provide you with an information not available through Robert Marsh. I recently finished my dissertation which included a chapter on Crane. I'll list below some of the works I found most useful. My general impression, however, was that Crane had never received an adequate or discriminating treatment. The other questions you raise about the influence of the Chicago school are interesting. McKeon rather than Hutchins was the intellectual centre of developments at Chicago. In criticism, however, Crane felt himself independent of McKeon but I doubt it. The effect of the Chicago school on practical criticism has been small and confined largely to U of Chicago products. To see two interesting developments out of Crane see Wayne Booth, *The Rhetoric of Fiction* & Sheldon Sacks, *Fiction & the Shape of Belief.* No practicing novelist, including fellow, has been directly influenced as far as I know.

The following items may provide bibliographical aid on Crane:

R. McKeon, *Thought, Action & Passion* (U of C Press)
Kenneth Burke, *A Grammar of Motives* (U of Calif. Press)
Husch, E.D., *Validity in Interpretation* (Yale Press)

Eliseo Vivas, *Creation & Discovery*—contains a vicious attack

Wimsatt, *The Verbal Icon* - „ „ „

Elder Olson, *The Theory of Comedy* (U of Indiana Press)— the most recent work in the Chicago school.

When *Critics and Criticism* first came out there were a number of debates in the reviews but I never followed up this information since reviews are generally trivial. In short, the area is still open for serious inquiry. Good luck.

Sincerely,
Sd/- Walter A. Davis

Tel. No. 26536
Department of English
Nagpur University, Nagpur

No. PGTD/
Dr. P.S. Sastri,
M.A., Ph.D.,
Professor & Head of the
Department of English,
Nagpur University, Nagpur.

New Library Building
North Ambazari Road
Nagpur
Dated 7-2-1972

My dear friend,

Your kind letter.

1. "Neo" does not refer to nay revivalist trend. Kenneth Burke used it only to refer to the "revival" of the Aristotelian methodology and to its possible extension by finding our analogues. Only the method is accepted and to that extent they can be called Modern Aristotelians. The method takes up the work of art as *a synola* and seeks to find its matter, manner, medium and *dynamis*. Of course the basic concept is that of mimesis. They are not bound by Aristotle's conclusions(?) if there are any. They reinterpret the old terms and show (1) that the method applies only to mimetic works, not to allegory, satire, didactic verse etc; and (2) that a few questions alone can be answered within the framework of this method.
2. Olson's paper will be found in a volume entitled *Aristotle's Poetics* in English edited by him.
3. After C please add—
   Imitation;
   Whole;

4. Rajnath published his *Essays in Criticism*—Doaba House, 1688 Nai Sarak, Delhi-6.

My best wishes.

Ever yours,
Sd/- P.S. Sastri

October 8, 1972

Dear Mr. Shrivastava,

Your letter dated Aug. 27, '72 came to me only a few days ago a very long time for air mail to take, even from India. I am afraid my answer will disappoint you, but I am unable to send any of the books you mention. But I have a few suggestions:

1. For *English Literature, 1660-1800*, write Princeton University Press, giving the author or editor, dates, etc. I do not have the volumes—in fact I never heard of the work.
2. For Hutchins's book write the University of Chicago Press.
3. For Howard Mumford Jones's book, write Mr. Jones in Ithaca, or the press which published it.
4. The University of Chicago professors you write to—except Keast—are still on the faculty here. Perhaps they did not receive your letters.
5. I know nothing of Michael Ruddick. Ronny Eckrcis address is 5459 S Dorchester Arc., Chicago, Dc., 60615.
6. As to a bibliography, you have all of the critical works that Mr. Crane wrote. As to reviews he did, you might see these Journals, *The Philological Quarterly* for April, 1935, April 1937 and July 1958.
7. Write to Mr. Bruce Bashford State University of New York, Stony Brook, Long Island, New York, 11790.

He wrote his Ph.D. dissertation on The Humanistic Criticism of R.S. Crane in 1970, and he may be able to help you in your research. The journals I mentioned for reviews are some that I know Mr. Bashford used. He might also answer some specific questions that may be troubling you.

Good luck on your dissertation.

Sincerely,
Sd/- Julia F. Crane.

(Mrs. Ronald S.)
5536 Dorchester Arc.,
Chicago Dc., 60637

STATE UNIVERSITY OF NEW YORK
AT STONY BROOK

Stony Brook, Long Island, New York
Zip Code 11790
Department of English

College of ARTS
AND SCIENCES

November 4, 1972

Professor R.N. Shrivastava
Arvind Institute Lane
Kadamkuan
Patna-3 (Bihar)
India

Dear Professor Shrivastava,

In response to your recent letter, I am going to suggest that you order a copy of my dissertation from the dissertation copy service in Michigan. I am including an order form and some related information.

I make this suggestion for two reasons: the nature of your questions and your interest. Your questions cover so much ground that an adequate response would, in effect, duplicate my dissertation. In addition, given your project, I am sure you want of know as much as possible about what an earlier worker in the same area discovered; my dissertation will give you both my findings and my bibliography in a way I obviously cannot do in a letter.

I would enjoy hearing from you after you read the dissertation. You may well want to take issue with some of my points. Also, I think you will discover areas which apparently interest you but which I have never investigated, for instance, the relation between the "humanisms" of Crane and Babbitt.

The order number for my dissertation, "The Humanistic Criticism of R.S. Crane," is 71-1790. It is available in two forms: on microfilm for four dollars (you must have access to a viewer) or as a xerox of the original for ten dollars. You will be charged for postage.

I wish you good luck with your project and look forward to hearing from you again.

Yours truly,

Sd/- Bruce W. Bashford,
Assistant Professor of
English

XEROX

University Microfilms
A Xerox Company
Ann Arbor, Michigan 48106
Telephone 313 761-4700

June 27, 1973

Prof. R.N. Shrivastava
Kachharia Kothi, First Floor
R.K. Avenue
Patna-4
Bihar (India)

Your purchase order number: Your order card

Dear Customer,

Thank you for your order. It has been received at our offices in Ann Arbor, Michigan, and is being processed now.

In the future please send your orders and direct your inquiries to

University Microfilms, Ltd.
St. John's Road
Tylors Green
Penn, Buckinghamshire
ENGLAND

University Microfilms, Ltd. is responsible for serving all countries in the Eastern Hemisphere of the world and is prepared to meet your needs and answer your inquiries. In order to obtain the best possible service for yourselves, may we suggest you direct all orders in the future to that office.

Sincerely,
Sd/-
Order Department

Select Bibliography

Ahmad, K., *Psycho-analysis and Literary Criticism*, Patna: Shri Ajanta Press (Year of publication not mentioned).

Aristotle, *Metaphysics*, translated by W.D. Ross in *Encyclopaedia Britannica*, Inc. (Chicago: The University of Chicago, 1952).

—, Meteorology (*Meteorologia*), Translated by E.W. Webster, *Ibid.*

—, *Nicomachean Ethics* (*Ethica Nicomachea*), translated by W.D. Ross, *Ibid.*

—, *Physics* (*Physica*), translated by R.P. Hardie and R.K. Gaya, *Ibid.*

—, *On the Parts of Animals* (*De partibus animalium*), translated by William Ogle, *Ibid.*

—, *On the Soul* (*De anima*) translated by J.A. Smith, *Ibid.*

—, *Poetics* (*De Poetica*), translated by Ingram Bywater, *Ibid.*

—, *On the Soul* (*De anima*) translated by J.A. Smith, *Ibid.*

—, *Poetics* (*De Poetica*), translated by Ingram Bywater, *Ibid.*

—, *Posterior Analytics* (*Analytica posteriora*), translated by G.R.G. Mure, *Ibid.*

—, *Rhetoric* (*Rhetorica*), translated by Ingram Bywater, *Ibid.*

Arnold, Edward, *Contemporary Criticism* (London: Edward Arnold Ltd., 1970).

Baker, John Ross, "From Imitation to Rhetoric"; The Chicago Critics, Wayne C. Booth and Tom Jones." Novel: *A Forum of Fiction* (Spring, 1973), 197-217.

Bayn, Max Issac, *A History of Literary Aesthetics in America* (New York: Frederick Ungar Publishing & Co., 1973).

Bethell, S.L., *Literary Criticism and the English Tradition* (London: Dennis Dobson Ltd., 1948).

Black, Edwin, *Rhetorical Criticism* (New York: The Macmillan Company, 1965).

Blackmur, R.P., "A Critic's Job of Work," *Literary Opinion in America*, edited by Morton Dauwen Zabel (New York: Harper & Row, 1962).

—, "A Burden For Critics," *Hudson Review* (Summer, 1948), 170-85.

Bodkin, Maud, *Archetypal Patterns in Poetry* (Oxford: Clarendon Press, 1934).

Booth, Wayne, *The Rhetoric of Fiction* (Chicago: University of Chicago Press, 1961).

Brooks, Cleanth, "The Formalist Critics," *Kanyon Review*, XIII (1951), 72.

—, "The Humanities: An Appraisal," *The Humanities*: An Appraisal, edited. Harris Julian (Madison: University of Wisconsin Press, 1962).

—, *The Well Wrought Urn* (New York: Reynal and Hitchocook, 1947).

—, *Modern Poetry and Traditions* (New York: Oxford University Press, 1965).

—, "Literature and the Professors," *Kenyon Review*, II (Autumn, 1940), 403-21.

—, Warren and Robert Penn *Understanding Poetry* (New York: Appleton-Century Croft, 1943).

—, Heilman Robert B., *Understanding Drama* (New York, Henry Holt, 1948).

Brower, Renben I.A. Richards, *Essays in His Honor* (New York: Oxford University Press, 1973).

Burke, Kenneth, *A Grammar of Motives and Rhetoric of Motives* (New York: Meredian Books, 1962).

—, *The Philosophy of Literary Form* (Baton Rouge: Louisiana State University, 1957).

Butcher, S.H., *Aristotle's Theory of Poetry and Fine Art* (4th ed. New York: Dover Publications, 1951).

Bywater, Ingram, *Aristotle on the Art of Poetry* (Oxford: Clarendon Press, 1909).

Cargill, Oscar, *Toward A Pluralistic Criticism* (Carbondale: Southern Illinois University Press, 1965).

Carney, James D., *Fundamentals of Logic* (New York: The Macmillan Company, 1968).

Chamberlain, T.C., "The Method of Multiple Working Hypotheses," *The Journal of Geology* XXXV (February-March, 1931), 155-65.

Clark, H.H. *et al.*, *Development of American Literary Criticism* (Chapel Hill: Carolina Press, 1955).

Cowden, Roy W., ed., *The Writer and His Craft* (Michigan: Univ. of Michigan, 1954).

Crane, R.S., ed., *Critics and Criticism* (2nd abridged edition, Chicago: University of Chicago Press, 1957).

—, "The Department of English Language and Literature," The University of Chicago Bulletin (Chicago, 1946), 115-19.

—, *The Idea of the Humanities*, edited by Wayne C. Booth, 2 vols. (Chicago: University of Chicago Press, 1967).

—, *The Languages of Criticism and Structure of Poetry* (Toronto: University of Toronto Press, 1953).

Croce, Benedetto, *Aesthetics as Science of Expression and General Linguistics*. Trans. Douglas Ainslie (New York: The Noonday Press, 1955).

Daiches, David, *A Study of Literature* (Ithaca: Cornl. Univ. Press, 1948).

—, "Principles of Literary Criticism," *The New Republic*, 98 (March, 1939), 95-98.

—, *Critical Approaches to Literature* (London: Orient Longmans, 1957).

Dewey, John, *Art as Experience* (New York: Capricorn Books, 1958).

—, *Logic: The Theory of Inquiry* (1st edition 1938, New York: Holt, 1966).

Eliot, T.S., *The Use of Poetry and the Use Criticism* (London: Faber & Faber Ltd., 1964).

—, *The Sacred Wood* (London: Methuen, 1966).

Eliot, T.S., *Selected Essays* (New York: Harcourt Brace, 1960).

—, *On Poetry and Poets* (New York: Farrar, 1957).

—, *Selected Prose* ed. John Hayward (London: Penguin Books, reprinted in 1953).

Fergusson, Francis, *Aristotle's Poetics* (New York: Hill and Wang, 1961).

Fisher, J.A., *The Humanities in General Education* (Dubuque: W.C. Brown Co., 1960).

Fowler, Roger, ed., *Essays On Style and Language* (London: Routledge and Kegan Paul, 1970).

Friedman, Norman, "Newman, Aristotle and the New Criticism," *PMLA*, LXXXI (June, 1966), 266-71.

Frye, Northrop, *The Stubborn Structures: Essays on Criticism, and Society* (London: Methuen, 1960).

Gardener, Helen, *The Business of Criticism* (Oxford: The Clarendon Press, 1959).

George, A.G., *T.S. Eliot: His Mind and His Art* (Bombay: Asia Publishing House, 1962).

Glicksberg, C.I., The Character of Modern Criticism, *Antioch Review*, 7 (September, 1947), 435-46.

—, American Literary Criticism, 1900-1950 (New York: Hendricks House Inc., 1951).

Gomme, Andor, *Attitudes to Criticism* (Illinois: Southern Illinois University Press, 1968).

Grebstein, Sheldon Norman, *Perspectives in Contemporary Criticism* (New York: Harper & Row, 1968).

Guerin, Wilfred, *A Handbook of Critical Approaches to Literature* (Harper, 1966).

Hagstrum, Jean H., *Samuel Johnson's Literary Criticism* (Chicago: The University of Chicago Press, 1967).

Handy, William J., *A Symposium on Formalist Criticism*, with an Introduction by Mark Schorer (Austin Texas: The University of Texas, 1965).

Hirsch, E.D., *Validity In Interpretation* (New Haven: Yale University Press, 1967).

Hutchins, Robert Maynard, *The Higher Learning in America* (New Haven: Yale University Press, 1967).

James, F.A., ed., *The Humanities in General Education* (Iowa: Win. C. Brown Company Publishers, 1960).

Jones, Howard Mumford, "Literary Scholarship and Contemporary Criticism," *English Journal* (College edition) 23 (1934), 740-58.

Knights, L.C., "Shakespeare and Historical Scholarship," *The Sewanee Review* (Spring, 1955), 223-40.

Krieger Murray, *The Play and Place of Criticism* (Baltimore: The John Hopkins Press, 1967).

—, "Literary Analysis Evaluation—and the Ambidexterous Critic," *Contemporary Literature*, 9 (1968), 290-310.

Langer, Susanne K., *Philosophy in a New Key* (New York: Mentor Books, 1950).

Leavis, F.R., "A Retrospect," Scrutiny XX (1963).

Lee, Brian, "The New Criticism and the Language of Poetry," *Essays on Style and Language*, ed. Roger Fowler (London: Routledge and Kegan Paul, 1970).

Lemon, Lee, T., *The Partial Critics* (New York: Oxford Univ. Press, 1965).

Lentricchia, Frank, "The place of Cleanth Brooks," *The Journal of Aesthetics and Art Criticism*, 2 (Winter 1970), 235-51.

Lodge, David, "The Critical Moment," *Critical Quarterly* VI (Autumn, 1964).

Lu-Fei-Pai, *T.S. Eliot: The Dialectical Structure of Poetic Theory* (Chicago: Univ. of Chicago Press, 1962).

Maclean, Norman, "Personification But Not Poetry," *A Journal of English Literary History*, XXIII (1956), 163-70.

—, and Elder Olson, "Two Essays in Practical Criticism," Prefactory Note by R.S. Crane, *The University Review* (Spring, 1942), 199-203.

Magner, James E., *John Crome Ransom* (The Hague Paris: Moulton, 1971).

Marsh, Robert, "Historical Interpretation and the History of Criticism," *Literary Criticism and Historical Understanding*, ed. P. Damon (Columbia Univ. Press, 1967).

Mckeon, Richard, ed., *The Basic Works of Aristotle* (New York: Random House, 1941).

—, "The Nature and Teaching of the Humanities," *Journal of General Education*, 3 (1949), 290-303.

—, "Philosophy and Method," *Journal of Philosophy*, XLVIII (October, 1951), 653-862.

—, *Thought, Action, Passion* (Chicago: Univ. of Chicago Press, 1954).

—, "Actions and the Uses of the Humanities," *Comprendre*, 15 (Venice, 1956), 69-83.

—, "The Battle of Books," *Knowledge Most Worth Having*, ed. Wayne C. Booth (Chicago, 1967), 173-202.

—, "Communication and Community as Philosophy," *Ethics*, XLIII (April, 1953), 190-206.

—, "The Liberating Arts and the Humanizing Arts in Education," *Humanistic Education and Eastern Civilization: Essays for Robert M. Hutchins*, ed. Arthur Cohen (New York, 1964).

—, "The Nature and Teaching of the Humanities," *The Journal of General Education*, ed. R.M. MacIver (New York, 1964).

—, "The Nature and Teaching of the Humanities," *The Journal of General Education*, ed. R.M. MacIver (New York, 1952), 105-32.

—, "The Philosophic Bases of Art and Criticism," *Critics and Criticism: Ancient and Modern*, ed. R.S. Crane (Chicago: Univ. of Chicago Press, 1952), 463-546.

—, "Richard Mckeon," *Thirteen Americans: Their Spiritual Autobiographies* (New York, 1953), 77-114.

—, "Semantics, Science and Poetry," *Modern Philology*, XLIX (February, 1952), 145-59.

Mencken, H.L., "The Critical Process," *Literary Criticism in America*, ed. Nostrand (New York: The Liberal Arts Press, 1957).

Morris, Wesley, Toward A New Historicism (New Jersey: Princeton Univ. Press, 1972).

Mudrick, Marvin Jane Austen, *Irony as Defence and Discovery* (Princeton, 1952).

Narsimhaiah, C.D., ed., *Better Literary History and Better Criticism* (Mysore: Rao & Raghavan).

Nath, Raj, "The Chicago Critics," *The Literary Criterion*, VIII (1967).

—, *Essays in Criticism* (New Delhi, Doaba House, 1971).

Nostrand, Albert D. Van, ed., *Literary Criticism of America* (New York: The Liberal Arts Press, 1957).

Olson, Elder, ed., *Aristotle's Poetics and English Literature: A Collection of Critical Essays* (Chicago: Univ. of Chicago Press, 1965).

—, "Criticism" *Encyclopaedia Britannica* (Chicago: William Benton, 1959), 727-29.

—, "Hamlet and the Hermeneutics of Drama," *Modern Philology*, LXI (1964), 225-37.

—, *The Poetry of Dylan Thomas* (Chicago: Univ. of Chicago Press, 1954).

—, "The Poetry of Wallace Stevens," *Modern Philology*, XL (1943), 275-83.

—, *Tragedy and Theory of Drama* (Detroit: Wayne State Univ. Press, 1961).

—, "Verse," *Encyclopaedia Britannica* (Chicago: William Benton, 1959), 96-98.

—, ed., "University Classics," edition of *Longinus and Reynolds* (Chicago: Packard 7 Co., 1945).

—, "The Dialectical Foundations of Critical Quarterly," *The Texas Quarterly*, IX (Spring, 1966), 202-30.

—, "An Outline of Poetic Theory," *Critics and Criticism: Ancient and Modern*, ed. R.S. Crane (Chicago: Univ. of Chicago Press, 1952), 546-67.

—, "Education and the Humanities," *Pedagogia*, VI (1953), 85-93.

—, "The Argument of Longinus on the Sublime," *Modern Philology*, XXXIX (1952), 225-58.

—, "The Symbolic Criticism of the Ancient Mariner," *Modern Philology*, XLV (1948), 275-83.

Olson, Elder, ed., "The Poetry of Marianne Moore," *Chicago Review*, XI (1957), 100-04.

—, "A Dialogue on the Function of Art and Society," *Chicago Review*, XVI (1964), 57-72.

—, "Rhetoric and Appreciation of Pope," *Modern Philology*, XXXVII (1939), 13-35.

—, "Sailing to Byzantium: Prologomena to a Poetics of the Lyric," *University Review*, VIII (1942), 209-19.

—, *The Theory of Comedy* (Bloomington: University of Indiana Press, 1968).

Petock, S.J., "Dewey and Gotshalk on Criticism," *The Journal of Aesthetics and Art Criticism* XXV (Summer, 1967), 387-94.

Prasad, S.K., *The Literary Criticism of Sri Aurobindo* (Patna: Bharati Bhawan, 1974).

Prior, M.E., *Science and Humanities* (Evanston: Northwestern Univ. Press, 1962).

Pritchard, J.P., *Returns to the Fountains* (New York: Octagon Books, 1966).

Rackin, Phyllis and Hulme Richards, *The Development of Contextualist Poetic Theory*, XXV (Summer, 1967), 413-25.

Ransom, John Crowe, "Humanists at Chicago," *Kenyon Review*, XIV (Autumn, 1952), 647-54.

—, "*The Bases of Criticism*," *Sewanee Review*, LII (1944), 556-71.

—, *The New Criticism* (Norfolk: New Directions, 1941).

—, *The Worlds Body* (New York: Charles Scribner's Sons, 1938).

—, "Strategy For English Studies," *Southern Review*, 6 (1940), 234.

Richard, I.A., *Practical Criticism* (New York: Harcourt Brace & Co., 1929).

—, *Principles of Literary Criticism* (London: Routledge and Kegan Paul, 1924).

Sacks, Sheldon, *Fiction and the Shape of Belief: A Study of Fielding* with Glances at Swift, Johnson and Richardson (Berkley: Univ. of California Press, 1964).

Sahai, Y., "New Criticism and the Aesthetic Experience," *The Literary Criterion*, IX (Winter, 1969).

Sastri, P.S., "The Chicago School," *Nagpur University Journal*, 1967, 145-57.

—, "The Poetics of Lyric and Olson's Approach," *The Literary Criterion*, IX (Winter, 1969), 70-78.

Sarag B. Lawall, *Critics of Consciousness* (Cambridge; Massachusetts: Harvard University Press, 1968).

Scott, Wilbur, ed., *Five Approaches of Literary Criticism* (New York: Collier Books, 1968).

Seidler, Ingo, "The Iconolatric Fallacy: On the Limitations of the Internal Method of Criticism," XXVI (Fall, 1967), 9.

Stallman, R.W., ed., "The New Critics," *Critiques and Essays in Criticism* (The Ronald Press Co., 1949).

Tate, Allen, "The Present Function of Criticism," *Southern Review*, 6 (1940), 246.

Thomas, Russel, *The Search for a Common Learning: General Education, 1800-1960*, ed. James A. Fischer (Iowa: Brown Company, 1960).

Thorpe, James, Relations of Literary Study Essays *On Interdisciplinary Contributions* (New York: MLA, 1967).

Vivas, Eliseo, *The Artistic Transaction* (Ohio: State University Press, 1963).

Waggoner, Hyatt H., "The Current Revolt Against the New Criticism," *Criticism, I* (Summer, 1959), 211-25.

Waston, George, *The Literary Critics* (Baltimore: Penguin Books, 1963).

Weinberg, Bernard, *The Art of Jean Racine* (Chicago: Univ. of Chicago Press, 1963).

—, Critical Prefaces of the French Renaissance (Evanston: North-Western Univ. Press, 1950).

—, ed., "French Poetry of the Renaissance," *Dictionary of World Literature*, ed. Joseph T. Shipley (New revised edition, Patterson Littlefield: Adam & Co., 1964).

Weinberg, Bernard, ed., *The Limits of Symbolism* (Chicago: Univ. of Chicago Press, 1967).

—, The Poetic Theories of Minturno Studies in Honor of Frederick W. Shipley (St. Louis: Washington Univ. Press, 1942).

—, "Scaliger Versus Aristotle on Poetics," *Modern Philology*, XXIX (1942).

Wellek, Rene and Austen Warren, *Theory of Literature* (New York: Harcourt, 1949).

—, *Concept of Criticism* (New Haven: Yale Univ. Press, 1963).

—, *Discriminations* (New Delhi: Vikas Publications, 1970).

White, F.R., "Historical Studies and the Humanists," *College English*, II (February, 1941), 571.

Wimsatt, W.K. Jr. and Cleanth Brooks, *Literary Criticism—A Short History* (New York: Alfred Knoff, 1964).

—, "The Chicago Critics," *Comparative Literature* (Winter, 1953), reprinted in *The Verbal Icon* (Lexington: Univ. of Kentucky Press, 1954).

—, ed., Explication as Criticism (New York: Columbia Univ. Press, 1965).

Winter, Yvor, *The Function of Criticism* (Denver: Swallon Press, 1957).

Zabel, M.D., *Literary Opinion in America*, 2 Vols. (New York: Harper Torchbooks, 1962).